The American Foreign Policy Library

Edwin O. Reischauer, Editor

By the same author:

*Education & Enmity: The Control of Schooling in
Northern Ireland*
*The Church of Ireland, 1800–1885: Ecclesiastical Reform
and Revolution*
*The Irish Education Experiment: The National System of
Education in the Nineteenth Century*
The Changing Uses of the Liberal Arts College
(with L. F. Stevens)

The United States and Ireland

Donald Harman Akenson

Harvard University Press

Cambridge, Massachusetts

1973

To J. V. K.

Foreword

Ireland is a relatively small and thinly populated island, and its people comprise little more than one-thousandth of the total population of the globe. Its history, however, has been extremely complex; it presents the world with one of its most disturbing current trouble-spots; the problems it faces present often unique variants of the quandaries of modern times; and it deeply involves the emotions of Americans, particularly of those who proudly trace their descent from the emerald isle. Ireland thus, despite its minuscule size, looms large to Americans. It is a land that we need to understand better.

There is, of course, considerable knowledge about Ireland in this country, and feelings tend to run deep. But both knowledge and emotions are commonly derived from somewhat shadowy family traditions relating to an earlier period or from fragmentary news accounts that can be more confusing than enlightening. For all the bonds between the United States and Ireland, there is little real comprehension of actual conditions there or of the extraordinary complexity of the intertwining forces that over time have woven the present tangled web of realities. Americans have a deep sense of concern about Ireland, but, impeded as much as aided by their fragmentary knowledge and emotional involvement, they have relatively little understanding.

It is no easy task to present a well-balanced but also comprehensive view of any society, with its endless complexities and inevitable contradictions. When partisan passions are aroused, as is the case with Ireland, the task seems well nigh impossible. But Professor Akenson has achieved it with outstanding success. He leads the reader with skill through the intricate paths of historical background. He presents a broad view of the many sides of modern Ireland, complete with the warts as well as the strong points. He explains the conflicting attitudes of the Irish without prejudicial distortion of any point of view. In sum, he draws a picture that not only is richly informative but also deepens true understanding. While this volume, as a part of the American Foreign Policy Library, is designed primarily for the American reader, it should prove as enlightening to others, including possibly the Irish themselves.

Edwin O. Reischauer

Preface

Several years ago when I was spending a good deal of my time as an adviser to pre-medical students in Harvard College, the head of medicine of the university health services told me that he thought historians should adopt the policy which works so splendidly for the medical profession: never let on that anything one does is not perfect. As much as I appreciate this advice, it is only fair to state that this book would be a much less imperfect object had it been possible for Professor John V. Kelleher, of Harvard University, and Professor Thomas N. Brown, of the University of Massachusetts at Boston, to co-author the volume as originally was intended. Heavy academic commitments, however, forced first Professor Kelleher and then Professor Brown to drop the project. Both men have been extremely generous with time and advice, and I have incorporated a large number of their suggestions into this volume.

This is a book about Ireland written for Americans in general and Irish-Americans in particular. It is not a chronicle of formal diplomatic relations, because those relations are not important enough (despite their interesting moments) to fill a book for the general reader. The most important relations of Americans to Ireland always have been informal, spontaneous, and familial. The degree to which Americans have been involved in the political, economic, and social affairs of Ireland has been a function of how they perceived Ireland. Therefore, in presenting a picture of Ireland to Americans, this book is intended to be not only a discussion of the circle of relations between the two nations but an active link in that relationship.

The organization of this book implicitly suggests that the history of Ireland in the last century and a half can best be seen as revolving around the pivotal years 1920–23. Up to that time all the key themes in Irish history seemed to point toward the Irish nationalists' achievement of political independence from Great Britain. A substantial form of independence was obtained for the southern three quarters of the country in late 1921. But what usually is forgotten is that at approximately the same time two other events of almost equal importance took place. First, in 1920, Northern Ireland was formally separated from the rest of the country, and second, in the south during 1922 and 1923 the revolutionary nationalists fell into a fratricidal conflict, the wounds from which still scar Irish society. From the years 1920–23 sound the dual tones which pervade Irish society, north and south, to the present day. One is conscious both of the island's considerable achievements and, simultaneously, made vaguely uneasy by the awareness that many other things are not as they could have been.

Most Irish-Americans probably will find modern Ireland a disappointment, especially if they know the country chiefly through grandfathers' stories and Aer Lingus tours. But disappointment and disillusionment are not the same thing. Modern Ireland is chiefly disappointing in terms of what the island could have been—its failures stand in sharp relief when held against the standard of the country's great potential. But disillusioning, never. The nation's potential, like the prismatic lines hidden in an uncut gem, can be unlocked at any time.

DONALD HARMAN AKENSON

The Bell Farm
Gananoque, Ontario

Contents

One.   Toward The Watershed

I The Geographic and Historical Framework

From a statistician's viewpoint the physical framework in which Ireland's history has unfolded is not impressive. The country is small. The land area presently governed by the Republic of Ireland is somewhat over seventeen million acres, that under the government of Northern Ireland between three and four million. The total, approximately 20.4 million acres, is about the size of South Carolina.

Ireland has relatively few of the conventional natural resources. Large deposits of the minerals upon which the industrial revolution in Europe was based, coal and iron, are absent. Peat, Ireland's predominant fossil fuel, is too inefficient for most industrial applications. Precious metals have been mined in small quantities since prehistoric times, but never in sufficient supply to permit broad industrial workings. The lack of mineral resources means that the land as a primary economic resource has been, and continues to be, much more important to Ireland than to other European nations.

Fortunately, Ireland's general climate is mild and, by the standards of the northern United States, allows a long growing season. For the winter months (December–March) the average temperatures usually are in the low-to-middle forties, Fahrenheit. Snowfall is limited (Dublin averages well under twenty snow days per year), and year-round livestock grazing is possible. The chief climatological limits on everyday agricultural life are twofold. First, the average summer temperatures range only from the high fifties to the low sixties, and this makes it difficult to grow those grains and legumes which require a good deal of sunshine and warmth; second, the average rainfall is high and in some places prodigious. It rains about 175 days a year in the "dry" southeast. In the waterlogged west certain areas will have as many as 250 rain days yearly. Four-fifths of the country has from 30 to 50 inches of rain annually, in comparison with England, where four-fifths of the country has 20 to 40 inches.

Obviously, in an agricultural country the amount of rainfall is more than a matter of mere conversation. Excessive moisture limits the nation's economic productivity, for waterlogged pastures and sodden furrows are just as crippling to an agricultural nation as rusting tools and poorly maintained machines would be to an industrial economy. Naturally, the individual farmer tries to overcome the handicaps of the climate by his own drainage efforts, some of them truly heroic in scale, but here the country's physical geography is deceptively cruel. Those apparently gentle rolling hills are perfectly situated for the tourist but devilishly ill-placed for the farmer. The country is shaped like a saucer, the coastal areas tending to be higher than the interior. This means that Irish rivers generally are short, meandering affairs and that the overall drainage pattern is far from efficient. According to the best estimates, two-thirds of Ireland is improved agricultural land, and most of the remainder is grazing land. But the inherent drainage problems, when combined with high average rainfall, result in a limited agricultural productivity of which the visitor who sees only the green fields is unaware.

In thinking about the historical geography of Ireland four points are worth remembering. The first is visual: the great events of the distant past did not happen in the country of small hedged fields and close settlements which we know today. A modern Irishman, set down in the midst of his home parish even as late as 1700, would have trouble recognizing where he was; and much earlier he would have been bewildered, literally, for the countryside was a wilderness. Drainage and turf-cutting for fuel has greatly reduced many of the once mammoth bogs. The old woods are gone too, most of them cut by the seventeenth century or earlier. Roads, like hedgerows, are mostly modern developments, and there are fascinating seventeenth-century travelers' accounts of journeys through trackless wastes where there was no grass for the horses, only heather and bog;

and where one could not find a house to buy fodder because the towns did not have steeples, only little low houses, so one could be within a mile of a town and not know it was there. Much of Ireland, especially the center, must have looked like a great park. The Curragh of Kildare is the best remaining example of this phenomenon—a great wide grassland plain with little woods, small lakes, and, in early times, never a fence.

Second, one of Ireland's most important physical characteristics is so obvious that it is easy to overlook, namely, its location in relation to the rest of the British Isles and to continental Europe. As the accompanying map indicates, Ireland has a strategic significance in relation to England which is out of all proportion to its own size. From a military point of view, Ireland stands poised as a knife in England's back. After the long-distance sailing ship was developed, England could ignore Ireland militarily only at great peril. English involvement in Ireland had begun in the twelfth century when Cambro-Norman knights conquered large portions of the country. England's hold was tenuous, however, and it was not until the reign of Henry VIII that a thorough conquest was initiated. During the seventeenth century the need for subjecting Ireland became all the more acute as it became clear that Ireland would not follow England in embracing Protestantism; in that era religious adherence and international politics were closely related. But English rule was never a success, for, as one writer has suggested, Ireland was too close to England to be ignored but too far away either to be assimilated or properly governed. Thus, Ireland's strategic location, ostensibly an asset, proved in the long run to be a national liability.

Third, Ireland's physical relationship to Scotland is very close and its cultural relationship even closer. From earliest recorded times there have been close trading ties between the two areas. In early Christian times the Irish influence upon the area which is now Scotland was great, involving as it did the conversion of the Scots to Christianity. Since the early sixteenth century the cultural influence has been chiefly the other way, with the dominant group in the north of Ireland springing from Scottish immigrants.

Fourth, the regional differences within Ireland are important. The four provinces of Ireland indicated on the accompanying map—Connacht, Leinster, Munster, and Ulster—have ancient origins and do not correspond either with present-day administrative units or with precise physical boundaries. They still are useful, however, because, like the counties, they allow one to describe locations accurately in a rural society without forcing one to fall back on the misleading expedient of relating all social geography to the nearest town or city. Dr. J. H. Andrews of Trinity College, Dublin, has convincingly argued that the two regional themes running through Ireland's historical geography are, first, the contrast between east and west, and second, the tendency of the north to stand apart from the rest of the country. Both of these themes run from earliest to modern times. As for the first, imagine an equilateral triangle with its base running from Dublin to Dundalk (or, since Belfast's growth in the nineteenth century, to Belfast). This triangle contains most of the best land in the country and a disproportionate share of material wealth. The rich land attracted first the Celts and then the English settlers. It was the first part of the country to become fully assimilated, during the eighteenth and nineteenth centuries, to the cash nexus and to the modern market economy. The polar contrast to the eastern triangle has been the far west, the provinces of Connacht and west Munster, comprising the worst land and least efficient communications. The west is the poorest section of the country and the least permeable to foreign influences. As a result, in material and cultural standards the average Dubliner of today resembles the average Londoner more closely than he does a Connacht small farmer. The second theme, the isolation of the north, stems from physical and spatial characteristics. Physically, the north is separated from the rest of the country by glacial drumlins, lakes, and small mountains. These obstacles are presently of no great moment, but before the nineteenth century's proliferation of roads they were of consequence and helped determine patterns of social geography which remain intact to the present. Spatially, the north has been distinct because, from most of Ulster and especially the coastal areas, Scotland is more accessible than Dublin.

Before turning from geography to history one caution is needed: any discussion of the geography of modern Ireland runs into the mystifying problem of what one should call it. The island considered as a geographic whole is, of course, properly called "Ireland" but the geopolitical names have varied. From 1801 until 1920 Ireland existed as an administrative unit but not as a sovereign political entity within the United Kingdom of Great Britain and Ireland whose capital was London. In 1920 "Northern Ireland" was hived off from the rest of the island. It acquired a home rule parliament of its own under the encompassing government of the "United Kingdom of Great Britain and Northern Ireland." Although the historical province of Ulster was considerably larger than the area actually under the control of the government of Northern Ireland, "Ulster" and "Northern Ireland" are generally used as synonyms. In some nationalist circles "the six counties" is used to refer to the north.

Then, in 1922, the remainder of Ireland became independent of the United Kingdom and became known as "Saorstat Eireann," which was translated as the "Irish Free State." This area often was, and still is, referred to as "southern Ireland" or "the twenty-six counties."

All this was reasonably clear, but in 1937 a new constitution was promulgated for the south, changing the name of the state to "Eire," or in the English language, "Ireland." Although the southern government controlled only the twenty-six counties, its constitution claimed sovereignty over the whole island. Whenever the state referred to itself in English it used the word "Ireland," but in administrative and statistical publications it used either the expression "Ireland (exclusive of the six counties)" or "Ireland" with a footnote referring to the exclusion of those counties. Thus "Ireland," and to a lesser extent its cognate "Eire," are well avoided in constitutional discussions, since the words either imply a prejudgment of the Irish unity question or the need for elaborate and awkward qualifying phrases.

When in 1948 the government of southern Ireland declared itself to be a republic, the English phrase "Republic of Ireland" was introduced to refer to a government which continued to claim sovereignty over the whole island, but which in practice still ruled only the twenty-six counties.

Because of the extraordinary confusion endemic in the name, it is best for our purposes to use "Ireland" only in two cases: to refer to the geographic entity of the entire island and to refer to the administrative unit which existed intact up to 1920. Thereafter, one of the appellations defined above will be employed. This is purely a matter of expository necessity and does not imply any judgment on the constitutional or moral legitimacy of any of the terms employed.

Ireland to most North Americans is a country from which emigration has originated, but, as Professor T. W. Freeman has pointed out, it is equally a culture which over the centuries has been shaped by successive waves of immigration. The first of these lies well beyond the realm of written history. Archaeological research indicates that sometime in the seventh millennium B.C. mesolithic peoples moved into Ireland, living presumably by hunting and fishing. Neolithic farmers succeeded the hunters in the fourth millennium B.C., and metal-working peoples arrived about 2000 B.C. The key immigrations, the ones about which we have literary knowledge, occurred in the first millennium B.C. Celtic-speaking, iron-using, warlike tribes from the continent invaded Ireland, displacing previous cultures and obliterating all but the most scattered traces of their existence.

By about 150 B.C. Ireland was dominated by "Q Celts," a linguistic group encompassing the cultures which came to dominate Ireland and Scotland. They were distinct from the "P Celts," who eventually dominated Wales and Brittany (the nomenclature derives from the use of "Q" or "P" in certain key situations, such as "equos" for horse among the Q Celts and "epos" among the P Celts). This Q Celtic culture was barbarian in the full sense of the word. It was gloriously self-confident, warlike, and heroic, and although coexistent in time with imperial Rome, its values were closer to those of Homeric Greece. Politically, Ireland now was a city state without cities. The basic unit was the "tuath," a petty kingdom, or tribal state.

In pre-Christian times there were 100 to 125 of these, each ruled over by a "ri," or king. Despite certain mythological assertions, it is now clear to scholars that there was no single "high king" over Ireland, which, in a monarchical society, is to say that ancient Ireland was not a single political entity. There existed instead a political kaleidoscope with one petty tribe coming for a time under the hegemony of another, which in turn was ruled by yet another, and so on—and then, suddenly, a realliance of some tiny tribe at the bottom of the pyramid would bring the whole system of relationships crashing down, and reconstruction would begin. Further to cause perpetual turmoil, within each tuath the succession to the petty kingship followed not a single line as it does in the case of modern monarchies, but descended to one of a number of eligible families. Each succession, therefore, was a potential quarrel, the more so because if a given noble family did not obtain the kingship within four generations, it descended into the peasantry. Not surprisingly, the great epics of the time are concerned chiefly with tales of combat and of military and physical prowess. Yet, the perpetual squabbling of the ancient Celtic world should not obscure its cultural richness. The poetic, legal, and decorative arts were highly developed. Unlike the vernacular cultures of most of Europe, Celtic Ireland was not bowed by Roman rule.

Thus, when Christianity was introduced into Ireland (St. Patrick's arrival is traditionally dated A.D. 432, but certainly other missionaries preceded him), the church met something it had not faced before: an unbroken barbarian civilization. The society's effect upon the church was as great as the church's upon the society. Christianity opened up a great vertical fissure in what previously had been a rigidly stratified social structure. Now a man who previously had been unworthy to hold the bridle of a court poet could become a Christian priest, learn a new language of incantation, and acquire even greater magical-supernatural powers than had the "druids" of old. Now an entire society which had lacked a time sense discovered that time was sequential, and suddenly the petty kings doggedly began to trace their genealogies back to Noah, and ultimately to

Adam. Now the work of metalcrafters, gold- and silver-smiths, focused upon Christian themes, and the Celtic visual sense, when combined with Christian piety, produced unique, other-worldly illuminated manuscripts and artifacts.

The church on its side gave up, for all practical purposes, its theory of episcopal administration on a diocesan basis. In a tribal society, with no towns, a diocesan system was impossible. Instead, a monastic system arose which in ecclesiastical matters was analogous to the tuath system in political affairs. The abbot, rather than the bishop, held real power, and the monasteries maintained complex relations with each other, usually spiritual, but often material. Not surprisingly, the same upper class that dominated a local tuath often came to dominate the local monastery. In many cases the abbacy became hereditary, passing from one member of a family to another and often being held by a layman. Only in the twelfth century, following the reform of the continental church, was the Irish church forced into line with continental practices.

If Christianity was an infusion of a new culture, rather than a new people, into Ireland, the Vikings constituted nothing if not a flesh-and-blood invasion. The Viking invasion occurred in two stages. The first began in the early ninth century and lasted into the 870's. Small bands of aggressive invaders swarmed about the Irish countryside, robbing, looting, and burning with indiscriminate ease. Ireland offered rich plunder because the island had not suffered physical invasion for a millennium, and its treasure was immense. The monasteries were especially tempting targets, the more so because their treasures were not guarded by fighting men, but men of prayer. Even the petty kings were no match for the Viking invaders, for Irish warfare had become formalized and was technically backward. More-over, the continual quarreling of the petty kings among them-selves precluded their forming military alliances against the quick aggressive raiders. Apparently at a few coastal places, notably Waterford and Dublin, the Vikings fixed settlements. Then, about 913–914, a whole new wave arrived. Once again they raided and plundered, but this time there was much more effective opposition from the Irish. In the face of this opposition the Vikings settled down in areas such as Limerick, Waterford, Wexford, and Dublin. They became in part agriculturists, in part extortionists. They employed stewards or bailiffs who went about the surrounding countryside demanding "black rents" from the native Irish which, if paid, bought peace. Otherwise a punitive raid followed. Once the Vikings became settled and reinforcements from home began to thin, they became targets for the Irish counterattack. When they became rooted to specific pieces of land they lost the advantage which an invader has and became just another warlike territorial faction. The great setpiece in the Irish resurgence—indeed, perhaps the greatest military victory in Irish history—was the battle of Clontarf in 1014, when Brian Boru brought a temporarily united Irish nation to success (and simultaneously led to his own death). Popular legend aside, the Vikings thereafter did not simply disappear from the Irish scene, but their importance was much diminished. Eventually, intermarriage with the native Irish resulted in their absorption into the dominant culture. Their greatest monument, besides the Irish plunder now found in Scandinavian museums, was the creation of towns, a new development in a totally agrarian society.

The Normans were quite another matter; their impact was permanent and far-reaching. In 1155 Pope Adrian IV, an Englishman, had "given" Ireland to King Henry II, the Norman French king of England. This commission was not taken up until 1169, after a displaced Irish petty king sought Henry's help in reasserting his rights to his Leinster kingdom. Henry responded by licensing a number of Cambro-Norman knights under "Strongbow" (or, more formally, Richard Fitzgilbert de Clare, second Earl of Pembroke) to move on Ireland in a combination military campaign and land speculation. Strongbow was spectacularly successful, and when King Henry came to Ireland in 1171, he found most of the south under conquest and almost all of the Irish kings willing to give homage (albeit insincerely) to the new monarch. Thereafter, the conquest of Ireland proceeded under the generalship of vigorous Norman marcher lords who carved out great hunks of land for themselves as vassals of the English crown. According to a leading authority, by the mid-thirteenth century three-quarters of the country had been overrun. In this conquest the Normans introduced a centralized administration, which, if not altogether pervasive or efficient, claimed to be national and promised to be permanent by virtue of its being independent of the personal authority of any given noble or petty king. Government, as distinct from personal monarchy, had arrived.

By roughly 1300 the Norman conquest had reached its height, and soon events turned against it. First Robert Bruce, having defeated the Norman-English at Bannockburn in 1314, turned to Ireland. In 1315 a force under his brother invaded Ireland. Although ultimately unsuccessful, the three years of attack by the Bruce sapped the Norman strength in Ireland. Second, the Normans in Ireland were further weakened by the great plagues of the time. There is no reason to think that they suffered more severely than did the conquered Irish, but the fabric of Norman rule was thin and the severing of any of its threads weakened the whole garment. Third, the Hundred Years War drew attention away from Ireland and denied needed resources to the Irish administration. Thus, the area under direct administrative control of Dublin continually shrank as resurgent Gaelic chiefs pressed continually forward. By the end of the fourteenth century the English government was reduced to "The Pale" on the eastern seaboard and to certain great earldoms which were ruled as independent princedoms. The result was an almost infinitely complicated social-governmental structure. In some areas the old Irish chiefs were in control, in others Irish leaders who had become Anglicized, and in still others descendants of Norman families which now were Hibernized. Intermarriage was common, and one could never be sure whether a given chief or lord was more English or more Irish (and to complicate matters further, at some undefined point in time the Normans in England had become the English; but back country lords in Ireland often acted more like their swashbuckling Norman forebears than their English contemporaries).

The governmental authorities tried unsuccessfully to shore up the slipping situation by defensive statutes: the Statutes of Kilkenny of 1366 proscribed the adoption by the English of a wide range of Irish customs, and Poynings' Laws of 1494–95 permitted the Irish parliament to pass statutes only after the measures had been vetted by the king and the English Privy Council.

Whether or not the Gaelic resurgence would ever have been complete is an intriguing but moot question for the exigencies of the Tudor world and the imperatives of the Tudor personality made a reconquest necessary. During the sixteenth century the strategic position of Ireland in relation to England changed. The wide-scale adoption of the long-distance sailing ship meant that England no longer could ignore Ireland militarily, but had to view the island as a threat, as a spot from which continental enemies could launch an invasion of the home country. The sharpness of the conflict with the continental powers which followed upon the Protestant Reformation in England underscored this fact. During the reign of Henry VII and the first part of Henry VIII's reign (accession 1509), the Tudors were content to assert their powers in Ireland through the intermediary of those great princelings, the Earls of Kildare. But a revolt by one of the younger earls in 1534 brought that policy to an end, and the Tudor conquest began in earnest. In 1542 Henry declared himself king of Ireland (previously Ireland had been a lordship of the king of England) and took over direct management of the Irish government.

Henry VIII's reconquest of Ireland had not proceeded far before his death in 1547, but his reign was a pivot upon which all subsequent Irish history turns: the Catholic-Protestant division was introduced into Ireland. The last thing one should believe is that Henry VIII was a thorough-going Protestant reformer or that a vigorous attempt was made to convert Ireland to Protestantism, but the ultimate tragic conclusion to Henry's religious revolution was that, over the next century, England became Protestant while the Irish people remained resolutely Catholic. In Ireland only the ruling and administrative classes became Protestant (and many of these individuals were simply temporary residents sent out from England). The majority of the Irish people, peasant and chief alike, remained Catholic. Inevitably, the natural tension between the central government and the baronies was heightened, for now it was not only a conflict between center and localities, but between Protestant and Catholic. The religious conflict wove a new and central strand into the identity of the Irish: to be Irish was to be Catholic. The "mere" (meaning pure) Irish, the "degenerate" (that is, Hibernicized) English, and the heirs to the old Norman lordships now were bound together by the strong cord of religion.

If the indigenous population was unreceptive to English rule, Elizabeth I reasoned, they could be displaced and loyal colonies established. Hence she supported the attempt to plant a colony in the midlands on confiscated land which is now the counties Leix and Offaly. Following a rebellion in Munster, a similar plantation was begun in the south. Although these two Elizabethan efforts were not permanently successful, that of the Stuart king, James I, was a success. Ulster was the one area where, decade after decade, the English government had made little progress. The native Irish civilization was vigorous and militarily strong, the landscape easily defensible, the leaders proud and unbending. Finally, however, the native chiefs were broken by the Elizabethan army in 1603 and, subsequently, by the barrenness of their own lives as a conquered people, so that in 1607 most of the great leaders of Ulster fled. Much of the north of Ireland now was open, and plantation, long meditated in London, quickly became a reality. Soon a large infusion of English and Scottish settlers was introduced. Culturally, these groups were distinct from the indigenous Irish, and they were Protestants. Like colonists throughout the world, they both despised and feared the native peoples whose lands they now held, and for their part the Irish were ever mindful that their patrimony had been seized by these hated aliens.

Not surprisingly, the Irish rebelled. This occurred in 1641 and the Irish situation quickly became intertwined in the complicated British contest between parliament and the monarchy. From 1641 to 1660 the contest in Ireland swirled about in a whirlwind of violence too complicated to summarize: there were as many as five or six factions and alliances among Irish groups, between Irish and English groups, and among the English groups, all of which were cemented and just as quickly tessellated. Two conclusions, however, are unavoidable. First, the Catholic Irish lost and lost heavily. One only has to think of Cromwell's massacre of the approximately 3,500 inhabitants (men, women, and children) of Drogheda in 1649 to comprehend this fact. Second, these two decades in the mid-seventeenth century, probably more than any equivalent period in modern Irish history, creased the lines of sectarian hatred deep into the Irish countenance. Hereafter the country might at times be quiet, but never at peace.

Ireland was battered once more before the seventeenth century ended. This time, it can be argued, it was hurt as much because of the actions of its ostensible friends as those of its recognized enemies. England's and Ireland's Catholic king, James II, was deposed in 1688 for his absolutist tendencies. He cared not a fig for the welfare of the Irish, but once he had fled England, he saw Ireland in a new light, as a stepping-stone to recovery of his English throne. For a brief time the Irish Jacobites controlled the island, but soon the competent, unflustered generals of William III of Orange and now of England, marched through the land. One victory in particular, the Battle of the Boyne of 12 July 1690 (new style), has rung down to the present, and is commemorated annually in the parades of the Protestant Orange Order. The immediate consequence of King William's victories was not as painful to the defeated Irish as they might have been, for William himself was a reasonably tolerant man and was opposed to large-scale victimizations of his former Irish enemies. He was not averse, however, to confiscating lands held directly by those enemies.

The real pain for most Irish Catholics began after William's death in 1702. Then, in three decades of self-serving legislation, the Irish Parliament, controlled by the Irish Protestant allies of the victorious English, wove an iniquitous "penal code." Strictly speaking, the code was not a code at all, but rather a tangle of overlapping, sometimes contradictory, statutes which penalized adherents of the Roman Catholic religion (and in some cases those of Presbyterian faith as well). Admittedly, penal codes were common in seventeenth- and eighteenth-century Europe and were invoked by both Protestant and Catholic governments.

The singular characteristic of the Irish penal code was that, in contrast to its continental counterparts, it was not imposed by a religious majority upon a minority, but by a minority upon a majority. Traditionally, the code is analyzed in three sections. The first segment comprises those laws aimed at making difficult the practice of the Roman Catholic religion. Bishops, regular clergy, and ecclesiastical dignitaries were banished from the country. Parish priests were required to register with the government and were limited in their activities by governmental fiat. The second section, the "disabling laws," prevented conscientious Catholic laymen from entering the higher trades or learned professions by requiring for admission certain oaths repugnant to their faith. The third category, the "punitive laws," prohibited (among other things) Catholics from practicing primogeniture, from buying land from Protestants, from leasing large parcels of land, and from acting as legal guardians of children. Catholic children who converted to Protestantism immediately became absolute heirs of their parents' landed property and the parents mere tenants.

What the actual motives were of those who framed the penal code, and of those who kept it on the statute books once it had been framed, is hard to say. Probably in the first quarter of the eighteenth century the Protestants actually were in fear of the Catholic religion and serious about the necessity of stamping it out. But by the mid-1720's it was obvious that the Catholic Irish were not going to rise to the rebellious notes of the Jacobite bugle, and the motives appear to have changed. Economic advantage, not fear of a Catholic uprising, seemed to be the chief motivation. Gradually the enforcement of the religious sections of the code cooled, and by mid-century Catholic functionaries were able to move about the countryside in safety if not in dignity. But as an instrument of economic discrimination against the Catholics the code continued to apply with remarkable efficiency. A good index of that efficiency is indicated in the following figures which trace the percentage of Irish land held by Roman Catholics, from 1641 to 1776: 1641 (59%), 1688 (22%), 1703 (14%), and 1776 (5%).

Against the dark backdrop of the eighteenth-century Irish

scene a triad of hopeful themes emerged involving religion, land, and national identity. In the 1770's, and with accelerating speed thereafter, sections of the penal code were repealed. By the mid-1790's the only major penal measure still on the books was an act which prevented Catholics from becoming members of Parliament. Eventually, in 1829, this provision was abolished, the movement for its repeal being known as "Catholic Emancipation." Second, the Catholics slowly began reacquiring land. Until the second half of the nineteenth century this reacquisition was through myriad individual purchases, but thereafter a series of land acts provided government aid for the small farmers who wished to purchase holdings. Thus, even before the Irish revolution of 1916–21 most of the land in Ireland was once again in Catholic hands. But that is to look far ahead, at the full embroidering of a theme which was only hinted at during the last quarter of the eighteenth century.

More clearly enunciated at that earlier time was the concept of national identity. A patriotic genealogy evolved, formed by a Protestant minority opposition to the Protestant Ascendency's willingness to subordinate Irish interest to English demands. Jonathan Swift, William Molyneux, Charles Lucas, and Henry Flood formed a chain of critics, stretching link to link over the first three-quarters of the eighteenth century, at times querulous, at times noble, but always active and hard to ignore. Most important was Henry Grattan, who, after entering Parliament in 1775, galvanized the Irish Parliament into asserting its independence as a legislative body of the English Parliament, an assertion that was formally recognized in law in 1782–83. This Irish Parliament still was composed only of Protestants, and despite its theoretical independence still was under severe restraints imposed by England, but undeniably it had taken a long step away from its traditional role of English lapdog.

Surveying Ireland in 1790, a contemporary observer probably would have concluded that although Ireland was not yet a happy country, things were getting better; in those palmy days just before the French Revolution, the western world was inclined toward optimism.

II The Rise of Nationalism

To understand the continuing impact of nationalism upon modern Ireland one must first realize that Irish nationalism of the nineteenth and twentieth centuries carried the seeds both of victory and of tragedy: victory because the southern Irish, who were politically and religiously opposed to British dominance, shook off alien rule; tragedy, because the nationalist ranks were fundamentally divided, a division which tore the fabric of southern Irish society in the civil war of 1922–23. In describing the rise of Irish nationalism it is best for our purposes to proceed at a fairly high level of abstraction and to delineate the two ultimately incompatible nationalist traditions. This is not to deny that for the land-hungry, rack-rented Irish peasant the fundamental issues were primarily economic, not constitutional. Nor is it to gainsay the complex forces of social change which made possible the creation of nationalist sentiment during the nineteenth century. But ultimately Irish nationalism came down to the concept of nationhood.

At the risk of oversimplification, Irish nationalism in the nineteenth and early twentieth centuries may be viewed as a response to the problem posed by the Act of Union which came into effect in 1801. Prior to that year Ireland had possessed its own parliament, which, if notably corrupt and highly unrepresentative, at least was Irish. During the last two decades of the eighteenth century this Irish parliament had shaken off some of its torpor and in certain instances had tried to defend Irish interests against the British. The increasing difficulty of controlling the Irish parliament, when combined with the impact of the abortive Irish rising of 1798, led William Pitt, the British prime minister, to suppress the Dublin parliament. Britain was at war with France, and could tolerate no difficulties on the home front. With the very reluctant consent of the Irish parliament, the Union of Great Britain and Ireland took place.

Ireland as a country possessing its own legislature disappeared. The most important articles of the Act of Union replaced the separate parliaments of Great Britain and of Ireland with a single parliament of the United Kingdom. In the new Commons Ireland was granted one hundred seats, a number which guaranteed that the Irish members would be submerged in the tide of English and Scottish M.P.s.

If the Union was the problem, from our vantage point in time we can see that for the nationalists there were two competing answers: the home rule solution and the republican prescription. The first of these is the easier of the two to deal with because most home rulers defined their goals with a reasonable degree of explicitness. This is not to say that they were a monolithic body. Each home rule proposal was a compromise taped at the seams to satisfy as many potentially divergent supporters as possible; but most home rule attempts were mooted in the United Kingdom's parliament, and this meant that eventually the proposals were forced into the tight phraseology of the legal draftsman. The nature of the legislative process forced the most Utopian-minded home rule advocate to press for a measure that actually would work if it were put into service. The myriad details of the home rule bills of 1886, 1893, and of 1912–14 bear testimony that the home rulers were dealing with the real world and not with an attempt to create the constitutional equivalent of the kingdom of God on earth.

The realism of the home rule proponents meant that they played the nationalist game within well-defined rubrics. They accepted the rules of the political process as it focused upon Westminster. The home rulers obtained power by orthodox political means, namely, through the creation of a political machine which produced electoral victories. Once having achieved political power they exercised it in the traditional British manner, that is, by trying to influence the course of legislation in parliament. Disruptive and heretical as the behavior of Charles Stewart Parnell may have seemed to contemporary Englishmen, he, unlike the dynamiters and extreme republicans, was satisfied with using political means to influence political events; in that sense he was an orthodox politician.

The realism of the home rule tradition dictated that its supporters were willing to accept a subordinate status for Ireland in whatever arrangements were made with Great Britain. While demanding control of specifically Irish affairs, the home rule advocates repeatedly affirmed Ireland's subordination to the crown. None of them pressed for complete separation from Great Britain, and most recognized that the United Kingdom parliament had to hold sway over Ireland in matters of defense and foreign affairs. Home rule sympathizers of all shades of opinion, however, agreed that Ireland's wrongs could be righted only by persuading the United Kingdom government to confer some of its authority upon a popularly elected Irish legislature. But there agreement ended.

Basically, three forms of home rule were possible. The first of these may be termed the "federal" solution, since advocates of this plan pointed to the government of the United States of America as a prototype. Under a federal system of government the countries within the British Isles would be joined into a single nation on the basis of complete equality in domestic affairs between the partners. As in the United States, each unit would have a legislature for purely regional affairs and would also send representatives to a national parliament that was charged with control of defense, diplomatic affairs, and other issues of common concern.

The second alternative was to create a subordinate legislature responsible solely for Irish matters, while not otherwise interfering in the constitutional arrangements of the rest of the British Isles. Such a solution had the virtue of specificity, for the fact that Ireland wanted to control its own affairs through its own parliament did not mean that the arrangements for governing Scotland, Wales, and England had to be altered. The Home Rule Bills of 1886 and of 1893, as well as the Home Rule Act of 1914, were measures of this sort. (The only example of such an arrangement in the present-day United Kingdom is the government of Northern Ireland.)

Third, home rulers had the option of simply demanding repeal of the Act of Union and a return to the "constitution of 1782." If the Union were repealed, Ireland would be joined to Great Britain solely by the nations' common allegiance to the crown. In theory this was the most radical of the home rule solutions, for it postulated that Great Britain and Ireland would have nothing in common save the monarchy. Not only would Ireland gain political equality, it would be independent of Britain in most matters. In actuality, as distinct from theory, Ireland's subordination to the British crown probably would have implied subordination to British ministers in important domestic matters and most diplomatic affairs, but the national orators skipped quickly over such reflections.

The chief proponent of repeal was Daniel O'Connell, who was, however, far from explicit or consistent in what he meant by repeal. O'Connell at one time had intended that repeal of the Union would follow the carrying of Catholic Emancipation achieved in 1829. During the 1830's, however, repeal slipped to the back of O'Connell's mind, and during much of the decade he was in alliance with the British Whigs, an entente that prevented open agitation for repeal. Then in 1838 O'Connell began preparing a repeal campaign and early in 1843 he promised his followers that the year of repeal had dawned. His agitation was constitutional and nonviolent, but nonetheless frightening to the United Kingdom government. One mass meeting after another lit up the countryside as O'Connell marched through Ireland. The great Catholic majority appeared to be united behind O'Connell, and it seemed as if the British government would grant repeal just as it had granted Catholic Emancipation. But then the bubble burst. In October 1843 the Prime Minister, Sir Robert Peel, called O'Connell's bluff. Faced with the threat of a confrontation with government forces, O'Connell backed down and canceled a scheduled mass meeting. This retreat was a grave symbolic defeat, and the repeal movement never recovered its lost momentum, but although the tack O'Connell took was unsuccessful, his agitation was the first call to the Irish people to seek through constitutional means the management of their own affairs.

Whereas O'Connell spread the gospel of repeal, Isaac Butt

preached federalism. Although Butt's domination of nationalist politics did not last long—roughly from 1870 until 1878—these years were of crucial importance in determining the direction of the home rule movement. Two developments were central. First, Butt replaced O'Connell's vague goals with a reasonably precise formulation of federal home rule. Second, Butt shifted the focus of the agitation. He realized that the hub of power in the British Isles was in the House of Commons. He therefore replaced mass meetings in the fields and hills of Ireland with efforts to influence directly the men in London who made policy. In their substance Butt's federal proposals were straightforward. He proposed that England, Scotland, and Ireland, united as they were under one sovereign, should have a common executive and a common Imperial parliament. Reporting to the Imperial parliament would be the secretaries of war, foreign affairs, India and the colonies, as well as the chancellor of the exchequer and the Home Secretary. He further proposed that England, Scotland, and Ireland each have a domestic administration and a domestic parliament governing its own internal affairs.

Butt's successor, Charles Stewart Parnell, is often seen as a great innovator in the methods of home rule agitation. Actually, his innovations were more apparent than real; the reason the originality of his methods is frequently overemphasized is that his parliamentary obstructions stood in marked contrast to the almost obsequious good manners of Butt. But it is a great mistake to allow the drama of Parnell's parliamentary truculence to obscure the central fact that it was inside the House of Commons that he chose to focus his energies. (Indeed, so firm was his mastery of some aspects of the Westminster political game, such as his discipline over his followers, as to invite imitation by British politicians.) Actually, if Parnell is to be regarded as a major innovator in the home rule tradition, it is for his insistence that greater realism replace abstract constitutionalism. Butt's federalism had been detailed but abstract and unnecessarily complicated. There was no reason to confuse an already difficult issue by demanding that not only Ireland, but Scotland and England as well, be given home rule parliaments. Under

Parnell, therefore, the Irish home rule tradition settled into a more focused and purely Irish pattern, unclouded by extraneous details.

Fortunately we do not have to speculate about what kind of home rule measure Parnell and his followers were willing to accept; the Home Rule Bill of 1886 speaks for itself. Gladstone's bill proposed the creation of a subordinate Irish legislature whose powers were to be stringently limited: Articles 3 and 4 listed no fewer than twenty subjects, ranging from military and diplomatic matters to the regulation of trade, upon which the Irish parliament was forbidden to legislate. A bicameral Irish parliament was to control domestic matters, but the Irish lord lieutenant was to be appointed by London and was to have veto power over all Irish legislation. Baron Thring, the draftsman of Gladstone's 1886 bill, explained that "the object of the Irish government bill is to confer on the Irish people the largest measure of self-government consistent with the absolute supremacy of the Crown and Imperial parliament and the entire unity of the empire." Significantly, the Parnellites and presumably the great bulk of the Irish people were willing to accept the supremacy of the crown and of the Imperial parliament. During his speech on the second reading of the bill, Parnell explicitly recognized the subordinate nature of the proposed Irish legislature and accepted it as the "final settlement" of the Irish government question. The willingness of Parnell and of the Irish people to accept a subordinate status for Ireland later gave great embarrassment to nationalist orators, but the fact of their acquiescence remains. Indeed, given the general acceptability to Irishmen of the 1886 bill, it is probable that Gladstone's measure would have proved a satisfactory and lasting solution to the problems posed by the Union of 1801. Thus, the bill's failure to pass its second reading, due to the opposition of the Tory party, stands as one of the tragedies of modern Irish history.

The Home Rule Bill of 1893 was an anticlimactic postscript to the 1886 proposal, from which it differed in several details, the most important change being that whereas the first home rule bill had made no provision for continued Irish representation in the London parliament, the second did. Although the bill was not ideal, the Irish representatives still were willing to accept the grant of a subordinate parliament as satisfying Irish national aspirations. The reaction of Michael Davitt, a staunch nationalist leader, may be taken as typical of that of most Irish members. "This bill," he said, "is the result of reform and not the consequence of revolution, and, therefore, the friends of peace in Ireland and in Great Britain can accept it, and do accept it, as containing all the terms and conditions of an honourable and lasting compact and union between the people of Ireland and Great Britain." But once again peace in Ireland was narrowly averted; the bill passed the House of Commons and was kept off the statute books only through the resolute efforts of the House of Lords.

Before turning to the final episode in the home rule sequence —the Home Rule Act of 1914—mention should be made of an important variant of the home rule tradition: the Sinn Fein movement in its pre-1916 form. Because Sinn Fein later became the front for violent nationalism, it is easy to forget that throughout its first decade it was a relatively conservative organization belonging to the home rule, rather than the republican, tradition. Sinn Fein was formally instituted in 1905 largely through the exertions of Arthur Griffith, a journeyman compositor, editor, and highly original nationalist thinker. The organization's goals were reminiscent of those of Daniel O'Connell: the restoration of the dual monarchy under the "constitution of 1782." Sinn Fein rejected the idea of a subordinate legislature as embodied in the home rule bills and demanded a parliament for Ireland with powers equal to that of Great Britain. Allegiance to the crown was not questioned, although under the theory of dual monarchy allegiance was made somewhat more palatable: the crown was really the Irish crown which only coincidentally was held by the same person who held the crown of Great Britain. The Sinn Feiners, obviously, did not seek a republic, and in refusing to press for one they were also refusing to adopt the violent methods of the republicans. "We believe," wrote Griffith, "that the four-and-a-quarter millions of unarmed people in Ireland would be no match in the field for the British Empire. If we did not believe so, as firmly as we believe the eighty Irishmen in the British House of Commons are no match for the six hundred Britishers opposed to them, our proper residence would be a padded cell." As this statement implies, Sinn Fein approved of the Irish parliamentary party as little as it approved of the Irish Republican Brotherhood. In a landmark book entitled *The Resurrection of Hungary,* Griffith used the example of Francis Deak and his colleagues to suggest how Irish M.P.'s should act. They should withdraw from Westminster and spend their time in Ireland creating an Irish nation. In particular, they should spend their time working out a scheme for the development and protection of Ireland's infant industries so that national independence and economic self-sufficiency could be achieved simultaneously.

But no Irish members of parliament gave up their seats. The real drama still was in Westminster's halls, and there the Third Home Rule Bill was debated. Because the general election of 1906 had given the liberals such a large electoral majority, they were able to ignore their longstanding pledges to the Irish nationalists until, in 1909–10, they came into conflict with the House of Lords. After the Liberals' majority slipped in the election of January 1910 they made a simple bargain with the Irish nationalists: if the Irish would help the Liberals strangle the House of Lords, they would pass a home rule bill for Ireland. The Lords were overcome in August 1911, and in the spring of 1912 Prime Minister Asquith began to pay his political debt. The bill itself was in no way dramatic, being similar to its predecessor of 1893, but the debates in both houses were spectacularly ill-mannered. During these debates John Redmond, head of the Irish nationalist party, kept reassuring the Commons that his followers were not radicals: "We deny that we are separatists and we say we are willing, as Parnell was willing, to accept a subordinate parliament created by statute of this Imperial legislature, as a final settlement of Ireland's claims." Redmond must have breathed easier when the third reading was safely passed by a vote of 367 to 257. The Lords, of course, did not accept the measure, and it was passed by the Commons in identical form the following year. Under the Parliament Act of 1911, the bill had to be passed a third time before becoming law. During the first seven months of 1914 Asquith tried desperately to wriggle out of having to pass the unamended bill a third time, for if it passed, civil war in Ulster was more than a mere possibility. But if the measure were altered too much the nationalists would balk. After a series of fruitless negotiations Asquith was saved by the Great War. The bill was passed unamended, but before it could become effective it was suspended until after the war. As is well known, during the war years the tide of Irish nationalism changed. The republican element became dominant, and home rule ceased to have any promise as a solution to the situation known by the British as "the Irish question."

Because the home rule tradition ultimately failed, its importance in shaping modern Ireland often is overlooked. Despite the home rule advocates' lack of success they were crucial in developing a set of reflexes among southern Irish leaders which lasted long after most of them had given up the formal concept of home rule through imperial devolution.

The republican habit of mind was incompatible with the home rule temperament, although the two cooperated for short periods of time. Precisely defined, a republic is a governmental arrangement in which supreme power lies with the citizen and in which there is no monarch. It usually connotes a state with a wide electoral franchise. But the Irish republicans were far from precise in the way they used the word, and many of them never bothered to define it at all. Most of them were more familiar with what a republic was not than with what it was—a failing that became tragic when the Irish nationalists turned from fighting the British to shaping a nation that had to exist upon its own merits. The republicans were all agreed that in any Irish republic there would be no deference, symbolic or real, paid to the British crown. Nothing would be permitted in fact or in theory to interfere with Ireland's handling of its own affairs. The republicans were thoroughgoing separatists, demanding that all ties with Great Britain be severed. Moreover, they were impatient with political methods; they rejected the decorous behavior of the home rulers and employed physical force to gain their cherished goal.

For most republicans the republic was as much a mystical and magical concept as a political one. Even the word itself held extraordinary emotive power; perhaps defining it precisely would have destroyed that power. Behind the mystical concept of the republic there grew up a genealogy that reinforced the magical power of the word "republic"—Theobald Wolfe Tone, Robert Emmet, the more radical of the Young Irelanders, and the Fenians of the 1867 rebellion.

Hence, to understand the republican mentality as it operated in the early twentieth century one should begin not with the 1916 Rising, but with the man whom the men of 1916 saw as their original forebear, Theobald Wolfe Tone. Although Tone was the founding figure in the republican genealogy, he differed from most of his political descendants in having a well-defined and complex political philosophy, a mixture of advanced French radicalism and a sense of Irish nationality. Tone desired an Irish republic with Irishmen in complete control of their own affairs, subject neither to the British crown nor to the British parliament. In 1791 he became a member of the Society of United Irishmen, a group founded by Belfast Presbyterian radicals. The society spread, all the time becoming increasingly radical, and Tone rose to be its leader. The organization was suppressed by the government in 1794, a move which only made it more conspiratorial and more closely allied with the French. Tone tried to use the French connection to liberate Ireland, heading a small French force which invaded Ireland in September 1798. The invasion and the Irish peasant rising, which had begun in May, were unsuccessful. Tone was captured even before leaving his ship. He chose suicide rather than the indignity of a felon's death and inflicted a penknife wound in his neck from which he died after a week of intense pain. His death was a martyrdom but, more than that, a serious loss, for he was one of the few leaders in the republican genealogy who had not only impressive courage but an ability to act in pro-grammatic terms. Tone, like his spiritual heir, James Connolly, knew not only what he was striving against, but what he was striving for.

Tone soon was followed by Robert Emmet, who stands as the great prototype of the nineteenth-century republican, for he was brave, romantic, unrealistic, and unsuccessful. Unlike Tone, Emmet had a distrust of ideology and refused to deal with the everyday political decisions that inevitably would need attention following a successful revolution. Emmet's rebellion, which took place in July 1803, was a sad affair. It was ill-planned and well advertised, and the government put it down with ridiculous ease. If that had been all there was to it, Emmet never would have become a republican hero. However, instead of fleeing Ireland, which he could have done easily enough, he stayed in the country, chased through the Irish countryside by the British hounds, thereby giving rise to a score of heroic anecdotes. Moreover, when finally placed on trial, Emmet was superb. He entered no plea of defense, was dignified and patriotic of mien, and he made a speech from the dock which remains a classic. He was hanged and then beheaded with a butcher's knife. He joined Tone as a republican martyr of high renown.

A gap intervened in the republican tradition until the Young Ireland rising of August 1848, which serves as an important link in the republican genealogy, spanning the years between the Tone–Emmet period and the Fenians. In the 1840's, a group of what today would be called "liberal intellectuals" coalesced around a new nationalist newspaper, the *Nation*. The Young Irelanders were not at first given to advocating physical force; neither were they willing to reject completely the possibility of its use. For a time they aligned themselves with Daniel O'Connell and repeal, but, frustrated by the failure of the campaign, they split with the repeal forces, and the more militant members of the group turned to physical force. Inspired by the French revolution of 1848, a rising was begun which rivaled Emmet's in its want of intelligent planning and in its lack of success. The leaders were transported, but none were martyred. Despite the almost farcical nature of the proceedings, the event was a significant one, for its reality proved to be of much less importance than the way it was interpreted by later republican patriots. To later generations the Young Ireland rebellion was presented as another noble example of Irishmen risking their lives to sever the chains binding Ireland to Britain.

Much less cultured and more to the point than the Young Irelanders were the Fenians. The "Fenians," or, as alternatively known, "the Irish Republican Brotherhood" (IRB), gradually coalesced in the decade after the '48 rising and were formally instituted in 1858. The body had an American as well as an Irish branch, the former serving as an important source of funds. The Fenians' message was simple and compelling: the British were foreign interlopers on Irish soil; they had to be driven out and all connections between the two nations severed; an Irish republic was the only acceptable form of government, and physical force the only means of establishing it.

An insurrection was attempted in March 1867 but was so incompetently organized that it scarcely lasted a day. Significantly, however, the Fenians did not collapse with the debacle. They remained strong from 1867 until the 1880's, when Parnell attracted away most of the rank-and-file. Thereafter, the remnant survived in a weak and straggly line until the time came for the Fenian creed to inspire the leaders of the 1916–21 revolution. Although, according to a responsible estimate, there were in 1900 no more than a dozen effective Fenians, the twentieth century saw a steady growth in their ranks. Young organizers such as Denis McCullough, Bulmer Hobson, and Sean MacDermott replaced the phalanx of garrulous, nostalgic old Fenians with young recruits given to action rather than words.

One of the most fascinating of the new generation was Patrick Pearse, whose commitment to past Irish glories was combined with a confusion about the nature of a republic that was all too typical of many young Fenians. In a political pamphlet revealingly entitled "Ghosts," he went so far as to describe the Irishmen who opposed the "English" landing of 1169 as "separatists." In his parade of ghosts he even managed to declare that Parnell was a separatist, a bit of wishful thinking strongly contradicted by Parnell's own testimony. In three well-known sequels to "Ghosts," namely, "The Separatist Idea," "The

Spiritual Nation," and "The Sovereign People," Pearse developed his historical argument and also made it clear that the separatist republic of the future was to be a democracy. But he gave no indication of the practical workings of the proposed new constitution. Pearse, like most Fenians, did not—or perhaps could not—face the unpleasant and unromantic business of planning the prosaic details of the new government that would be established after the victorious revolution.

The words of the young Fenians became more than rhetoric with the founding of the Irish Volunteers in 1913. The Volunteers were headed by the relatively moderate Professor Eoin MacNeill, but many of the ranking leaders were secret members of the IRB. At the outbreak of the First World War a split occurred among the Volunteers, the most moderate members following John Redmond in maintaining loyalty to Great Britain. From the Fenian viewpoint this split strengthened the organization; the most troublesome of the moderates were now gone, and the remainder, still headed by MacNeill, could be easily manipulated.

Meanwhile, a group known as the "Irish Citizen Army" was drilling. Originally formed in 1913 as a protection squad for strikers, it soon became an organ of republican socialism. The group was confined almost entirely to Dublin and had a small following compared to that of the Irish Volunteers. The ICA gained in intensity what it lacked in size, for it included the only group of modern republicans who thought in ideological rather than historical terms and who had practical plans for the new government. Its leader was James Connolly, an orthodox socialist of the British Independent Labour Party stamp. Originally Connolly was interested primarily in social reform and only secondarily in nationalism, but he turned increasingly nationalistic when it became clear that the Home Rule Act of 1914 would not take effect unamended. Connolly changed from espousing nationalism as a mere tactic to a conviction that the establishment of a republic was an absolute prerequisite for a socialist Irish society. As he turned to separatism so he turned to physical force, and the ICA stood ready to take to the streets to battle the British.

All this was unnerving to the leaders of the IRB who would have preferred to maintain their monopoly on revolutionary dogma. The Fenians were perturbed especially by the possibility that the ICA might upstage them and begin a rising before the Fenians could. Hence, the Fenians decided to act as soon as possible. In the actual event, however, Connolly agreed to the IRB's plans and coordinated action took place.

The Easter Rising of 1916 is the one event in Irish history which is well known to the informed public throughout the English-speaking world, and its drama and heroism need no emphasis. Three comments are in order, however. First, the 1916 Rising should not be interpreted primarily as a military episode, but as a symbolic event. Although the IRB was defeated in the streets, it won the hearts of a new generation of Irish nationalists. Second, despite their ultimate success, it is hard to say what the republicans thought they were achieving. Their proclamation was impressive in its fervor but extremely vague in content. And there was even some serious talk among the leaders, most notably Pearse, of placing a German prince upon an Irish throne, which, in some unexplained way, would serve to prevent a British reconquest of Ireland. Indeed, in the last analysis it is impossible to discover whether or not the republican leaders expected the rising to succeed militarily or even if they wished it to succeed. The desire for self-immolation was strong among several of the leaders. Third, the great irony of the 1916 Rising was that, despite the heroic contributions of the republican socialists, it led to the near-extinction of Irish republican socialism. Connolly was executed, and no leader of stature stepped forward from the socialist ranks to replace him. The republican program, which might have assimilated the precise demands for social reform espoused by Connolly, became more than ever a purely separatist program; the republicans knew that they did not want any connection with Great Britain, but only that.

Whatever the intentions behind the rising and despite the ironies associated with it, the ultimate effects of the men of '16 were profound. The use of physical force now replaced the parliamentary bargaining of the home rule party. In the eyes

of the Irish public the British execution of the leaders of the
Rising converted them from a despised rabble into national
martyrs and so sanctified and revitalized the republican tradition. The complacency of 1914, with its Home Rule Act, was
replaced by a nationalism in which the ruthless urgency of the
Fenians was dominant.

Although orthodox home rule was dead after 1916, the habits of mind formed by generations of the home rule tradition
did not suddenly disappear. Republicanism was in the ascend-
ant, but if the republicans were to bring about national independence they had to work with other nationalists of more
moderate stripe. While a common enemy existed, the two styles
of nationalists could gloss over their differences. Eventually,
however, they would have to face each other and resolve the
dissonance.

Whenever that confrontation took place a civil conflict among
Irishmen was nearly inevitable. This becomes apparent when
we polarize the mental habits of the nationalists into republican
and home rule categories (while fully granting that the majority of nationalists were not found at either of the far extremes).
The situation was potentially explosive, because, in the first
place, the republicans refused to think in terms of specific political arrangements for their beloved republic while the advocates
of home rule almost reveled in the intricacies of governmental
planning. Further, the overriding negativism of the separatists'
mentality meant that doctrinaire republicans were apt to be
highly critical of any and all arrangements for the government
of Ireland; men who had spent their lives denouncing governments have a hard time constructing them. Obviously, the unbending separatism of the republicans was in direct conflict
with the home rule proponents' willingness to maintain some
form of tie with Great Britain.

Indeed, the intellectual and temperamental reflexes of the
two traditions were fundamentally incompatible. The republicans dwelt on Ireland's past glories and upon the need to re-
dress ancient wrongs. Men of the home rule mentality thought

in terms of the present and they negotiated in the present about precise details concerning Ireland's political future. Whereas the republicans were courageous, emotional firebrands, men of the home rule stamp usually preferred peace and negotiation to conflict, and they preferred compromise to unbending adherence to abstract principles.

As we shall see in Chapter IV, the opportunity for welding these two traditions together was lost during the years 1916–21 and the Irish nationalist movement remained an admixture that could separate at any time into its individual and irreconcilable components.

III The United States and Irish Nationalism

Citizens of the United States of America assumed significant roles in the development of nationalism in Ireland. When playing a part in Irish events, Irish-Americans were responding both to the situation in Ireland and to their own circumstances in America.

In referring to "Irish-Americans" one means the Roman Catholic Irish and their descendants whose mass exodus from Ireland began with the Great Famine of the late 1840's. Undeniably, there were Americans of Irish Protestant stock who had a notable impact on American society well before the mid-nineteenth century. These immigrants and their descendants were mostly from Ulster and were rarely associated with Irish nationalism. Separate both in politics and religion from their Catholic nationalist counterparts, by mid-nineteenth century the Protestant Irish had taken to calling themselves "Scotch-Irish" in a determined effort to distinguish themselves from the more recent arrivals. Thus, it is not only convenient but necessary to postpone discussion of the Scotch-Irish in America and here to focus on Irish-Americans in the limited sense of the term.

In the four and a half decades between 1846 and 1891 more than three million Irish came to America. Although precise figures on the religious composition of this mass are not available, it is clear that the overwhelming majority (about three quarters) were from Catholic backgrounds. Why did these millions come to America? In large part because they were expelled from their homeland by economic circumstances. Ireland was a chronically overpopulated country having almost no industry and subsisting on a narrow agricultural base. The years of and immediately after the Great Famine saw hundreds of thou-

sands of Irish come to the United States, almost 220,000 in
1847 and somewhat over 254,000 in 1851 (the latter being the
peak figure in the entire history of Irish immigration). Great
surges of migrations also occurred in the years 1863–66 and
1880–83, which were periods of agricultural distress in Ireland.
But if economic necessity was the chief force pushing the Irish
from their home, there was also a pull from the American side.
The economic vitality of the United States undoubtedly was
attractive, and even had there been no Famine and no depres-
sions in Ireland, there would have been at least a steady stream
of migrants from Ireland just as there was from the more prosperous European countries. The "American wake" for depart-
ing emigrants was an Irish custom born of despair, but always
hinting of opportunity, an occasion for tears which might perhaps nurture the seeds of success.

Those left behind, and their descendants, often argued that
the migrants to America were the worst of Irish society—and
the Irish-Americans have suggested just the opposite. The argument is profitless. What can be noted with profit, first, is that
the Irish migrant was usually from a rural area, most often
from the provinces of Connacht and Munster. This rural origin implied a second characteristic. When translated into the
occupational structure of urban America—the Irish, it must
be remembered, settled mostly in the cities—the new Irish-
Americans became unskilled workers and domestic servants.
They brought with them none of the trades or skills which would
have led to rapid advancement in an industrial metropolis. Only
slowly, and then not until the early twentieth century, did the
average Irish-American lift himself from the lowest rungs of
the occupational ladder where, perforce, his rural background
had placed him. A third point: in contrast to most other groups
of migrants, the Irish sent almost equal numbers of men and
women to the United States. This made the formation of families within the ethnic group much easier and undoubtedly
contributed to the great cohesiveness of the Irish-Americans,
both by reducing the incidence of marriage with Americans of
non-Irish descent and by making it easy for the new arrivals
to form a family unit whenever they desired. Thus, despite the

rigors of the new industrial life, the Irish-American family remained remarkably stable and secure.

To keep a sense of proportion one must realize that the great migration to America was more important to Ireland than to the United States. Granted, between 1821 and 1851 Irishmen comprised 42 percent of all immigrants into the United States (largely as a result of the exodus following the Great Famine), but between 1851 and 1860 they dropped to 35 percent, and German immigration rose to 37 percent. The Irish proportion continued to decline thereafter, being 11 percent between 1891 and 1900 in comparison to 14 percent for the Germans and 10 percent for the Scandinavians. At their peak, immigrants from Ireland comprised only 5 percent of the total American population and that in 1860. In 1920 the combination of Americans born in Ireland and those of Irish parentage was 4 percent of the total United States population. Yet the impact of the Irish-Americans upon their new society was greater than these statistics would suggest, in large part because they did not disperse throughout the larger population. Instead, they tended to settle in the cities of the Eastern Seaboard (plus Chicago) where their numbers gave them both social impact and political leverage.

If the political and social advantages of the Irish-Americans stemmed from their being a compact urban group, so did many of their problems. They formed an ethnic urban proletariat which awakened the fears of a dominant "native" American society still agrarian and "Anglo-Saxon" in outlook. The turbulent populace of the burgeoning industrial cities increasingly was viewed as a threat to the American Way of Life. In the nativist mind factories, slums, crime, and riot became associated with the Irish immigrants, and the nativists struck hard at the new arrivals.

But American nativism above all else was religious in nature, which is to say anti-Catholic. American anti-Catholicism has a long and dishonorable history stretching back to Puritan times. It took especially virulent form in the nineteenth century. One need only mention the no-Popery crusade of the 1820's, the church and convent burning of the 1830's, the Native American agitation of the 1840's, the Know-Nothing movement of the 1850's, and the recrudescence of anti-Catholicism in the 1870's to realize how deep this stain in the American culture ran.

The dissonance between the newcomers and American society reinforced their cohesiveness. Because they were alienated from that larger community, Irish-Americans turned increasingly inward as a group, and it was a rare Irish-American who took his cues from the larger society rather than his ethnic cohorts. Quite consciously Irish-American cultural leaders rejected the values of the dominant Protestant, nativist tradition. Editorials in Irish-American newspapers attacked the values and character of the older society as feckless, cowardly, and pretentious. Yet, for all their apparent reluctance, at heart most Irish-Americans wished to become middle class and respectable.

Just as the Catholicism of the Irish-Americans was at the heart of the nativist American hostility, so was Catholicism a central component of the Irish-American self-identification. The church served both as a cause of their alienation from American society and as an instrument of cultural self-affirmation. Predictably, Irish-American influence upon the Roman Catholic church in America increased in direct proportion to the flow of migrants from Ireland until by the early 1850's bishops of Irish birth or extraction dominated the American hierarchy. (The only potential rivals to the Irish were the Germans, but their influence upon the national Catholic polity was limited by language difficulties.) The Irishmen who dominated the American Catholic church were staunch in defense of the church's traditional separatism. Admittedly, during the later nineteenth century there was a movement to adapt the church to American society, a development which led to the famous "Americanization controversy." The Americanizing faction, led by Archbishop Ireland of St. Paul, was convinced that there was nothing in American social and political arrangements which could not be reconciled with the church's teachings. Significantly, both the German-American Catholics and several bishops of Irish-American dioceses fought hard for the separatist practices which precluded the melding of the various

Catholic minorities into the American mainstream. In the end, Pope Leo XIII condemned Americanism, thus affirming that to be a Catholic is the United States was to be set apart from one's fellow citizens.

If Catholicity was one enduring touchstone of the Irish-American identity, the other was the group's involvement in politics. For the Irish-Americans political organizing on ethnic lines was simultaneously a sign of their alienation from the larger society (if they had been integrated into the general culture such ethnic voting would not have been necessary) and a means of gaining at least partial control over their own destinies. The leading historian of the Irish-Americans, Professor Thomas N. Brown, has noted that nothing is so striking to the historian as their drive to wield power. Irish-Americans entered politics for all the "wrong" reasons. They were not concerned primarily with public service or with maximizing the general welfare, or any of the other high-flown motives espoused by political purists. Politics was about power, about money, and about secure government jobs. Its methods were the well-oiled ward machine and the patronage list, its vices factionalism and corruption, its virtues the protection of vital ethnic interests and, eventually, national eminence for the group's leaders. Two key dates in the rise of Irish-Americans to political power were the election in 1880 of William R. Grace as the first Irish Catholic to be Mayor of New York, and Hugh O'Brian's victory in 1884 in the campaign for the Boston mayoralty. By the end of the 1880's Irish-American politicians controlled the government of sixty-eight Massachusetts cities and towns.

Daniel Patrick Moynihan has noted that the American Irish introduced several new characteristics to political life in the United States. First, they were indifferent to Yankee proprieties and replaced the idea of government run upon principles and by gentlemen with a personal concept of government based upon human relationships. Second, and closely related, the Irish brought with them a tradition of distrust for formal and a respect for informal government, an instinct ingrained by centuries of foreign rule of their homeland. They tended to trust Tammany Hall and distrust city hall and to prefer to deal with ward captains rather than with higher civil servants. Third, because the Irish arrived with a collective memory of the great Catholic Emancipation movement of the 1820's, they arrived already imbued with a sense of the possibilities of concerted group action. Fourth, Moynihan notes that the Irish-Americans possessed an extraordinary capacity for political bureaucracy, a capacity which interwove and reinforced the other three characteristics. To this one might add a fifth point —that having become attached to the Democratic party in most cities soon after their arrival, Irish-Americans stayed with the party. It is, indeed, impossible to conceive of the Democratic party in our own century without the great Irish-American machine upon which it so long depended.

To succeed in politics is not, of course, the same thing as gaining social equality, and the Irish-Americans controlled the government of several cities long before their leaders were admitted into the best homes and clubs of those same cities. By the beginning of the twentieth century, however, it was clear that a large body of Irish-Americans was becoming established as solid, comfortable middle-class Americans.

The relationship between Ireland and Irish-Americans was not a simple, one-way transaction. One need only note the estimate that yearly in the mid-1850's one out of every two families in Ireland received a letter from the United States (a proportion which actually increased in the next two decades) to realize how directly the experience of the new Americans fed back into Irish society. The cultural effects of this American material ranged from the introduction of American slang into Irish speech to the adoption of higher standards of economic expectation among those left behind. But money was the most important thing the new Americans sent back to Ireland. The flood of migrants which came with the Famine did not forget the misery of those left at home, and the regular remittance to the old country became a striking and continuing feature of Irish-American life. The best available figures show that between 1848 and 1887, inclusive, remittances from North America to the United Kingdom exceeded £34 million (equal to over $170 million). All but a small portion of this money came from the United States, and the great bulk, perhaps nine tenths, was sent by Irish-Americans to Ireland. The total magnitude of these remittances becomes clear when it is compared with the total amount of government expenditure on poor relief in Ireland in those same years: which it exceeds by nearly £1.75 million! Irish tenant farmers on small uneconomic holdings came to depend on the remittances of their emigrant children to pay the rent and to square their accounts with local shopkeepers. In the poorer areas of the west of Ireland whole parishes depended upon the American money to erase their annual debts.

Within the circle of remittances from America to Ireland there was yet another loop. Approximately 40 percent of the remittances in the post-Famine years was in the form of prepaid tickets of passage, usually intended for some other member of the previous migrant's immediate family. In these instances remittance money spurred further migration, which in turn produced additional remittances from the latest crop of migrants—and so on and on in a social spiral which continued strong well into the twentieth century.

Significantly, despite their continuing familial ties with Ireland, Irish-Americans returned permanently to Ireland only in very small numbers. Although precise figures are not available, it is clear that the Irish-Americans were wedded permanently to their new homeland.

Committed as most Irish-Americans were to life in America, a significant minority maintained an intense interest in the nationalist movement in Ireland. Obviously, for many of the new migrants this involvement in Irish nationalist affairs was simply a continuation of political commitments they had had in Ireland. But the striking thing about the nationalist interests of the American Irish was that they were shaped as much by the group's American experience as by its Irish inheritance. The loneliness of life in the New World drew the new migrants together, and for some community life metamorphosed into nationalist politics. Significantly, even second and third generation

Irish-Americans responded to the prejudice and hostility of American society by venting their spleen not upon the Yankee establishment but on the British domination of their ancestral homeland.

In the story of Irish-American nationalism the first body of importance was the American Fenian movement founded in 1858 by John O'Mahony and paralleled by its Irish sister organization. The American Fenians mushroomed during the Civil War when in both the Confederate and Union armies there were Fenian groups learning the use of arms in preparation for a future attack on the British. In 1866, veterans of these units made a ridiculously unsucessful invasion of Canada. Ironically, the Fenian organization failed to send more than a handful of men to participate in the 1867 rising in Ireland, and after a final silly raid into Canada in 1870 the American Fenian movement fell to pieces.

A more effective nationalist organization was forming even before the Fenians' decline. This was the Clan na Gael founded in 1867. In 1877 this group was tied directly to Ireland by the establishment of a joint revolutionary directory binding the Clan and the Irish Revolutionary Brotherhood. At that time Clan na Gael's membership was approximately ten thousand. The Clan's most important single activity was to gain control over a "skirmishing fund" which had been established in 1875 by nationalists to subsidize terrorism against the British Empire. By 1877 the fund, which comprised $48,000 and was the largest nationalist treasury in America, was under the control of Clan trustees who used its resources more for propaganda than for terrorism.

While the Clan continued to be the leading nationalist organization among Irish-Americans, the Land League and the "New Departure" in Irish politics of the late 1870's and early 1880's drew most of the headlines. The New Departure was a nondoctrinaire mixture of demands for Irish land reform, social welfare programs, educational concessions, and political independence. It was remarkably attractive, drawing together conservative Irish farmers, nationalist M.P.'s and republican revolutionaries. From the viewpoint of American history the signal point about the New Departure is that far from issuing in full splendor from the prison meditations of Michael Davitt, as is usually claimed, it actually was the product of the confused interaction of Davitt and some of the leading Irish-American nationalists. In this case Irish-Americans were the cutting edge of Irish nationalist politics.

While the Irish-Americans made direct contributions both in money and method to the nationalist movement in Ireland, they also interjected their nationalist concerns into American domestic politics. During the early twentieth century Irish-Americans entered into a fascinating series of alliances aimed at influencing the foreign policy of the United States government toward recognition of Irish nationhood and away from diplomatic association with the United Kingdom. Thus, Irish-Americans led the pro-Boer phalanx in the United States during the United Kingdom's war in South Africa (one Irish-American ambulance corps was sent from Chicago, and took up arms upon arriving in South Africa!). In 1904–1905, during the Russo-Japanese war, Irish-Americans conducted mass meetings with Russian flags replacing those of the Boers. The same Irish-Americans opposed the major power arbitration treaties of 1905 because the agreements hinted of increasingly close ties between the United States and the United Kingdom. This opposition helped delay until 1908 the United States' ratification of the treaties.

These Anglophobic pressures ran very much against the grain of American foreign policy. The years 1895–1914 have been described by a leading diplomatic historian as the years of "the great rapprochement" between the United States and the United Kingdom. The mutual animosity which had characterized nineteenth-century Anglo-American diplomatic relations was replaced by a new spirit of friendship which implied an informal alliance between the two nations and, eventually, a full wartime commitment to mutual security. The outbreak of World War I placed the Irish-Americans in a vulnerable position because it evoked a pro-Central Powers response among the more extreme nationalists, while simultaneously stimulating a pro-Allied response in the larger American population. The

Clan na Gael, the most extreme group of any size, responded to the war by sending a secret address to the Kaiser expressing their hopes for the success of the German people in the struggle which faced them. Other more moderate Irish-American organizations expressed sympathy with the Central Powers and complained that the American press had a pro-Allied bias. Such opinions reverberated through the American population and rendered the Irish-Americans almost as suspect as were the German-Americans. Ironically, recent scholarship has shown that the overwhelming majority of Irish-Americans was, if anything, hyperpatriotic and that the American Catholic church itself was formally neutral while emphatically demanding that its adherents be loyal to the United States.

The Irish-Americans were especially vulnerable because the Easter Rising of 1916 stimulated anti-British sentiment among Irish-Americans at the very time a presidential election was in the offing and when, simultaneously, it was obvious that America would be entering the European war on the side of the United Kingdom. Naturally, the executions which followed the Easter Rising outraged Irish-Americans, but it was the case of Sir Roger Casement upon which Anglophobic sentiments were most sharply focused. Casement had been arrested on the west coast of Ireland in mid-April 1916 just prior to the Rising, after being landed by a German submarine. (Ironically, Casement himself was opposed to the planned Rising.) A great movement for clemency for Casement arose among Irish-Americans, but the State Department and President Wilson held an opposite view: that the United States had no grounds in international law for intervening in the internal affairs of the United Kingdom. Eventually, in late July, the United States Senate passed a resolution asking for clemency for Irish political prisoners—Casement, although not specially mentioned, being the case at issue. Casement, however, was adjudged guilty and was executed early in August. Wilson was widely attacked in the Irish-American press.

The disenchantment of Irish-American nationalists with Wilson was matched by the president's dislike of them, and on both sides hostility went much deeper than the specific issue of the

Casement affair. During the 1916 presidential election campaign Wilson referred disapprovingly to "hyphenism," that is, to groups with hyphens in their names because their hearts were still on the other side of the Atlantic. Doubtless he was most concerned with the German-Americans, but the Irish-American nationalists were also in his mind. He sent a telegram to Jeremiah A. O'Leary, the Irish-American president of a German-financed political front organization, stating, "I would feel deeply mortified to have you or anybody like you vote for me," a statement widely publicized in the Irish-American press. The Democratic national platform incorporated an "anti-hyphenism" tone, declaring that "we therefore condemn as subversive . . . the activities and designs of every group or organization, political or otherwise, that has for its object the advancement of the interest of a foreign power. . . ."

Yet, despite the antihyphenism campaign and despite the denunciations of Wilson by leading Irish-American nationalists, recent scholarship has shown that the majority of Irish-Americans voted for Wilson. (One must emphasize the word "recent:" it previously was thought that because Wilson lost six of the eight states with the highest concentration of Irish-Americans that they had turned against him; actually this was a psephological freak; Wilson lost the states despite the continued loyalty of the Irish-Americans to the Democratic party.) In this voting pattern we have a synecdoche of the dilemma of the Irish in early twentieth-century America. They had to choose between their own interests as Americans (which in this case lay with the continued support of the Democratic party), and the interests of Ireland as articulated by the leaders of Irish-American nationalism. Their interests as Americans prevailed.

Once America entered World War I the great bulk of Irish-Americans joined the effort without reservation, and the nationalist leaders turned grumblingly to planning ways to further Ireland's interests in the eventual European peace settlement. Nationalist hopes were raised by President Wilson's elegant statements on the idea of self-determination for small nations. Unfortunately, Wilson's polished rhetoric far outdistanced what could be done in reality. Although he never made a specific promise to fight for Ireland's self-determination, he had allowed the general concept of self-determination to be so interpreted, to his distinct political advantage among Irish-Americans. By the time the Peace Conference officially opened at Versailles in January 1919, however, it was clear that Wilson would be doing little or nothing on the question of an independent Ireland. His viewpoint was now practical: the French were not at all interested in the Irish question, and the British would not permit it to be introduced, and for the United States government to force the issue would have been to destroy the Anglo-American understanding and, perforce, to scuttle Wilson's dream of establishing a League of Nations. In response, the Third Irish Race Convention was convened in Philadelphia in mid-February 1919, and despite internal bickerings a strong lobby was formed to press for Ireland's future to be placed on the agenda at Versailles.

All to no avail. Ireland went unmentioned, and the Irish-American nationalists turned their anger upon Wilson and his proposal for a League of Nations. If Ireland could not have nationhood, the world could not have internationalism, especially through an organization that would guarantee existing territorial borders. Republican isolationists and Irish-American Democrats formed a temporary alliance which denied Wilson his necessary two-thirds' Senate majority for the amended League treaty. For the Irish-American nationalists the bitter months spent on Versailles and the League netted little. As one historian has astutely observed, "Both Wilson and the Irish lost."

IV From Apparent Unity to Civil War

Let us return now to events in Ireland. For most of the years from 1916 through 1921, the Irish nationalists worked reasonably well together. Divergencies in style, motivation, and methods were submerged in the common opposition to United Kingdom rule. Ideally, these were the years when the nationalists could have ironed out their differences and prepared themselves to assume independence as a united people, at least in southern Ireland. Unhappily, while headway was being made during these years toward the goal of Irish self-government, little progress was made in erasing basic antipathies between nationalist groups. Major differences were only papered over, and as soon as a truce was arranged with the United Kingdom government, the underlying rifts among the Irish nationalists came to the surface.

The rising in Dublin in Easter Week, 1916, made it clear once and for all how great the distance was between the orthodox home rule advocates and those willing to take up arms. The reaction of John Redmond, head of the Irish nationalist party in the Westminster parliament, was swift, self-pitying, and politically suicidal. "This attempted deadly blow at Home Rule," Redmond said in referring to the Rising, "is made the more wicked and the more insolent by this fact—that Germany plotted it, Germany organised it, Germany paid for it." This wicked move of the republicans "was not half as much treason to the cause of the Allies as treason to the cause of Home Rule." Momentarily, the bulk of Irishmen probably agreed with Redmond, but within a year the executed men of '16 were enshrined as national martyrs, and when released the republican prisoners were welcomed as heroes in Dublin. As the political beatification of the republican martyrs took place, John Redmond and his party plunged into political oblivion.

During 1917 there was a great whirling around of nationalist alliances, with the unexpected result that Sinn Fein became the national front behind which all other organizations operated. On its own merits Sinn Fein was becoming more popular. In February a Sinn Fein candidate was returned for north Roscommon, and in May the Redmondite candidate at a by-election was defeated in a straight fight with a Sinn Fein candidate. That Sinn Fein deserved increased attention is evidenced by the endorsement of its program by several Irish newspapers. Then, at the instigation of Count Plunkett, a convention was convened in Dublin in April 1917 with the hope of forging a single nationalist front. The meeting was attended by representatives of over seventy groups. As one might predict from an acquaintance with the divergent strands comprising Irish nationalism, the convention delegates could not agree on a single program. But one positive result did come of the conference: the appointment of a "National Council" to plan future arrangements for coordinating nationalist activities. This National Council prepared a draft constitution for a pan-nationalist organization. Significantly, the new organization was to operate within the old shell of Sinn Fein. Hence, it was the Sinn Fein convention of November 1917 to which leaders from all the major nationalist groups, including the IRB, flocked.

This Sinn Fein convention was a troubled one for two reasons: the republicans were split among themselves about the proper position in the new movement of the IRB and its secret apparatus. Some, such as Michael Collins, preferred to continue working through the clandestine network, while others, like Cathal Brugha, felt that the time had come to work above ground with all those who sought the republic. The second rift was deeper. At one end of a spectrum were nationalists such as Arthur Griffith who would not promise to seek a republic and nothing else; at the other end, the more enthusiastic Fenians would settle for nothing less than Pearse's spiritual nation, pure and unsullied by the realities of the twentieth cen-

tury. The situation was all the more complicated because among
the republicans the two lines of disagreement intersected. For
example, Cathal Brugha was ideologically closer to pure republicanism than were the men of Michael Collins' camp, in
spite of the fact that Collins and his men clung to the IRB
apparatus while Brugha did not.

After considerable disagreement the solution was to eviscer-
ate Sinn Fein and to place a new compromise constitution
within the old Sinn Fein framework. The new constitution
was a masterpiece of concise vagueness. The aim of Sinn Fein
was declared to be the securing of international recognition of
Ireland as an independent republic. The right of the British
Parliament or crown to legislate for Ireland was denied, and
the use of any means to render impotent the power of Britain
to subjugate Ireland was condoned. But what was a republic?
No answer was given. The new Sinn Fein constitution declared: "Having achieved that status of Ireland's being recognized as an independent republic, the Irish people may by
referendum freely choose their own form of Government."
Thereafter, eleven clauses reaffirmed the resolutions of the Sinn
Fein convention of 1905 which described the system of economic protection that would be introduced by Sinn Fein
M.P.s, individuals who would take their seats not in the Imperial Parliament, but in an Irish parliament.

There was something here for everybody and just enough
imprecision to allow all sides to ignore the basic difference di-
viding Irish nationalism. While everyone said that an Irish
republic was the common goal, the provision for a referendum
after the republic was internationally recognized allowed everyone to maintain his own conception of what a republic actually
was. The apparent blessing on the use of physical force was a
concession making the new Sinn Fein constitution acceptable
to the diehard Fenians. On the other hand, the reiteration of
the old Sinn Fein program of withdrawing Irish members from
Westminster to form an Irish parliament and the reaffirmation
of the industrial protection program kept the moderates within
the fold.

But by itself a new Sinn Fein constitution was not enough to
create even the appearance of unity. A national leader was

needed. Eamon de Valera was perfect for the role. As one of the most competent military leaders of the Easter Rising he was respected by even the most extreme republicans. Because of his refusal to join the IRB he was trusted by the moderates. He was a man of dignity and presence, and as a speaker he combined sincere fervor with an ability to obscure issues behind rhetoric of the sort not heard in the British Isles since the passing of William Ewart Gladstone. De Valera's choice as president of Sinn Fein was as important as the drafting of the new Sinn Fein constitution for, as Cathal Brugha remarked, "Who else but Eamon de Valera could have kept Arthur Griffith and myself together?"

Before the new Sinn Fein could become truly effective it needed to broaden its base of support. David Lloyd George inadvertently did this for the Irish when in the spring of 1918 he introduced a Conscription Act making Irishmen liable for compulsory service in the United Kingdom military. This was the one move that would unite all sections of Irish nationalist opinion. Members of the Irish Parliamentary Party stomped out of Westminster and returned to Dublin to join the opposition. They joined with labor and Sinn Fein in a conference summoned by the Lord Mayor of Dublin. This Mansion House Conference denied the right of the United Kingdom government to impose compulsory military service on the Irish people against the general will of that people. The passing of the Conscription Act was regarded as an act of war upon the Irish nation, and Irishmen were called upon to resist by all means at their disposal. To this impressive degree of unity among laymen was added the backing of the Roman Catholic bishops, a surprising fact since most of the bishops had been unenthusiastic heretofore about the nationalist cause. The nationalists could only have been pleased to read the section of the bishops' manifesto that stated, "In view especially of the historical relations between the two countries from the very beginning up to this moment, we consider that conscription forced in this way upon Ireland is an oppressive and inhuman law, which the Irish people have a right to resist by every means that are consonant with the law of God." But the bishops then went on to explain what they meant by consonant with the law of God. They advised the people to attend more fervently to their religious duties and to secure domestic peace through a national novena in honor of Our Lady of Lourdes—hardly the thing the IRB had in mind. Instead, Sinn Fein and the parliamentary nationalists were drawn together with the election of Eamon de Valera as President of the Irish Volunteers. The IRB continued to have a strong independent influence on the Volunteers, but Sinn Fein and the Volunteers were united at least nominally.

Sinn Fein now was ready to move forward. The election of December 1918 was a golden opportunity. The truce between Sinn Fein and the Irish Parliamentary Party had proved to be temporary, and Sinn Fein went out to win seats at the price of their former allies. The Sinn Fein election manifesto was a mixture of the old pre-1917 Sinn Fein policy with a republican veneer. Sinn Fein, the manifesto said, aimed at establishing the republic through the withdrawal of Irish representatives from Westminster and by creating an Irish constituent assembly as the supreme national authority. The present Irish M.P.s, the manifesto flatly stated, stood in the way of that goal. In line with the Sinn Fein constitution of 1917 the manifesto promised an appeal to the Peace Conference at Versailles for its recognition of Ireland as an independent nation. Fervent republicans were kept happy by the affirmation that a republic—undefined as always—was the national goal and that every available means was to be used to render British rule nugatory. It was a splendid manifesto, and the election campaign was a success, even though the majority of Sinn Fein candidates were either in jail or fleeing arrest (the government had moved against Sinn Fein leaders in May). Seventy-three of the 105 Irish seats went to Sinn Fein, with the Irish Parliamentary Party maintaining only six. Sinn Fein appeared to have a national mandate.

Actually, the election results must be interpreted with greater caution than the distribution of parliamentary seats might indicate, for almost a third of the Irish electorate did not vote and only 47 percent of the votes cast were for Sinn Fein candidates. Many of these votes were not cast for the Sinn Fein program but against conscription. Eamon de Valera realized this and stated in the Dail (the self-established independent Irish legislature) that he interpreted the vote for Sinn Fein as a vote not "for a form of government so much, because we are not republican doctrinaires, but it was for Irish freedom and Irish independence, and it was obvious to everyone who considered the question that Irish independence could not be realized at the present time in any other way so suitably as through a republic." Sean O'Faolain has noted that those who voted for the republic in 1918 were not voting for a concrete political program but for a symbol. As a symbol the republic represented the opposite of everything wrong with the Irish situation. It was freedom and happiness and the land of saints and scholars all wrapped into one. Of course no real political constitution could live up to this symbol.

Dail Eireann, the new constituent assembly, first met on the seventh of January 1919 and almost immediately adopted a provisional constitution and declared itself to be the sovereign national government. In many respects the Dail's achievements were impressive. Its declared aim was to replace the United Kingdom administration with Irish governmental bodies. In the administration of justice, for example, this meant that by Dail decree courts were established throughout the country. At first they handled only civil matters, but later criminal proceedings also were conducted. In most areas the United Kingdom system of justice was supplanted and official courtrooms were vacant. Almost equally successful was the Dail program of local administration. After the election of 1920 most of the local administrative bodies were pledged to the Dail and refused to act as part of the United Kingdom administration. Instead, they constituted themselves Irish administrative bodies, responsible only to the Dail and to the electors. Two points are worth noting about this self-government campaign. The first is that most members of the Dail were under arrest orders by the United Kingdom government, and the Dail met only three times during 1920 and only four times the following year. Thus, the self-government campaign was not a master plan directed from the center, but a grassroots campaign. Second, it is easy to forget that there was nothing uniquely republican or Irish about the judicial and local government administrations which came under Dail auspices. Even when directed by republicans, affairs were conducted along lines determined by United Kingdom legal and governmental practice.

As for the Dail itself, its activities were more verbal than governmental. It published a declaration of independence, dispatched a message to the international Peace Conference, and drew up "Ireland's Democratic Programme," a document remarkable for its lack of specificity. Various Dail emissaries were sent to America to raise funds, the most interesting of these being Eamon de Valera.

Meanwhile, the republican army was in the field. After the Dail was established, each member of the former Irish Volunteers, which now was commonly known as the "Irish Republican Army," took an oath of allegiance to the republic as declared by the Dail. Despite this oath and the overlap of personnel between the Dail and the army, the IRA was not controlled by the Dail, which could not have restrained the activities of the extreme republicans even if it had wished to do so.

In 1920 the United Kingdom Parliament passed the Government of Ireland Act, usually known as the "Partition Act," separating northern from southern Ireland. In theory the southern republicans still were fighting the United Kingdom government for independence for a united Ireland, but in reality the battle now was for indigenous control of the southern three quarters of the country. Militarily a stalemate developed, the British Army being unable to put down the republicans and the republicans clearly unable to obtain a military victory. Finally, truce feelers were put out, the primary initiative coming from private individuals and from the United Kingdom government, which was increasingly anxious to have the Irish matter settled. Lloyd George and de Valera eventually met in July 1921. The truce they arranged became effective on 11 July 1921.

Lloyd George and de Valera now began negotiating about negotiations—that is, they began bargaining over the ground rules for arranging a two-nation treaty. These negotiations were important because a point given away in the preliminary negotiations could not easily be regained. A further reason for the importance of these preliminary negotiations is that they shed considerable light on the outlook and abilities of Eamon de Valera. In these preliminary bargainings, de Valera showed himself to be a skillful, resourceful, and very subtle negotiator. The letters between Lloyd George and de Valera, which we will examine below, clearly indicate that de Valera drove a much harder bargain than did his Welsh opponent—no small achievement. Indeed, the preliminary negotiations give one the rare pleasure of feeling somewhat sorry for the outmaneuvered Lloyd George. According to the British prime minister, arguing with de Valera was like chasing a man on a merry-go-round while seated on the horse behind him.

In approaching the correspondence between the two men we must continually bear in mind that we are viewing a game of collective bargaining. In this game each side consistently overstates its demands in order to obtain terms for which it will actually settle. Therefore, neither the proposals of de Valera nor of Lloyd George are to be taken literally, but must be interpreted as moves within the negotiation process. This caution, which is so obvious as to seem almost gratuitous, is necessitated by the tendency of certain republican historians to forget that bargaining proceeds by overstatement. If the demands in de Valera's bargaining process are read as policy statements of the Dail, rather than as cards played in the game with the United Kingdom, then the treaty between the two nations appears to be a break with the previous governmental policy. Actually, the treaty was a logical continuation of developments begun by de Valera in the summer of 1921, and the contents of the treaty were those which an external observer would have predicted given a knowledge of the de Valera–Lloyd George correspondence.

The post-truce correspondence began with a letter of 20 July 1921 which followed upon private conversations between Lloyd George and the Irish leaders. The letter from Lloyd George to de Valera was an outline of the United Kingdom's terms.

The fact that the British rather than the Irish had been forced to make the first substantial proposal was a point for the Irish. Moreover, even that initial action contained a massive concession to Ireland. The letter formally presented an offer that had only been briefly mooted previously, namely, that Ireland would be granted dominion status:

> By the adoption of a Dominion status it is understood that Ireland shall enjoy complete autonomy in taxation and finance; that she shall maintain her own courts of law and judges; that she shall maintain her own military forces for home defense, her own constabulary and her own police; that she shall take over the Irish postal services and all matters relating thereto, education, land, agriculture, mines and minerals, forestry, housing, labour, unemployment, transport, trade, public health, insurance and liquor traffic; and, in sum, that she shall exercise all those powers and privileges upon which the autonomy of the self-governing Dominions is based.

But the United Kingdom government had to protect its bargaining position. It therefore quickly added restrictions upon dominion status, allowing the term to remain but considerably restricting the meaning. Six provisos were added: first, that the Royal Navy would continue to control the seas around Ireland; second, that the Irish army should be roughly the same proportion as the military establishments of the other parts of the British Isles; third, that the Royal Air Force would have the use of Irish facilities; fourth, that voluntary recruitment for the United Kingdom Army would be permitted in Ireland; fifth, that free trade would exist between the United Kingdom and Ireland; sixth, that the Irish would assume a just share of the public debt of the United Kingdom as determined by an independent arbitrator.

Granted, each of these stipulations touched an area with which the United Kingdom government had a vital concern, but taken as a whole they should be viewed more as a move in the bargaining game than as demands the British expected to be fulfilled. If we assume for a moment that the most radical final solution the United Kingdom government would accept was dominion status for Ireland, then the reason for the stipulations becomes clear: if they offered dominion status without provisos as their first move, the natural process of compromise implicit in the negotiating process would force them to go beyond mere dominion status before the negotiations were concluded. On the other hand, if they offered dominion status with qualifications, the qualifications would probably have to be given up during the course of the negotiations, but the acceptable solution, dominion status, would remain.

Having allowed Lloyd George to make the first move, de Valera slapped his face. The proposals were rejected as self-contradictory, the principle behind them not being easy to determine. Naturally, the specific qualifications to dominion status were found unacceptable. But dominion status was not dismissed out of hand. In a very subtle passage de Valera declared:

> Dominion status for Ireland everyone who understands the conditions knows to be illusory. The freedom which the British Dominions enjoy is not so much the result of legal enactments or of treaties as of the immense distances which separate them from Britain, and have made interference by her impracticable. The most explicit guarantees, including the Dominions' acknowledged right to secede, would be necessary to secure for Ireland an equal degree of freedom. There is no suggestion, however, in the proposals made of any such guarantees.

Herein is the gist of de Valera's reply. In veiled diplomatic language he was offering a very broad hint that he would welcome a proposal of dominion status, without qualification, and with Ireland's right to secede from the Commonwealth specifically guaranteed.

Lloyd George understood the message, even if he did not yield to it, as indicated in his next letter, in which he countered: "We must direct your attention to one point upon which you lay some emphasis, and upon which no British Government

can compromise, namely, the claim that we should acknowledge
the right of Ireland to secede from her allegiance to the King.
No such right can ever be acknowledged by us."

The exchange continued, de Valera's position being in essence not a demand for the British recognition of the Irish
republic, but for acceptance of "the broad guiding principle
of government by the consent of the governed," and Lloyd
George's the position that "we can discuss no settlement which
involves a refusal on the part of Ireland to accept our invitation to free, equal, and loyal partnership in the British Commonwealth under our Sovereign." In reality the two positions
were very close, the only crucial difference being whether or not
the right of the governed to choose their own form of government included the right to repudiate allegiance to the crown.

De Valera remained cool, but Lloyd George was becoming
restless. Once again he was maneuvered by de Valera into
making a first move. In early September, Lloyd George wrote
that the correspondence had lasted long enough and invited a
definite reply "as to whether you are prepared to enter a conference to ascertain how the association of Ireland with the
community of nations known as the British Empire can best be
reconciled with Irish national aspirations. If, as we hope, your
answer is in the affirmative, I suggest that the conference should
meet at Inverness on the 20th instant." De Valera gave a quali-
fied acceptance, the qualification being his note that the Irish
representatives would be negotiating as representatives of an
independent and sovereign state. He was doing his best to have
things both ways, for acceptance of Lloyd George's invitation
implied that the Irish accepted a position within the British
Empire, and, undefined though that position was, it necessarily
implied some limitation on national independence. Lloyd
George was unnerved by de Valera's double shuffle and replied
that the Inverness arrangements had to be canceled. Later he
explained that recognition of Ireland as a sovereign state would
entitle her to belligerent status before the nations of the world
should the conference break off, and he again stated, "We
cannot consent to any abandonment, however informal, of the
principle of allegiance to the King, upon which the whole fab-

ric of the Empire and every constitution within it are based. It is fatal to that principle that your delegates in the conference should be there as the representatives of an independent and sovereign State. While you insist on claiming that, conference between us is impossible."

Harsh words from Lloyd George, but de Valera knew he had the Welshman well pinioned on the merry-go-round and that one more whirl would leave him completely off balance. He therefore gave the maddening reply that "I have only to say that we have already accepted your invitation in the exact words which you re-quote from your letter of the 7th instant. We have not asked you to abandon any principle, even informally, but surely you must understand that we can only recognise ourselves for what we are. If this self-recognition be made a reason for the cancellation of the conference, we regret it, but it seems inconsistent." In other words, while the Irish representatives agreed to work within a framework of the Empire that implied some limits on their sovereignty, they would think of themselves as representatives of a sovereign power, but without asking the British to recognize them as such. Lloyd George sputtered in reply that he and his colleagues would accept the Irish representatives as the chosen spokesmen of Ireland to discuss the association of Ireland with the British Commonwealth. He soon regained his composure and invited the Irish to negotiate, this time in London in October. The Irish accepted and made preparations for a conference whose purpose would be to determine "how the association of Ireland with the community of nations known as the British Empire may best be reconciled with Irish national aspirations."

What were the results of this most ungraceful, but entertaining, bartering between the United Kingdom and Irish nationalist leaders? In practical terms the victory was all de Valera's. As the price for getting the Irish even to sit down at the bargaining table, Lloyd George had to promise in advance to yield dominion status. He was not even able to force de Valera to give the six British stipulations more than passing notice. The United Kingdom prime minister soon gave up any discussion of these stipulations and had to settle for the subject of the association of Ireland and the Commonwealth—an association which implied none of the six stipulations. De Valera, it is clear, did an excellent and hard-headed job of gaining the maximum possible recognition of Ireland's right to govern her own affairs.

But disaster lurked. While gaining his practical victory, de Valera had to surrender on symbolic matters. The republic, in the sense of a government with no connections with the United Kingdom and no limits on its sovereignty, had to be sacrificed. The military situation dictated that the achievement of a pure republic was impossible. As a price for maximum freedom in the real world, de Valera had to surrender the theoretical republic. During the negotiations he did not mention the republic. He only pressed for the principle of the consent of the governed, a weak substitute. Indeed, the very existence of the Lloyd George–de Valera correspondence implied that a totally independent republic was not feasible, for if the republic was already in existence, as the Dail claimed, no negotiation was required.

The closest de Valera came to the pure republican position was to state that dominion status should explicitly guarantee the right to withdraw from the Commonwealth. This point Lloyd George rejected, and de Valera did not raise it again. In any event, it would have been a strange form of republic which needed a written guarantee from a foreign government stating that it had the right to become a republic. Most important, the agreement to center negotiations on the question of how Ireland would be associated with the Commonwealth was an admission by de Valera that total separation from the United Kingdom was not being demanded. It was taken for granted on both sides that Ireland would, in some as yet undefined way, remain a part of the Commonwealth. And the one point on which Lloyd George was unequivocal was that membership or association with the Commonwealth implied an allegiance to the crown.

With our knowledge of nationalist thought, it is easy to see the trouble ahead. With keen practicality, de Valera had laid the groundwork for a treaty with the United Kingdom which would give Ireland almost total control of her own affairs, but which would necessitate the abandonment of the symbol of the republic. Although an oath of allegiance and some kind of association with the Commonwealth might have little bearing on Irish government as it functioned day by day, it was an emotional pill the doctrinaire republicans would find hard to swallow. Trouble from the doctrinaire republicans was all the more likely because they had always known what they did not want in the way of an Irish government, but had rarely given serious thought to what they actually wanted. Given their mentality, it was inevitable that when specific treaty arrangements were made, they would not focus their attention upon the very real freedom provided by the new governmental machinery, but would stare fixedly at the limitations as embodied in dominion status and the oath of allegiance. There was thus a latent fissure in the nationalist movement. On the one side were the pragmatic republicans and the milder nationalists, and on the other were the doctrinaire republicans. This was a split that had been developing since the rivalry of the Fenians and the Parliamentary Party. It was a split between idealists and realists, between men who would protect the symbol of the republic whatever the price, and those who preferred peace and were satisfied with the everyday control over their own affairs even if their symbol were tarnished.

Unhappily for the Irish nationalists, the treaty negotiations with the United Kingdom government were as disastrous as the preliminary bargaining had been successful. The following men were sent to London: Arthur Griffith (Chairman), Michael Collins (Deputy Chairman), Robert Barton, E. J. Duggan, and George Gavan Duffy; Erskine Childers was selected as secretary. The fact that de Valera placed Griffith and Collins in charge of the delegation deserves more than passing notice. Before 1917, Griffith was a dual monarchist, and he made it clear before going to London that he would never break with Britain on the issue of loyalty to the crown. To Griffith allegiance to the crown was an acceptable part of a treaty. De Valera was fully aware of this fact but nevertheless placed him in charge. Given our knowledge of the preliminary correspondence conducted between de Valera and Lloyd George, it may be suggested that Griffith was chosen as head, not in spite of his willingness to compromise on the issue of allegiance to the crown, but partially because of it.

Michael Collins' presence was also important. Despite Collins' public image as a romantic and fanatic republican, he was a realist and recognized how weak the military resources of the cause were; Collins therefore was willing to compromise on the symbol of the republic in order to gain the substance of Irish freedom. Futher, the pragmatists were strengthened by exclusion as well as by inclusion. Neither Austin Stack, nor Cathal Brugha, the most doctrinaire republicans in the cabinet, was included in the delegation (admittedly both men were reluctant to have anything to do with the negotiations anyway).

There are only two ways to interpret de Valera's appointment of a delegation dominated by men of pragmatic mentality, men willing to compromise to attain lasting peace. One of these is that de Valera himself favored compromise and therefore appointed men who would negotiate in a way he himself desired. This interpretation meshes well with the evidence of the Lloyd George-de Valera correspondence, in which de Valera showed himself to be far from a doctrinaire republican. The other interpretation is that de Valera was playing some kind of demoniacally Machiavellian game; that he was using the negotiations as an instrument for besmirching the pragmatists, and that he would then march in and save the republic from the compromisers. The chief problem with this latter view is that the evidence—and again the Lloyd George–de Valera correspondence is crucial—indicates that de Valera himself was on record as willing to negotiate and compromise, and the record of the correspondence would inevitably tie him to the pragmatists whom he allegedly wished to ruin. Thus, we can forget the spy-novel implications and conclude that de Valera sent a delegation in control of the moderate and pragmatic men to negotiate with the British because he himself desired a solution such men would naturally negotiate.

Another point about the composition of the delegation is obvious but crucial, namely, that de Valera was not a member.

His determination not to head the delegation split the cabinet, and de Valera prevailed only by employing his own casting vote on the matter. Explanations for his refusal to serve on the negotiating team are legion, and most of them are plausible. However unclear the motives behind de Valera's refusal to join the team of negotiators, the effects were obvious. For one thing, his absence robbed the Irish delegation of the most experienced of Irish statesmen. De Valera was the only cabinet member with experience in the rugged diplomacy practiced by Lloyd George and company. He had already proved himself Lloyd George's equal in international bargaining. Certainly the United Kingdom cabinet must have been gratified to learn that their most formidable opponent was not going to enter the lists.

Yet another effect of de Valera's staying at home was to make possible the intra-Dail split on the treaty. If de Valera had headed the delegation with Collins and Griffith as his lieutenants, they would have held overwhelming power in the cabinet and in the Dail, and any treaty acceptable to them would have been instantly acceptable to the great majority. In the face of a united front by these three outstanding leaders, any opposition, from whatever source, probably would have been ineffective. Furthermore, by refusing to go to London, de Valera unwittingly cut himself off from any direct influence in shaping the constitutional structure of the new Ireland.

If de Valera did not take charge of the negotiations in person, he at least could have made certain that the delegates received explicit instructions about their role. But here he failed miserably. The powers and responsibilities of the delegates were defined in cloudy and self-contradictory terms, so that individual cabinet members could have conflicting views of the delegates' authority and each would have evidence to back his contention. Before leaving, the delegates received (1) tacit instructions dictated by de Valera's own position and the structure of the negotiating transactions; (2) explicit statements of their powers as plenipotentiaries stated in their diplomatic credentials; (3) equally explicit, but contradictory, cabinet instructions to guide their behavior; and (4) a copy of a document usually known as "Draft Treaty A," which was an outline of a treaty that would be acceptable to the cabinet. These initial instructions were supplemented by communications from Dublin during the course of the negotiations.

The diplomatic credentials of the delegates were explicit enough. They stated that the delegates were appointed "Envoys Plenipotentiary" from the government of the Republic of Ireland "to negotiate and conclude on behalf of Ireland with the representatives of His Britannic Majesty, King George V, a treaty or treaties of settlement, association and accommodation between Ireland and the community of nations known as the British Commonwealth." By definition a plenipotentiary has full power to transact business on behalf of another individual or group of individuals. The more extreme republican members of the Dail attempted to limit the power of the delegates, but de Valera himself insisted that the envoys' powers must be unrestricted. His argument resulted in the withdrawal of a resolution the intent of which was to restrict their authority.

But almost simultaneously with the issue of the official credentials and the public declarations that the delegates were indeed plenipotentiaries, de Valera issued a set of private instructions contradicting the credentials and his public declarations. These instructions declared, in the first place, that the plenipotentiaries had full power as defined in their credentials, but the remaining points of the instructions contradicted this first point as well as the content of the official credentials and de Valera's statements before the Dail. The delegates were instructed to keep the cabinet regularly informed of the progress of negotiations and, before any decision was reached on major questions, to dispatch such word to the cabinet and wait for a reply from the Dublin cabinet before making final commitments. Further, a complete text of the draft treaty was to be submitted to Dublin for approval before it was signed. In case of a break in negotiations, the text of the final Irish proposals before severance was to be submitted to Dublin for approval before being handed to the British.

Arthur Griffith declared that he would not accept these instructions as binding, and made it clear that he interpreted them only as guiding principles, not as mandatory practices. There is no evidence of de Valera's having disputed this point with him. Therefore, the Irish delegates left for London publicly charged with full responsibility for negotiating the treaty, but privately given a set of restrictions which clashed with their public instructions.

The only potentially useful marching order given the delegates was in the form of Draft Treaty A, already referred to, which, unfortunately, was so full of holes as to be almost valueless. The document left out more than it covered. It provided for British recognition of Ireland as a sovereign independent state but did not once use the word "republic." Matters concerning the structure of the Irish constitution were left to be drafted by Griffith, hardly an indication that a republic was contemplated. Drafting of provisions for Ulster were also left completely undefined and in Griffith's hands. The financial article was a blank check to be filled in by the Minister of Finance, and the trade article was to be left to the Minister of Economic Affairs to draft. In other words, aside from the implicit surrender of the republic through silence, the Dail cabinet did not know its mind about Ulster, and was totally up in the air on such crucial matters as the economic and financial relations of their new country. The only area in which significant proposals were made was that regarding the relationship of Ireland to the Commonwealth, and here Childers and de Valera spun out their scheme for "external association." Ireland was to be equal with the sovereign dominions, such as Canada, but somehow different. The best explanation is that while the dominions, in theory at least, granted the crown authority, an external association recognizes the crown as taking precedence without, however, granting it authority.

Clutching an incomplete draft treaty and confused by sets of instructions that clashed with their credentials, the delegates set off to face the strongest team of negotiators the British government could muster.

The chronology of the negotiations is deceptively simple. The Irish delegation arrived in London on 8 October. On the eleventh they met an impressive United Kingdom team consisting of David Lloyd George, Lord Birkenhead, Austin Chamberlain, Winston Churchill, Sir Worthington Evans, Sir Hamar Greenwood, and Sir Gordon Hewart. Negotiations proceeded slowly as the Irish gradually defined their position and dealt with the relatively uncontroversial topics of trade and finance. On 24 October the Irish delegation presented a memorandum based on Draft Treaty A, stating that Ireland's goal was not dominion status; but a republic was not mentioned. "On the one hand," the memorandum stated, "Ireland will consent to adhere for all purposes of agreed common concern to the League of Sovereign States associated and known as the British Commonwealth of Nations. On the other hand, Ireland calls upon Great Britain to renounce all claims to authority over Ireland and Irish affairs."

Negotiations continued, and de Valera was kept fully informed. In a subcommittee meeting on the twenty-fourth of October, Griffith showed himself amenable not only to external association but to a limited recognition of—although not allegiance to—the British crown. Apparently de Valera had somehow thought that the Irish, in associating themselves with the Commonwealth, would not have to recognize the head of that association. He therefore responded with a stiff note enjoining nonallegiance to the king (he said nothing about recognition). The delegation bridled, claiming that he was trying to limit their negotiating powers, to which he replied that his note was not an order but a presentation of cabinet views.

On 2 November the entire delegation signed a note attesting to their willingness to recognize the crown "as head of the proposed Association of Free States." The British handed in a draft treaty on 16 November. The Irish countered with a draft memorandum of their own on the twenty-second. The British document afforded dominion status; the Irish draft stuck to external association. In late November the Irish delegation returned to Dublin.

Suddenly, the British made a brilliant tactical concession. They offered to allow the Irish to insert any phrase they wished into the treaty to insure that the position of the crown in Ireland would be no more in practice than it was in Canada or any of the other dominions. This offer caught the Irish off balance, since they had been arguing against dominion status on the basis that the United Kingdom team was offering them the name of dominion status but were hedging it with practical restrictions. Here was an explicit guarantee that the power of the crown in Ireland would be limited to the almost purely symbolic position it occupied in Canada.

The befuddled Irish returned to London to be handed, on 1 December, a detailed draft treaty by the British delegates. Ireland was offered full and unfettered dominion status as it existed in Canada, the most constitutionally advanced of all the dominions. In practice the only significant limitations on Irish sovereignty were that United Kingdom forces were to have access to Irish harbors for defense purposes, that the size of the Irish military forces was to be limited to proportional equality with that of the other countries in the British Isles, and that the crown should be represented in Ireland by a governor-general whose appointment and duties would be the same as those of the governor-general of Canada.

All this was a considerable British concession. But there remained the question of the oath, which was a matter of symbol and therefore harder to deal with than questions of reality. The oath to be taken by members of Parliament was to be as follows:

> I . . . solemnly swear to bear true faith and allegiance to the Constitution of the Irish Free State; to the Community of Nations, known as the British Empire; and to the King as Head of the State and of Empire.

De Valera and his cabinet now had to face some hard decisions that they had heretofore avoided. The delegation returned to Dublin divided in counsel. Arthur Griffith and Eamon Dugan were convinced that the issues of allegiance to the crown and the distinctions between dominion status and external association were too abstract to warrant a renewed war. Collins was not ready to make a final decision, although he approved of the English proposals generally. Duffy and Barton opposed acceptance as did de Valera and a majority of the Dail cabinet. De

Valera wanted the following oath inserted in place of the one proposed by the British:

> I . . . do solemnly swear true faith and allegiance to the Constitution of the Irish Free State, to the Treaty of Association and to recognize the King of Great Britain as head of the Associated States.

But the confused delegates were still split among themselves and as a group did not receive precise instructions from the cabinet on exactly what was expected of them in London. Collins is reported to have complained on the way to the docks, returning to London after the cabinet meeting, "I've been there all day and I can't get them to say Yes or No, whether we should sign or not." Barton and Duffy believed the cabinet wanted them to make another attempt to achieve external association, while Collins and Griffith were equally convinced that this was not the case. Robert Barton pleaded with de Valera to accompany the expedition, but he adamantly refused.

In such a situation it was child's play for Lloyd George to split the delegation, play on their weaknesses, and browbeat them into signing a treaty which was certainly less than a united, confident, Irish negotiating team would have obtained. The Irish delegates signed the treaty on 6 December 1921, without reference to Dublin.

Before discussing the specific content of the treaty it is crucial to realize what the treaty was not. As signed by the delegates it was *not* binding. It had to be ratified by the Dail (as well as by the United Kingdom Parliament). Anyone who did not approve of it or of any specific article had only to garner a majority in the Dail to have either the entire treaty rejected or the offending article struck. Nevertheless, in fairness to those opposed to the treaty, it must be added that although it was not binding until ratified by the Dail, the weight of events was stacked strongly behind the pro-treaty party, since there always was the implicit danger that a rejection of the treaty would result in renewed hostilities with the United Kingdom.

A second thing the treaty was not: it was not the formal constitution of the Irish Free State. The treaty would serve as the foundation for the constitution, but the specific frame of government was to be shaped later. This point is crucial if we are to understand later events, because Michael Collins and others felt that they would have a chance to nullify offensive articles of the treaty through the constitution which they would create. This fact goes a long way toward explaining why Collins supported the treaty so vigorously: he did not believe it was a final settlement, but merely a step toward a more satisfactory arrangement to be embodied in the constitution.

The treaty—or more properly the "articles of agreement for a treaty"— began by defining Ireland's constitutional status. It was to be the same as that of Canada, Australia, New Zealand, and South Africa—in other words, dominion status. The word "republic" was not employed. The new Ireland was to be called the "Irish Free State."

But whatever the name, it was to be a dominion and not a republic. As a dominion, however, Ireland was to be considerably in advance of the other dominions from the constitutional point of view, since its position was stated in law while the others' independence was established only by practice. Specifically, the basic status of the Irish Free State was to be that of the Dominion of Canada, generally regarded as the most independent of the dominions. Like Canada, the Free State was to have a resident representative of the crown in the form of a governor-general. In point of fact, Ireland was granted full self-government. Its internal sovereignty was guaranteed. Canadian practice meant that the Irish Parliament would have unrestricted legislative autonomy, and, in accordance with the recent concession of full diplomatic status to the dominions, the Free State would have the right to conclude its own treaties with foreign governments, and would not be associated in any treaties signed by the British Parliament, nor be obliged to participate in any British war unless specifically approved by the Irish Parliament.

The obligations of the Irish government to the United Kingdom were few. The most important symbolically, but least sig-

nificant in terms of the day-to-day conduct of Irish affairs, was
the requirement that an oath be taken by members of the Free
State's Parliament:

> I . . . do solemnly swear true faith and allegiance to the
> Constitution of the Irish Free State as by law established and
> that I will be faithful to H. M. King George V, his heirs
> and successors by law, in virtue of the common citizenship
> of Ireland with Great Britain and her adherence to and
> membership of the group of nations forming the British
> Commonwealth of Nations.

The oath is an interesting compromise between Irish and United
Kingdom positions. The Irish clearly gave up the idea of recognizing the king only as head of the association of states of
which Ireland was to be an external member, and were forced
to withdraw their objections to common citizenship. On the
other hand, it is easy to forget that the oath was a significant
deviation from that taken in the Imperial Parliament and by
M.P.s in the dominions. In those cases, the M.P.s took an oath
of unqualified allegiance to the king, whereas faith and allegiance in the Irish oath was to be given only to the Constitution
of the Irish Free State; only faithfulness was to be sworn to
the king.

The other sphere in which the Irish Free State's freedom of
action was to be significantly limited by the treaty was in military matters. Until arrangements could be made for the Free
State to provide for its own coastal defense, the British Navy
was to continue to defend Irish coastlines. In peace time United
Kingdom forces were to be allowed to keep harbor facilities
at Berehaven, Queenstown (Cobh), Belfast Lough, and Lough
Swilly, as well as coastal defense airfields. In wartime, or periods
"of strained relations" with a foreign power, the United Kingdom was to have access to other facilities it might require.
This proviso meant that although Ireland might remain neutral
in a future war, it was effectively impossible for her to give
comfort to Britain's enemy; indeed, the use of its harbors and
soil would almost inevitably link her with the United King-

dom's diplomatic and military position despite any Irish desire for neutrality.

Although most nationalist Irishmen would have rejected the idea, it now was inevitable that the Ulster solution would leave the country divided. This had been decided in 1914 when the Home Rule Act was suspended, and only through military force would it have been possible to force Ulster to accept an all-Ireland government. Yet the treaty team seems to have let wishful thinking get the better of its judgment and accepted a scheme which Lloyd George said would provide a good chance of uniting Ulster and the south. These arrangements were found in Articles 11–17 of the treaty. Until one month after Parliament passed the act ratifying the agreement, the Government of Ireland Act of 1920 (the Partition Act) would remain in force in the north. If, in that month, the Ulster Parliament formally rejected a union with the rest of the country, the Act of 1920 would remain effective for the north. A boundary commission would be set up to determine: "in accordance with the wishes of the inhabitants, so far as may be compatible for economic and geographical conditions, the boundaries between Northern Ireland and the rest of Ireland." Each of the governments concerned—Northern Ireland, the Irish Free State, and Great Britain—was to appoint one commissioner.

News of the delegates' signing the treaty was published on the morning of 6 December 1921, and that night Eamon de Valera saw it for the first time. On the eighth the cabinet met. It split. Collins, Griffith, Cosgrave, and Barton were for the treaty, de Valera, Brugha, and Stack against. The following morning de Valera published a letter to the Irish people, stating that "the terms of this agreement are in violent conflict with the wishes of the majority of this nation as expressed freely in successive elections during the past three years. I feel it my duty to inform you immediately that I cannot recommend the acceptance of the Treaty, either to Dail Eireann or to the country." The Dail was convened to pass verdict on the agreement.

Why de Valera refused to accept the treaty remains a mystery to the present day, despite scores of attempts at explanation: certainly not because he was a doctrinaire republican and certainly not because he was opposed to some kind of compromise with the United Kingdom. Personal factors clearly played a large part, but in exactly what way is uncertain. In any case, de Valera and Erskine Childers spent the night before the Dail meeting of 14 December hurriedly writing an alternative to the treaty, usually referred to as "Document No. 2" to distinguish it from the first document, the Anglo-Irish treaty. Significantly, the word "republic" was not mentioned in Document No. 2, and by no stretch of the imagination could its proposals be considered as a demand for a republic. Instead, the idea of external association was propounded. Ireland should not be part of the Commonwealth, but associated with it. No oath to the king should be taken by members of the Irish Parliament. There should be no governor-general as the crown representative in Ireland.

In general, however, Document No. 2's departures from the Anglo-Irish treaty were more apparent than real. The London agreement was tied to the prevailing practice in Canada under which the crown had no practical rights of interference in everyday governmental business, and Ireland would be no more free under external association than under dominion status. The only practical ways in which the London treaty and Document No. 2 differed were that the latter limited to five years British access to Irish harbors for military purposes and essentially ignored the Ulster problem, stating that Ireland was prepared to give the north privileges and safeguards no less substantial than those provided in the London treaty. Not without justice the contemporary press described the difference between the Anglo-Irish Treaty and Document No. 2 as the difference between Tweedledee and Tweedledum.

Dail Eireann assembled on 14 December 1921. The details of the session will not detain us, but three points are worth noting. The first is that the concept of the republic played a surprisingly small part in the discussions. Most members focused their attention on the oath of allegiance and on the exclusion of Ulster. Second, de Valera got nowhere with his Document No. 2. Eventually he withdrew it, stating that its contents should be kept confidential; he made strenuous, but unsuccessful, efforts to collect all existing copies. Third, the tone of those debates of which there is public record was bitter, vindictive, and divisive almost to the point of violence. The climactic moment came on 7 January 1922 when the vote on the Treaty was taken. The speaker announced the decision: "The result of the poll was sixty-four for approval and fifty-seven against, a majority of seven in favour of approval of the treaty."

De Valera resigned as president the next day and was narrowly defeated when proposed for re-election. Arthur Griffith was elected as the new president of Dail Eireann, an ironic twist, since de Valera had replaced him as president of Sinn Fein in 1917. Michael Collins was chosen president of the Provisional Government of Ireland, the legal body to which the United Kingdom would transfer control of Southern Ireland's affairs.

At this point most accounts of Irish history during the 1920's jump to the civil war, a great mistake since the first six months of 1922 were filled with feverish albeit near-secret activity aimed at heading off the conflict. This activity centered on the drafting of the new constitution for the Free State. If the leaders of the Provisional Government could draft a document sufficiently radical to detach de Valera and his followers from the extreme republicans, civil war would be avoided, because the combined powers of Collins, Griffith, and de Valera would overwhelm any opposition. But the new constitution also had to be acceptable to the United Kingdom government. The extremely difficult task of threading the constitutional needle, of obtaining the approval both of the British and the de Valera faction, fell to the head of the Provisional Government, Michael Collins.

In late January, Collins appointed a drafting committee. He was the titular chairman, but in the actual event he was so busy with other preparations for the transfer of power from London to Dublin that in its early stages the committee acted by itself. His instructions, however, were clear. The committee was to proceed from an Irish viewpoint and produce a short, simple document which would stand independently of the Anglo-Irish Treaty.

Because the framing of the constitution was as much a diplomatic as a legal exercise, Collins had to obtain room for his committee to maneuver. On the one flank he dealt with the British. If his committee was to produce the kind of independent constitution he wanted, Collins had to induce the United Kingdom government to ratify the Anglo-Irish Treaty before it saw the constitution. But when he approached Lloyd George with the request for ratification he was turned down. Collins cannily responded by implying that his government might fall unless the treaty were ratified, and thereupon Lloyd George gave in, with the specific proviso that the final draft constitution would be shown to the British cabinet before it was made public. Collins agreed, and the Westminster Parliament ratified the treaty which received the Royal Assent on 31 March, 1921.

Next, Collins cleared the other flank by coming to an agreement with de Valera postponing the scheduled general election for three months and agreeing that the new constitution would be published before the polling took place. The committee went to work, and although the nature of the American presidential system precluded a direct application of American precedents to a country steeped in the British style of democracy, the United States' influence in drafting the constitution was clear. C. J. France, a lawyer from Seattle, was a member of the committee. Two other members, James Douglas and James MacNeill, had served together with France on the Irish White Cross, a civilian relief agency created to funnel American funds to Ireland. Kevin O'Sheil, another member, had written a book on the framing of the Constitution of the United States.

Despite the care with which Collins had chosen his drafting committee its members fell to squabbling among themselves, with the result that in mid-March Collins was handed not one draft constitution, but three. Thus, the whole matter was back on his shoulders, and it was not until mid-May that he was nearly done conflating his final draft constitution. In mid-May one of the most enigmatic events in the history of the period occurred: the announcement of the "Collins-de Valera" pact. The public version of the pact, which was approved unanimously by the Dail, provided that the general election scheduled for mid-June would be an "agreed election" that would result in a coalition cabinet consisting of five pro- and four anti-treaty ministers. Despite its specificity this agreement must be described as enigmatic because it is probable (although by no means certain) that it was predicated upon some kind of agreement about the nature of the constitution Collins was to present to the British.

In any event, the pact was catalytic. The United Kingdom cabinet viewed it as the first step in the repudiation by the Irish Provisional Government of the Anglo-Irish Treaty arrangements and demanded an immediate explanation. Collins' attempt at explanation led almost at once to his presenting to the British cabinet the final version of the draft constitution of the Irish Free State.

The constitution was handed to the British on Saturday, 27 May, and by Monday the twenty-ninth the United Kingdom cabinet had prepared a memorandum summarizing its objections. The British, it became clear, were not going to accept the proposed constitution. Why not? The fundamental point, they held, was that Collins' draft violated the provisions of the Anglo-Irish Treaty and was well outside of dominion precedents. The Irish draft declared that Irish sovereignty rested in the people of Ireland and made no mention of the crown. The draft's complicated arrangement for an executive council (cabinet) seemed to allow certain members of the Free State government to avoid taking the oath of allegiance to the crown. Further, the draft's judicial provisions gave ultimate appellate jurisdiction to the proposed Irish Supreme Court and not to the United Kingdom Privy Council, and the section on foreign relations seemed to give Ireland complete control of all aspects of its foreign relations. Michael Collins, in other words, had produced a constitution which, although not republican, would satisfy the demands of all but the extreme minority of Irish nationalists.

But it certainly would not satisfy the British. Lloyd George entertained no suggestion of compromise. Instead, he flatly demanded that the constitution be redrafted to fit the United Kingdom view of the treaty. Once again the Irish broke under pressure: on 3 June they promised to amend their constitution to fit within the treaty. Years later Winston Churchill, who had been closely involved with breaking the Irish, wrote that "the form of the constitution to which the Free State leaders had agreed, was such as to preclude Mr. de Valera and his followers from sharing in the Government. A pernicious duality in the Executive was thus avoided." Which is to say that a civil war in Ireland now was inevitable.

On 14 June, two days before the general election was to take place, Michael Collins told his constituents that he was no longer bound by the pact with de Valera. The final version of the draft constitution was published two days later on election morning, and the pro-treaty bloc won overwhelming control of the legislature.

At this juncture the militants among the anti-treaty phalanx, who had been champing at the bit for months, broke free of political restraints. On their side the men with the guns, not the politicians, were once again making the running. The anti-treaty militants (who preferred to be called "republicans" and whom the government soon was to call as "irregulars") seized the Four Courts buildings in Dublin, and the provisional government decided to attack if the insurgent garrison did not surrender by four o'clock on 28 June. When no white flag was hoisted, the government bombarded it into submission. By so doing they forced many previously moderate anti-treaty politicians into the arms of those who violently opposed the new regime. Among those men was Eamon de Valera.

Irish nationalists now fought each other. Men who had been comrades in arms only short months earlier now hunted and ambushed each other. The civil war ended in mid-1923 with the new government firmly in control, the opposition crushed. As a military sequence it is of scant interest, but as a social trauma its effects were incalculable. The scars it left are still visible upon Ireland's countenance.

V The Creation of Northern Ireland

The government of Northern Ireland has been so controversial that few Irish-Americans and fewer native Irishmen are without opinions about it, the fervor of which usually exceeds their insight. This is a great shame, for the events leading to the establishment of the northern government must be viewed dispassionately if one is to draw any valid conclusions. The point at issue here is not *whether* the northern government should exist but *how* it came to exist. Viewed coolly, the course of events leading to the partition of Ireland had a certain logic, indeed almost a predictability. Long-term historical trends, not individual conspiracy, were at the heart of the matter.

Merely because two areas are geographically contiguous does not mean that they must be culturally merged or geopolitically united (the coexistence of Canada, the United States, and Mexico on the North American Continent illustrates both these points). Ulster always has been distinct from the rest of Ireland. Southern Ulster is separated from the rest of the country by a line of drumlins, low mountains, and lakes, reinforced in earlier times by forests. After the Norman conquest Ulster was the province least permeated by foreign influence and most Celtic in its social organization and culture. The line of forests and mountains served as a frontier between the Anglo-Norman culture of the Pale and the Celtic culture of Ulster. Sporadically, the English tried to subdue the Ulstermen, but they achieved only humiliating defeats and meaningless victories. Aside from a few coastal settlements, most notably Carrickfergus, the Dublin authorities were forced to recognize Ulster as a troublesome native preserve. Long after most of Ireland was at least partially Anglicized, the great Celtic princes, especially the O'Neills, headed a vigorous and proud Celtic society.

All this changed radically in the decade after 1603. In that year the last great Celtic prince, Hugh O'Neill, Earl of Tyrone, surrendered to Lord Mountjoy, the English Lord Deputy of Ireland. This event marked a watershed in Irish history: the last of the independent Irish princes was subdued, and the links between Spain, the Counter Reformation, and Ulster, which had so bedeviled Elizabethan statesmen, were broken. England could now settle matters in Ireland permanently, or so it seemed. As the first step in this settlement the English government pardoned both O'Neill and his ally, Rory O'Donnell, and allowed the former to keep his English-style title of Earl of Tyrone and gave the latter the rank of Earl of Tyrconnell. Most of the Irish chiefs were pardoned and allowed to keep their lands, but they, like Tyrone and Tyrconnell, were granted the lands not as Irish chiefs but under new rules which converted them into English-style landlords; the superseding of the Irish system of land tenure by the English system rapidly undercut the Celtic social system.

Then, in August 1607, occurred one of the strangest events in Irish history. Humiliated by the continuing decline of their influence, and fearful of further harassment by the government, the Earls of Tyrone and Tyrconnell and nearly one hundred petty chiefs boarded a boat in Lough Swilly and fled to the Continent. In one brief moment the native Irish leadership of Ulster disappeared, and the province was left open to English manipulation. The Dublin authorities were quick to realize the possibilities and treated the earls' departure as evidence of treason. The crown thereupon seized all lands which had been under the control of the departed chiefs. Most of what are now the counties of Armagh, Cavan, Donegal, Fermanagh, Londonderry, and Tyrone were confiscated.

The Dublin and London authorities set to work at once to frame a scheme for the colonization, or "plantation" of Ulster. The scheme, which went into operation in 1610, was uneven and erratic in implementation. It may be summarized as follows. The confiscated lands in the six escheated counties were granted to individuals and groups whose duty it was to form British colonies. The most important single colonizing effort was

that made by the City of London Company, which agreed as a
financial speculation, to colonize what is now the County of
Londonderry and to rebuild the towns of Coleraine and Derry.
Most of the remaining five counties was parceled out to "undertakers," who undertook to colonize a given amount of land and
to build villages and fortified enclosures in return for title to
their lands. A relatively small amount of land was reserved for
Irish natives whose loyalty was certain and who promised to
adopt English social and agricultural customs. Originally, the
London Company and the other undertakers were required to
remove the native Irish from the land under colonization and
to bring in British settlers. However, although considerable
numbers of English and Scottish colonists were induced to migrate to Ulster, it was economically advantageous for the undertakers to allow large numbers of the native Irish to remain
as tenants, intermixed with the Scottish and English immigrants.

At this point we should note that simultaneously in the
counties of Antrim and Down, which had not been affected by
the confiscations, an influx of Scottish migrants was occurring.
At the nearest point, Scotland lies only thirteen miles from the
Antrim coast, and there had been since earliest recorded times
relations between the inhabitants of Scotland and the Antrim
coast. Now, after James VI of Scotland assumed the English
throne as James I of England, a number of aggressive Scottish
lords took the opportunity to begin private plantation ventures
in Antrim and Down and to a much lesser extent in Monaghan.
The two leaders of this movement were Hugh Montgomery
and James Hamilton, who acquired 40,000 acres from Con
O'Neill by securing a pardon for him on a charge of suspected
treason. They then proceeded to gull O'Neill out of most of
the remaining 20,000 acres he still held. Into their newly gained
land Hamilton and Montgomery introduced lowland Scots as
colonists. Other Scots lairds tried similar private ventures, and
soon Antrim and Down seemed more Scottish than Irish.

When we aggregate the plantation of Ulster and the immigration of lowland Scots to Antrim and Down it becomes clear
that overnight a radical transformation had occurred in the

Ulster social structure. Prior to 1603 Ulster had been a cohesive, independent bastion of Celtic culture. A decade later the province was characterized by a tripartite social division. One of these segments comprised the native Irish who had, until 1603, owned almost all the land and who had lived according to political and social customs which antedated the Norman invasions. These people were suddenly transformed into the lowest of tenantry. They held only the poorest land. The size of their landholdings was drastically reduced. The native Irish were leaderless, for their chiefs had fled. As the old Celtic social system crumbled, they held desperately to the one remaining badge of their identity, the Roman Catholic faith. The second group was the lowland Scots. The Scots dominated the counties of Antrim and Down, which they independently colonized, and among the planted colonies they comprised the majority of colonists in Donegal and Tyrone and a portion in Fermanagh and Cavan. The Scots were Presbyterians and were uncompromising in their religious beliefs. The third group was the English. Most of the original undertakers of the planted colonies were English, and therefore the Ulster upper classes were chiefly English in origin. There were, in addition, a considerable number of settlers brought from England who formed the bulk of the colonial population in Fermanagh and Cavan. The great majority of the English colonists were Episcopalians. Thus, in the early seventeenth century there was formed the social structure which characterizes Ulster to the present day. Racial (or if one prefers, national) background became nearly synonymous with religious preference. Even today, one is usually correct if one assumes that in Northern Ireland a person with an English surname is Anglican, a Scots name Presbyterian, and an Irish name Roman Catholic.

These were not merely religio-national distinctions; these were lines of hatred which were etched deeper with the passage of time. The Roman Catholics, understandably embittered at losing their patrimony to the conquerors, were constantly on the verge of rebelling against their masters. Twice, in 1641 and in 1689, the Catholics in Ireland rose, and foremost among them were the Ulster Catholics. Both times they were beaten

down. Both times more of their remaining lands were taken
from them. Worse yet, during the first third of the eighteenth
century the Irish Parliament, composed solely of Protestants,
framed a penal code which hampered the Catholics in the
practice of their religion, in the pursuit of education, and in
the practice of any livelihood other than the humblest tenant
farming. During the course of the century the Catholics lost
most of what little land in Ulster remained to them, partially
through continued confiscation and partially through Catholic
landowners turning Protestant in order to preserve their
landholdings.

The Presbyterians and the Episcopalians regarded the
Catholics with hatred equal to that of the Catholics for the
Protestants; that is obvious. What is not so obvious is that
during the seventeenth and eighteenth centuries many of the
Episcopalians and the Presbyterians bitterly disliked each other.
The Presbyterians, by and large, viewed the Established Church
as religiously moribund and tinged with Romanist elements.
The Anglicans, on the other hand, saw the Presbyterians as
Dissenters. In Ulster during the seventeenth century there were
clashes between Anglican bishops and Presbyterian ministers,
precipitated by the seizure by Presbyterian pastors of Anglican
benefices which were unoccupied because of the inefficiency
of the Established Church. Friction was especially rife during
the 1630's when the High Church policy of Archbishop Laud
in England led to a similar High Church regime in Ireland.
In the eighteenth century the Presbyterians were embittered
because of their inclusion under the terms of the Test Act of
1704, a penal measure designed to prevent non-Anglicans from
holding civil office. The Presbyterians were outraged; they had
fought loyally in 1689–90 against the Jacobite-Catholic threat,
only to be excluded from the spoils of victory.

The event which brought the Episcopalians and the Presbyterians into alliance—and thereby realigned Irish religious
divisions into the Catholic–Protestant split which prevails today
—was the rising of 1798. Under the combined influence of
Irish patriotism, French Jacobinism, anti-Protestantism, and
wracking poverty, the Irish Catholic peasantry revolted. The

rising in Ulster was not so serious as that in Leinster, and its leadership included several Protestants, but the effect was traumatic nonetheless. Most Presbyterians and Episcopalians concluded that, Protestant involvement in the rising notwithstanding, the real enemy was the Catholics and that their mutual differences were unimportant in the face of this enemy.

The Act of Union of 1800, which was the consequence of the '98 rising, was designed to preclude forever a Roman Catholic coup by merging the government of Ireland with that of Great Britain. On 1 January 1801 the government of Ireland ceased to exist and the United Kingdom came into being. The maintenance of the Union with Britain continues to lie at the heart of Ulster politics.

Implicit in the process of uniting Presbyterians and Episcopalians was a change of capital importance in the collective character of Irish Presbyterianism. Before 1798 many Irish Presbyterians had politically been radical. The democratic structure of the Presbyterian faith had been conducive to the development of demands for political democracy. The Presbyterians had been favorable to the cause of American independence. But after 1798, and the subsequent Act of Union, the Presbyterians did an about-face and, like the Anglicans, centered their attention on preserving the position of Protestants. The Catholic emancipation movement of the 1820's, and the repeal movement of the 1840's only served to reinforce the Presbyterians' fear of the Catholics and to convince them of the need to maintain the Union, which they believed protected them from Catholic domination.

During the 1790's an organization developed that was to be crucial to the Protestant defense of the Union with Great Britain. This was the Orange Order, formed in 1795 in the county Armagh, following a party fight between Catholics and Protestants (usually known as "the Battle of the Diamond"). At first the movement comprised chiefly lower-class Protestant farmers, but it spread quickly, and this growth coincided with the increasing desire of the Dublin authorities to establish a dependable militia in the north. The government allowed whole lodges of Orangemen to be co-opted into the yeomanry and

thus clothed this aggressively Protestant society with legal legitimacy. Simultaneously, the Orange Order received social legitimacy, for the officers of the yeomanry in most localities were
the Protestant gentry. The existence of a large band of organized
loyal yeomanry guaranteed that the 1798 rising had no chance
of success in Ulster. After the rising was suppressed, however,
the government had no use for the Orangemen, and the energy
and unity of the order declined. Eventually, in 1836, the original Orange Order was dissolved under government pressure, a
remnant going underground. But the memory of the Orange
system remained, and when, in the 1880's, Ulstermen were
threatened by the First Home Rule Bill, they quickly revived
the order. This time, the order had middle- to upper-class backing from the start. Initially the revived order served as an
efficient ward-level political machine. Always, of course, there
was the possibility of converting the machine to paramilitary
uses.

The three themes dominating Ulster's political history during
the nineteenth century were, first, the removal of the remaining causes of friction between the Episcopalians and Presbyterians. The disestablishment of the Church of Ireland in 1871
removed the last Presbyterian complaint against the Anglicans.
Second, this increasingly united Protestant phalanx remained
wholeheartedly and uncompromisingly opposed to repeal of the
Union with Great Britain. In practice this meant that Ulster,
unlike the rest of Ireland, supported the Conservative rather
than the Liberal party. Indeed, after the appearance of Gladstone's two Home Rule Bills in 1886 and 1893, the terms "tory,"
"conservative," and "unionist" became synonymous. The third
signal characteristic of Ulster politics in the nineteenth century
was the adhesion of the Catholic minority to, first, the Liberal
party and, later, the Irish Nationalist party as led by Charles
Stewart Parnell.

As much because of political necessity as because of principle,
the Tory party found itself pledged to unswerving unionism.
In the complex alliance of Tory groups the impact of the
Ulster unionist forces was much greater than their mere numbers would seem to justify. In the period just preceding the

introduction of the Third Home Rule Bill, the Tory alliance was composed of three elements. By far the largest component was the British conservative block, a body of men believing in the maintenance of the Union, but increasingly willing to compromise if necessary. The second element comprised southern Irish unionists, and the third, Ulster unionists. During the years immediately following the Liberal party's election victory of 1906 the viewpoint of the two Irish unionist groups came to dominate conservative thinking. One reason for this was that the unionists developed effective propaganda agencies whose services were in constant demand by British conservative associations, with the result that the unionist cause became an integral part of conservative political thinking. The other reason why unionism was so important to the Conservative party was that it was one of the few things upon which all wings of the party could agree. Thus, the political power of the Irish unionists was considerably magnified.

So bluff and truculent were many Ulster unionist leaders that it is easy to forget that Ulster unionism was born of fear, not of aggressiveness. It was a defensive reaction to the imagined horrors of living under a Roman Catholic government in a state which would be industrially backward and, in all probability, economically isolationist. If we examine these three fears, it becomes clear that they were not without substance. (Whether or not they were sufficiently substantial to justify the Ulster Unionists' activities is a question the reader will have to decide for himself.) First, note that an important strand in Irish nationalist thinking was that Ireland should become economically self-sufficient, and second, that the northeast part of Ulster was the only part of Ireland which had undergone the industrial revolution and which was tied into the international economic network created by that revolution. Hence, nationalist propaganda about economic self-sufficiency presented the Ulstermen not only with the prospect of being severely hurt economically through severance of their ties with industrial Britain, but also of becoming the economic dray-ox expected to pull the economically primitive remainder of the country in its van. Third, given the information with which they had to deal, the Ulster unionists (meaning Ulster Protestants) were not entirely irrational in concluding that they would be badly off in a Catholic-dominated Ireland. During the latter half of the nineteenth and early twentieth centuries the Catholic Church in Ireland and throughout the world had become increasingly aggressive on certain matters of concern to Protestant groups, especially on education, mixed marriages, and church-state relations. Moreover, one school of Irish nationalist thought formulated an equation of Irish nationalism with Irish Catholicism, a blend which was made all the more repugnant to the Anglophilic unionists when other nationalists added the Gaelic language to the equation. All this is not to say that the Protestant unionists would have done badly in an independent Catholic Ireland (personally, I think they were strong enough to defend their own interests) but that their fears were not solely a function of anti-Catholic prejudice and were in part a result of the religious events and nationalist rhetoric of the period.

Until the events of 1912–14 it was not clear precisely how strongly the Ulster Protestants felt about maintaining the Union. By late 1912 it was obvious that political tactics would fail and that the Third Home Rule Bill would become law. The Ulster Protestants thereupon decided to go beyond the bounds of conventional behavior and to introduce paramilitary tactics. As early as September 1911, 50,000 men representing the Orange Order and the Unionist Clubs had marched past the home of the Protestant leader Captain James Craig in a show of anti-Home Rule solidarity. "Home Rule is Rome Rule" epitomized Protestant beliefs. In September 1912 the Ulster Protestants were brought to a high pitch of excitement with the introduction of the Ulster Covenant. From a legal viewpoint the Covenant was a distinctly treasonable document. Its signers swore to use all means necessary to defeat the "conspiracy to set up a Home Rule Parliament in Ireland." Nearly half a million men and women signed the document. Throughout Protestant Ulster, companies were formed to hold regular military drills, using firearms whenever available. Early in 1913 the disparate paramilitary bodies were welded into a single organization as the Ulster Volunteer Force under the control of the Ulster Unionist Council. The Volunteers were successful in buying arms abroad and smuggling them into the country. By late April 1914 Ulster was an armed camp, its Protestant citizens pledged to frustrate the will of the Imperial Parliament at whatever the cost. The unionists' plan of action, in the event that Home Rule was thrust upon them, was for the Ulster Volunteer Force to seize control of the province. All British military barracks, ammunition, and equipment were to be captured. The existing civilian administration was to be replaced by a provincial government headed by members of the Ulster Unionist Council under the leadership of Sir Edward Carson.

Perhaps resolute action by the United Kingdom government could have quashed the Ulster paramilitary movement in its early phases, but Prime Minister Asquith was far from resolute, and by 1914 it was too late. Events in March 1914 revealed that the United Kingdom military no longer could be trusted to move against a unionist insurrection in Ulster. General Arthur Paget, Commander-in-Chief of the Army in Ireland, was ordered to move some of his forces from the Curragh to various barracks in the north which were deemed to be insufficiently manned. Paget disliked these orders and sent supplies to the designated barracks, but no troops. He then went to London to argue with the Secretary for War, Colonel Seely. Winston Churchill at the Admiralty moved quickly, dispatching warships and infantry transports, but adhesion of the army was necessary if any move against Ulster was to be successful. Meanwhile, Colonel Seely gave in to Paget and provided him with a written guarantee which Paget transmitted verbally to his officers, Paget told them about the planned army movements and added that those officers whose homes were in Ulster simply could disappear at the beginning of the operation and return when it was over, with no penalty whatsoever. Those who were not domiciled in Ulster but who were unwilling to take part in the operation could tender resignations from the service, although these resignations would not be accepted and the officers would suffer dismissal instead. The result was that

General Gough and fifty-seven officers of his Third Cavalry Brigade stated their preference for dismissal. The Ulster situation now was out of control.

During the spring and summer of 1914 Asquith desperately tried to negotiate a way out of the dilemma: he was pledged to carry a home rule statute for Ireland, but he knew that the measure's subtitle could well be "An Act for the Provision of Civil War in Ulster." Every conceivable compromise was suggested secretly to the parties involved, and solutions also were mooted in both Houses of Parliament, but to no avail. Only the European situation saved the liberals from having to choose between attempting to coerce Ulster and refusing to honor their pledge to the Irish nationalists. The liberals, however, were able to suspend the Home Rule Act for the duration of the war and, in addition, promised that the act would not come into effect until an amending bill was introduced to deal specifically with Ulster. As we now know, Ulster had won.

(The Ulster unionists, in preventing the application of the Home Rule Act, killed traditional home rule politics. Nationalists soon came to the conclusion that if constitutional methods did not work, physical force was the only alternative. But extreme unionists did not merely deflect the path of Irish nationalism from constitutional to violent lines, their organizations served as a model after which the more militant Irish nationalists could mold their own agencies. If one forgets for the moment the divergent causes to which the bodies were devoted, it becomes clear that the Ulster Volunteer Force, the Irish Citizens Army, and the Irish Volunteers were very similar associations, operating upon nearly congruent organizational principles.)

During the war Asquith initiated one final attempt to resolve the Ulster difficulty. After the Easter Rising the British cabinet came under considerable pressure to find a solution to the Irish problem, the more so because the brutality of the United Kingdom military in suppressing the Rising offended American public opinion at the very time Britain was seeking American war aid. In early May, Asquith announced that he would go to Ireland to survey the situation and to consult about the future government of the country. While in Ireland he visited unionist leaders in Belfast and found a number of them willing to accept the immediate invoking of the Home Rule Act of 1914 if Ulster were excluded from its operation. At the same time Asquith realized that the Irish nationalists in Parliament were receptive to any plan that would bring the Home Rule Act into effect. He therefore proposed to his cabinet that a minister be appointed to negotiate a settlement. His choice was a curious one in some ways, for he selected David Lloyd George, Minister of Munitions. Lloyd George, however, already had made contacts with Irish leaders so his choice was not so strange in fact as in appearance. Moreover, it already was painfully obvious to Asquith that Lloyd George had overriding ambition, and perhaps Asquith hoped that if given enough Irish hemp, Lloyd George might well destroy himself politically.

Lloyd George's first move was to draw up a set of proposals which he could present to Irish leaders. The backbone of these was that the Home Rule Act of 1914 was to come into immediate operation in southern Ireland through a special Irish Government Act designed to last at least for the duration of the war. During the war an Irish parliament was to sit in Dublin, but the 103 Irish M.P.s also were to continue to sit in the United Kingdom Parliament. Significantly, certain counties, namely Antrim, Armagh, Down, Fermanagh, Londonderry, and Tyrone, including the boroughs of Belfast, Londonderry, and Newry, were to be excluded from the aegis of the new Irish parliament. The proposed act was to remain in force until twelve months after the conclusion of the war, but could be extended by order in council if permanent provision for the government of Ireland had not been made. It was also understood that an Imperial conference was to be held at the end of the war to unite the dominions with the Imperial government. At that conference the permanent settlement of Irish matters was to be completed.

There was one obvious ambiguity in these proposals: they did not specify how long Ulster was to be excluded from the Home Rule Act and if the exclusion were to be permanent. This was intentional, for Lloyd George was fully committed to St.

Paul's command to be all things to all men. Armed with his plastic proposals, Lloyd George approached Sid Edward Carson, the Ulster leader. Carson was willing to settle for nothing less than a promise that the exclusion of the six counties would be permanent. Lloyd George gave him such a promise in writing but with the understanding that the letter would remain secret. Carson agreed to the proposals and conveyed them to a meeting of the Ulster Unionist Council in early June 1916. Only with considerable difficulty was he able to convince his fellow unionist leaders that the proposals should be accepted. They agreed only when Carson convinced them that if they did not accept Lloyd George's proposals the European war might well be lost.

After dealing with Carson, Lloyd George approached John Redmond and then Lloyd George met several times with Redmond, Devlin, and Dillon. He finally convinced them of the attractiveness of his proposals by assuring them emphatically and repeatedly that the exclusion of the six counties was to be only temporary and that Ulster would eventually be included under the home rule parliament that would sit in Dublin. Redmond, like Carson, had difficulty in convincing his followers. He persuaded the apprehensive northern nationalists only by threatening to resign from the leadership of the Nationalist party.

As long as Lloyd George's duplicity was not discovered by either of the other two principals (and it was not) it seemed as if the Welsh magician had worked the impossible and had gained agreement between Ulster unionists and Irish nationalists about the government of Ireland. The only trouble was that the United Kingdom cabinet was far from united, and Lloyd George clearly had overrun the mandate it had given him. Most of the British unionists in the cabinet found his activities unacceptable. Lord Selborne resigned from the cabinet, while Lord Lansdowne and Walter Long remained within, denouncing Lloyd George's plan. Faced with the possibility of his coalition crumbling, Asquith gave in to the vehement unionists and broke faith with the Redmondites. A bill was drafted to exclude

Ulster permanently from the working of any home rule measure. Such a bill was unacceptable to the nationalists, and the
whole business collapsed. The story is unattractive but instruc-
tive. It was the last hope for maintaining a united Ireland and
it was a chimera.

The final anticlimactic scene in the story was played in 1920.
David Lloyd George, now Prime Minister of the United Kingdom, framed the Government of Ireland Act, 1920, often
known as the "Partition Act." It was a mixture of realism and
hypocrisy and possessed the twin virtues, if such be virtues,
of being repugnant both to Ulster unionists and to Irish nationalists. In essence it was the Home Rule Act of 1914 bisected. It
provided for the establishment of home rule parliaments in both
Northern and southern Ireland, with powers roughly equal to
those allocated to the Irish Parliament under the ill-fated 1914
Act. Northern Ireland was defined as Antrim, Armagh, Down,
Fermanagh, Londonderry, and Tyrone, and the County Boroughs of Belfast and Londonderry. Both parliaments were to
have an upper and a lower house. All of Ireland was granted
forty-six representatives at Westminster. The act provided for
the creation of a "Council of Ireland," an institution that ostensibly was to bring about the eventual reunification of the
country. It was to consist of a president nominated by the Lord
Lieutenant (the crown representative) and forty other persons,
seven from the senate of Northern Ireland, thirteen from the
House, and an equal number from southern Ireland's institu-
tional counterparts. At any future date the council could be
replaced by a united Irish parliament through the passage of
identical affirming acts by the parliaments of Northern and
of southern Ireland.

Most of these provisions were fictitious. Lloyd George knew
that the only clauses which would be carried into effect would
be those for the creation of a parliament and government of
Northern Ireland. The nationalists were well beyond the stage
where they would accept home rule, and in no case would
they implicitly recognize the partition of their country. Like so
much of Ireland's history, the establishment of the Northern

Ireland government was fraught with irony, for it gave home rule to the one part of Ireland that never had wanted it. In 1921 Sir James Craig, head of the northern government, wrote to David Lloyd George: "As a final settlement and supreme sacrifice in the interests of peace the Government of Ireland Act, 1920, was accepted by Northern Ireland although not asked for by her representatives."

At this point a brief footnote is in order. During the eighteenth and early nineteenth centuries the Presbyterian emigrants from Ulster had a significant impact on the forming of American society. The major migration of the Ulster Scots to America began in 1717, during a period of economic hardship in Ulster. The tidal years of Ulster Scots' immigration into America were 1717–18, 1725–29, 1740–41, 1754–55, and 1771–75, each of which was coterminous with a period of economic difficulty in Ulster. Estimates of the total number of migrants to the United States vary, but 200,000 is the number chosen by the best authorities. In 1790 about one quarter of a million living Americans had Ulster Scots ancestry. The Presbyterian immigration into America being chiefly a phenomenon of the American colonial era, it is not surprising that the Ulster Scots' most important impact was in settling the inland area of the seacoast states. The westward expansion of the frontier in Pennsylvania, the Carolinas, and Virginia was energized by persons of Ulster Scots origin. During the early years of American independence, men of Ulster Scots descent were politically prominent. Andrew Jackson, James Buchanan, and Chester Alan Arthur were all first generation and all presidents of the United States. In addition, the following presidents were also of Ulster descent: James Polk, Ulysses S. Grant, Woodrow Wilson, Andrew Johnson, Grover Cleveland, Benjamin Harrison, and William McKinley. Immigration by the Ulster Scots diminished in the nineteenth century and was overshadowed by the massive immigration of Irish Catholics during the post-Famine years. In the atmosphere of prejudice which greeted the Catholic Irish immigrants, the Americans of Ulster Scots descent, who had previously not objected to being called "Irish," took to calling themselves "Scotch-Irish" in order to disassociate themselves from the newcomers. Hence, even in America the split between Protestant and Catholic Irishmen continued.

Two.   Past The Watershed

VI   Southern Politics in the Collectivist Age

In the south of Ireland, no less than in the north, politics was permanently creased by the events of the early 1920's. As in Northern Ireland, the line of demarcation between the major political organizations was based on constitutional issues. However, whereas the line of constitutional cleavage between unionist and nationalist has remained functional and prepotent, in the twenty-six counties the formal constitutional differences between the two major power blocs have disappeared almost completely. The original point of dispute between the two major parties in the Free State was whether or not the Anglo-Irish Treaty and its dominion constitution was acceptable. After the new constitution of 1937 was put into operation, the differences between the two groups effectively disappeared. Yet—and this is the crucial point—the party alignments which had been engendered by the constitutional cleavage of 1921–23 did not change. To our own day the two major political parties are distinguished primarily according to the way their political forebears responded to the crisis of 1921–23.

Here the reader might suggest that perhaps the cleavage between the two parties which once was constitutional now runs along ideological lines; but such is not the case. Both parties are conservative and respectable. Neither has ever presented a radical political program or become identified with the interests of a single social class. Indeed, a striking fact about political life in southern Ireland has been the weakness of ideologically based political movements. The party differences, it may be suggested, are more tribal and historical than anything else. Memories are long and loyalties strong, so that the grandsons of men who voted for de Valera in the twenties vote for the party of which he remains the figurehead in the seventies; and the same pattern holds to a remarkable degree for the opposition.

Since the historical differences between the two major parties stem from their response to the constitution of 1922, it is well to examine briefly that frame of government. Functionally, the 1922 constitution was essentially British (as was its successor, de Valera's constitution of 1937). The legislature—in Irish the "Oireachtas,"—was made up of two chambers, the lower one being "Dail Eireann," the upper "Seanad Eireann," or more commonly, "the senate." Members of the lower house were elected by the universal suffrage of those twenty-one years of age and above. The senate was elected by those thirty years and over from a panel of candidates chosen by the Dail. The senate had only a 270-day delaying power and no powers at all in respect to money bills. Cabinet government prevailed, although the dependence upon British precedents was to some extent masked by the introduction of the term "Executive Council." All bills which were passed by both houses had to be certified by the governor-general before becoming law.

This was not an unusual constitution and was not greatly different from that of any other nation whose political procedures followed British examples. But three innovative ideas were of note. The first was the adoption of proportional representation rather than the simple-majority method of choosing members of the legislature. Second, there was provision for "the referendum." Any bill passed by the legislature could be suspended for a period of ninety days upon the written demand of two fifths of the members of the Dail or of a majority of the members of the senate. During the suspension period the matter was to be submitted by referendum to the people for their decision, provided that three fifths of the members of the senate demanded the referendum, or that a petition of one twentieth of the registered voters asked for it. Third, there was provision for "the initiative." Should the legislature fail to frame a measure which the public demanded, a petition of 75,000 voters could force the legislature to do so, or compel it to put the matter up to the entire electorate for decision by referendum. Granted, in actual practice neither the referendum nor the initiative was utilized, but their introduction revealed a desire upon the part of the new government to go beyond British parliamentary practices and make the new political machinery directly responsive to the people.

Although it was based largely on United Kingdom precedents, one should note that the Free State constitution was of disputed parentage. This does not mean that the authorship was uncertain, but that it was unclear whether it assumed legal authority because of its passage by Dail Eireann or through its ratification by the United Kingdom Parliament. The Free State view was that the constitution had force because the Irish legislative body had given the document its sanction. The British maintained that the constitution of the Irish Free State derived its validity from the fact that it was passed as an Act of the Imperial Parliament. These views obviously were irreconcilable, and the best contemporaries could do when faced with the question of Free State sovereignty was to use the word "sovereign" enclosed in quotation marks.

The political party whose identity was tied to this constitution was Cummann na nGaedheal, the heir of the pro-treaty party. Following the deaths of Arthur Griffith and Michael Collins in 1922, it was led by William T. Cosgrave, who served as head of the executive council from 1922 through mid-1932. In 1933 Cumman na nGaedheal and various splinter groups merged into the Fine Gael party, which is today one of the two major parties in the Irish Republic.

The signing of the Anglo-Irish Treaty, it will be recalled, provoked vigorous opposition, and many members of the anti-treaty bloc eventually took up arms against the new government during the civil war. At war's end the "republicans" sank into sullen silence, but in 1926 a large group led by de Valera decided that refusal to recognize the new government was unproductive and that they should form a party, gain control of the government, and change the constitution from within. This party, named Fianna Fail, first took seats in 1927 and by 1932 had gained control of the Dail. This was a crucial moment in modern Irish history, for a party opposed to the nature of the existing constitution had gained power. Note, however, that it had done so by constitutional and peaceful means, and note further that the transfer of power from the Cosgrave to the de Valera administration took place pacifically. Thus, despite the past bitterness about the character of the written constitution, the Free State politicians had established the validity of the unwritten rule upon which the existence of any form of representative government must rest: that political battles are fought by nonviolent means and that control of government follows the popular mandate.

By the close of 1936 de Valera had removed from the original 1922 constitution everything connecting the Free State with the British Empire, save certain matters written into statute law relating to the accreditation of diplomatic officials. But de Valera was not satisfied with excising the evils of the old constitution; he wanted his nation to have a written constitution that was positively and uniquely Irish. Hence, in 1937 he presented to the electorate his "Bunreacht na hEireann," the Constitution of Ireland. This was a constitution for a republic, although the word was not used. It was a strange republic, one which was structurally very similar to British monarchical democracy, though wrapped in arcane terminology and Catholic theology, a weird but workable creation. Where previously the crown had appointed the governor-general as head of state, the people now elected a president. The actual head of the government, now called the "taoiseach," was directly analogous to the United Kingdom prime minister. The legislature remained bicameral although the senate was somewhat restructured in an attempt to introduce the principle of vocational representation. Significantly, the new constitution gave special recognition to the position of the Roman Catholic church and sanctioned the Catholic theology of family life. The Catholic tone of de Valera's constitution reflected accurately the outlook of the people of the twenty-six counties. Quixotically, the same document explicitly affirmed the right of the southern government to rule the entire island, including the Protestant north.

Substantively, then, the 1937 document was no great innovation, and the opposition party has not had any trouble working under its rubrics. Once de Valera had completed his mission of reforming the monarchy out of the constitution and writing Catholicity in, southern Irish politics settled down to a tussle over who controlled the power and patronage. De Valera stayed in office until early 1948. His administration was replaced by a coalition under John A. Costello of the Fine Gael party, whose government in 1948–49 made statute law of the point which de Valera's constitution had made only tacitly: that Eire was a republic. The Fianna Fail party led by de Valera returned to office from 1951 to 1954, was succeeded by another Costello coalition from 1954 to 1957, and then returned to power and remained until upset by a Fine Gael-Labour coalition in the spring of 1973. De Valera retired as taoiseach in 1959, when he assumed the role of president. He was replaced by Sean Lemass, who in turn was succeeded by John ("Jack") Lynch in 1966. Lynch was succeeded by Liam Cosgrave (son of William T. Cosgrave) in 1973.

Professor Samuel H. Beer in his seminal work, *British Politics in the Collectivist Age,* proposed that the notion of "functional representation" was the foundation stone of modern politics as practiced in the United Kingdom (and, he might have added, of politics in most continental European countries as well). Functional representation refers to political arrangements whereby the community is divided into various levels, each of which has a corporate integrity of its own—such as social classes, professional and vocational interest groups—and which imply that each group has a right to be represented in government as a group, not merely as a collection of individual citizens. Despite a brief flare-up of interest in vocationalism in the thirties and forties, the Irish Republic obviously has not yet entered the collectivist age. The two major parties, Fianna Fail and Fine Gael, are not very much different in political philosophy and are very close in terms of the social groups from which they draw their support (granted, Fianna Fail is somewhat stronger in the rural areas than is its counterpart). Both parties are coalitions bound together not by coherent philosophies or distinctive class interests, but by the desire to obtain political power and, once having obtained it, to keep it.

Yet, the southern Irish structure does not dissolve into the chaotically shifting alliances and continual power plays one might expect; indeed, political alignments are notable for their stability. Professor Basil Chubb has delineated several characteristics of Irish political behavior which, when placed within the context of the present discussion, indicate that certain ingrained social-political patterns serve to prevent political chaos in southern Ireland in the same way that ideology or functional interest act in most European democracies. Political behavior in the Irish Republic is characterized by an almost instinctive loyalty—loyalty to institutions and especially to individuals. This characteristic stems from a social structure which is still organized upon parochial and familial lines. Loyalty in politics is reinforced by the underlying authoritarianism of southern Irish culture. One respects one's superiors and expects them to give a strong and continuing leadership in response to the loyalty which is tendered them. Further, Chubb underscores the importance of the anti-intellectualism of Irish culture and especially of the Catholic church in Ireland. This anti-intellectualism makes it very difficult for ideological parties, which by definition are intellectual in their origins, to make inroads on the existing parties, groups which are bonded to their followers by the personal nonintellectual ties of history, loyalty, and deference to authority.

An observer with an eye to bellwether institutions should watch the development of the Irish Labour party. It has a coherent socialist ideology and aspires to become the representative of the interests of a specific social class. Since the late sixties it has provided political opportunities for bright, aggressive young politicians who are blocked by the seniority systems of the two major parties. At present the Labour party has substantial strength only in the Dublin City area and in the far south—Cork, Wexford, and Waterford. It seems far from able yet to shoulder aside either of the two older parties, but should that happen, the observer will know that politics in the Republic has crossed the line from the tribal to the collectivist age.

VII Southern Ireland and the
International Economy

The easiest way to understand the recent economic history of southern Ireland is to contrast two periods of time, the 1930's and the present era. The primary theme of Irish economic development from the 1930's to the present day is the evolution from very primitive roots of a complex advanced economy capable of competing in the international marketplace. From one perspective we can view the growth of an international economy in southern Ireland as part of a larger change in its life, namely the transformation of the nation's cultural and social life from a provincial to an international basis. From another vantage point the economic changes in southern Irish society can be seen as contributing to the social and diplomatic changes which have begun to transform it from its previous position on the far fringe of Europe into a thoroughly European nation. The causation has been reciprocal, for the loosening of the parochial bonds which once restricted southern Irish social and cultural life has made it easier for economic planners and industrial administrators to bring the economy into twentieth-century world exchanges. A secondary theme is that despite its growth the Irish Republic is vulnerable, sometimes seeming like a bewildered waif amidst the bustling traffic of the international marketplace.

The economic war of the 1930's, waged between Eamon de Valera and the government of the United Kingdom, provides an excellent baseline against which to measure Ireland's subsequent economic development. In order to understand the significance of the economic war it should be kept in mind that as a nation southern Ireland has been handicapped in the modern world by a paucity of the resources most needed for industrial development. Iron and coal, the mineral bases of modern industrial development, are not found in significant quantities.

Certain minor metals, silver, zinc, lead, and copper, are found in deposits large enough to make mining worthwhile, but not large enough to underpin economic development. Natural gas and oil may some day be found in quantity under the Irish sea, but so far wishful thinking has been the prospectors' chief reward.

During the 1920's, the government of the Irish Free State drew the correct economic conclusion from the data on resources: that the Free State, if it were to become anything other than an agricultural backwater, had to trade diligently and intelligently in the world market. Under the energetic leadership of Patrick Hogan, Minister for Agriculture, Free State farm exports won their way back into the English market. Taxes and public expenditures were kept low, and the government's budget was balanced in order to keep inflation from destroying the price advantage Free State products had in Great Britain. Tariffs were kept to a minimum (being used only to protect infant industries), because the erection of tariff barriers would have been ruinous to a trading nation. Large farmers were encouraged on grounds of productive efficiency. By these methods the Irish Free State established a precarious toehold in the highly competitive European market.

When Eamon de Valera came to office in 1932 he abruptly reversed the Free State's economic policy and propelled the nation into a period of financial instability and economic uncertainty. De Valera's economic program, it appears, was founded upon both metaphysics and economics. His policy, which de Valera himself described as "frugal self-sufficiency," was an integral part of his political program. De Valera's political position in the early 1930's was strongly nationalistic. He desired the removal from the Free State constitution of the oath of allegiance to the crown required of members of the Dail, the abolition of the provisions in the constitution which made the Free State constitution subject to the Anglo-Irish Treaty, and the abolition of the office of governor-general, the incumbent of which was chosen by the cabinet at Westminster. The economic analogue to this political nationalism was a desire for economic self-sufficiency for Ireland. His drive toward this goal echoed strains in Irish nationalist history having nothing to do with the contemporary economic situation. In talking about self-sufficiency, de Valera was sounding the same tones which underlay Arthur Griffith's *The Resurrection of Hungary,* the classic economic treatise of the nationalist movement. Simultaneously, de Valera presented economic self-sufficiency as the economic concomitant of the virtuous life. Citizens, in his view, should not value material wealth as the basis of their lives, but should be satisfied with frugal comforts and the cultivation of things of the spirit. And of course the reduction of external trade meant that southern Irishmen would have to traffic less with the money changers and usurers of England, Anglophobia being a sentiment easily mobilized by any shrewd politician.

De Valera had economic reasons as well as national-moralistic ones for preferring economic isolationism. In contrast to the preceding Cosgrave government, he viewed the economic interest of the small farmer as prepotent. Hence, the policies of the twenties which had maximized agricultural trade but had simultaneously left the small farmer at a disadvantage were reversed. (The situation was not unlike that in the United States under the various New Deal agricultural acts.) Further, economic isolationism was characteristic of many nations after the Great Crash. Although preferential treatment for Ireland by the United Kingdom no doubt could have been arranged, it was not unreasonable for de Valera to conclude that British economic barriers would continue to increase. In such a situation it was possible to argue that a well-conceived plan for economic self-sufficiency would turn an unfortunate international situation into an opportunity for national economic progress.

The Free State budget of March 1932 imposed forty-three new tariffs, a number which was regularly augmented during the succeeding four years. In 1934 a quota system limiting imports on specified items was adopted. Concurrent with the exclusion or inhibition of entry of foreign goods was the stimulation of domestic manufacture of products previously imported from abroad. With the introduction of the tariff on foreign manufactures the normal market mechanisms made it profitable for domestic industry to produce industrial goods which earlier had come from Britain or the Continent. In the agricultural sector, however, large state subsidies were necessary to induce the farmers to reallocate a significant portion of their lands from pasturage to cereal crops, cereals previously having been imported.

Conceivably, economic isolationism could have been a successful policy for the Free State (although this is doubtful), but de Valera enmeshed the new protectionism in an economic squabble with the United Kingdom on the issue of land annuities. The land annuities were the result of the land acts of 1891, 1903, and 1909 which had converted the Irish peasantry from insecure tenants to small landholders. Under the acts the United Kingdom government had bought out large estates and sold them in small parcels to the tenantry. To recoup its expenditures the Exchequer received small annual payments from the farmers, much in the manner a bank receives mortgage payments. After southern Ireland attained independence, the Irish Free State took over the collection of the annuities and transmitted the aggregate sum to the United Kingdom treasury. The annual sum of annuities collected by the Land Commission was roughly three million pounds. Although transmitted publicly to the United Kingdom each year, the obligations of the Free State Land Commission had been formulated in two international agreements which were made by the Cosgrave government without submission to the Dail for approval. De Valera argued that because the agreements lacked Dail ratification and because the money was paid to the United Kingdom National Debt Commissioners, and therefore fell under an agreement between the Cosgrave government and the British exempting Ireland from responsibility for any share of the United Kingdom's National Debt, the payments should cease. Consequently, roughly £3 million in land annuities due on the first of July 1932 were withheld by the Free State government (along with approximately £2 million owed the United Kingdom in miscellaneous compensations, the largest item being nearly £1 million intended for pensions for former Royal Irish Constabulary members).

Naturally, members of the United Kingdom cabinet were taken aback by de Valera's actions and favored a strict and literal interpretation of the Anglo-Irish Treaty and all subsequent agreements. When de Valera, who served as his own Minister for External Affairs, and J. H. Thomas, the Dominion's Secretary, met on the eighth of July 1932 it was a case of stone striking stone. Thomas offered to have the financial problem submitted to arbitration by a tribunal of Commonwealth members, but de Valera, remembering the boundary commission of 1925, refused arbitration unless non-Commonwealth nations sat on the tribunal. Neither de Valera nor Thomas would budge, and on the twelfth of July the United Kingdom cabinet imposed a 20 percent duty on Free State livestock, meat, bacon, butter, poultry, cream, and eggs. Soon thereafter the Free State escalated the conflict by abolishing the preference on British goods that had been maintained even under the original de Valera tariff policy and by adding a 20 percent duty on steel, coal, cement, and iron. (As a result of the coal duty, Jonathan Swift's eighteenth-century slogan "Burn everything British but their coal" became the half-serious, half-satirical battle cry of the Dublin working classes.) Import quotas were soon added by both sides and, with a slight slackening of tension in late 1934 and thereafter, the economic war was to continue until 1938.

What was the result of de Valera's program of protectionism and of economic hostility toward the United Kingdom? From the viewpoint of self-sufficiency the program was partially successful, for it drastically reduced southern Irish imports. Imports ran more than £50 million in 1931, but had been reduced to under £36 million in 1933, which represented a low for the decade. But from the viewpoint of anyone other than a doctrinaire economic protectionist, this success was more than offset by an even greater fall in exports: from over £36 million in 1931 to the decade's low of under £18 million in 1934. Hence, the trading position of Ireland actually deteriorated during the years of economic isolationism, the excess of imports over exports being about £14 million during the last full year of Cosgrave's administration and more than £21 million in 1934, the high noon of the protectionist period. In fairness to the government's policies, it should be noted that from 1932 to 1939 employment in Free State industries grew by about two thirds, thus providing the base for more extensive industrialization after World War II. Also, a quarter of a million acres more of wheat was harvested in 1938 than had been grown at the beginning of the decade, a step toward self-sufficiency which was to be appreciated during wartime. Nevertheless, it remains clear that thousands of persons were forced into poverty by the program and that the economy as a whole was weakened rather than strengthened by economic parochialism. In 1931 there were 30,000 persons listed on the unemployment register. By the end of the following year the number was over 100,000. Major relief works, chiefly in the form of a house-building campaign, were necessary. For a time the government was forced to alleviate widespread hunger by giving away meat and milk.

Fortunately for the material well-being of the southern Irish people, the extreme form of economic parochialism originally envisaged by de Valera soon was abandoned. In December 1934 a coal-cattle pact was signed under which the quota of Free State cattle allowed in Great Britain was raised by one third in return for giving the United Kingdom a virtual monopoly on coal importation into Ireland. Tariffs, however, were maintained on both sides. Because British coal was more expensive than that from other countries, many southern Irishmen viewed de Valera's coal-cattle agreement with the British as a form of near madness involving the Irish Free State's underwriting Britain's economic recovery. Nevertheless, the pact which was renewed in 1936 was a step away from economic isolationism and pointed to an eventual settlement of the economic war. This settlement was negotiated in the first four months of 1938. Under the Anglo-Irish trade pact that ended the economic war, the United Kingdom received a lump sum of £10 million in settlement of all claims against southern Ireland (save a relatively small sum for war damages which the Dail in 1925 had agreed to pay), an amount which represented only half of the amount due the British government on land annuities. The penal tariff arrangements which the two nations had enacted against each other were repealed. Southern Irish

farmers and manufacturers were once again able to trade freely
with their nation's oldest enemy and best customer.

Paradoxically, one of the results of the Second World War
was that southern Ireland, while isolated from both sides by
its neutrality, was brought once again into the European economic nexus. This occurred because its economy appeared to
have been damaged by the war despite the nation's being
physically unscathed. Although difficult to document statisti-
cally, agronomists argued that Eire's soil, its chief resource,
had suffered because of the unavailability of chemical fertilizer
during the war years. Livestock and poultry were reduced in
number. It was also argued that Eire suffered industrially
through plant deterioration for lack of replacement parts and
equipment. (It is difficult to square the claims of industrial
hardship with the fact that the value in current pounds sterling
of Ireland's industrial output was more than two and a half
times as great in 1948 as it had been in 1936.) Undeniably the
war had played havoc with Irish trade. Both imports and exports shrank drastically during the war years (see Appendix,
Table A.10). Immediately after the war, imports rose drastically while exports failed to keep pace. The result was a severe
trade imbalance.

In the actual course of events it was irrelevant whether or
not Eire had shared to a significant extent in European war
damage. The American government ignored the fine points
of the war damage debate and treated southern Ireland under
the same rubric as that prescribed for its allies, namely, through
Marshall Plan aid. The announcement by Secretary of State
George G. Marshall of a plan for European recovery in his
Harvard University speech of 5 June 1947 was quickly followed
by a meeting the next month of representatives of sixteen European nations (excluding Germany, but including Italy, plus
neutral countries such as Sweden and Switzerland). Ireland
was represented by Sean Lemass, then Deputy Prime Minister
and Minister for Industry and Commerce, and by Patrick
Smith, Minister for Agriculture. Eamon de Valera as External

Affairs Minister also was directly involved. The meeting's report, published in September 1947, was simple in its outlines: the United States would provide about $22 billion if the European countries would strenuously pursue the goals of increased production, financial stability, and economic cooperation among themselves. The immediate goal of the plan was to close the "dollar gap," the long-range goal to recreate a viable European economy.

The American act establishing the Marshall Plan was signed into law in April 1948. A vote of $5 billion soon followed. The headquarters of the European Recovery Program (ERP) were Washington, D.C., and Paris. The Washington organization was entitled the Economic Co-operation Administration (ECA) and maintained liaison with the European countries through a Special Mission to each nation. The coordinating body in Paris was the Organization for European Economic Cooperation (OEEC). Ireland's representative on the council of the OEEC was Sean MacBride, who ably pressed the case for a strengthening of the OEEC and for hastening economic cooperation between member nations.

While the OEEC coordinated the interests of the European nations vis-à-vis one another, each nation also dealt directly with Washington. Hence, in June 1948 the first major treaty between southern Ireland and the United States was signed, spelling out the two countries' obligations under the European Recovery Program. Under the agreement Eire received $18 million in gift aid. More than any other country in the ERP program, however, Eire participated on a loan rather than on a grant basis: $128.5 million was loaned to Eire by the United States at 2½ percent interest. The ECA special mission to southern Ireland which supervised these transactions was headed by J. E. Carrigan, Chief of Mission and Dean of the Agricultural College at the University of Vermont (Carrigan was succeeded by Dr. Paul Miller, Director of Agricultural Extension at the University of Minnesota, who, in his turn, was replaced by Albert J. Dexter, the Agricultural Development Agent of the Northern Pacific Railroad). The two key staff posts were filled by Dr. Paul K. Findlen, the economic adviser, and by William Howard Taft III, Special Assistant, who was later to be named United States Ambassador to Ireland.

Great as the direct economic influence of American money was in stimulating economic growth, it was of minor importance compared with the Marshall Plan's impact on the way the leaders of Southern Ireland viewed their nation's place in the world. In order to receive ERP aid, these politicians not only had to renounce economic isolationism and the nationalist dogma of self-sufficiency, but had to move convincingly into the European market place. This meant that the government, while continuing industrial development, had to accept southern Ireland's position as a specialized agricultural exporter, and, inevitably, as a breadbasket for England. Price subsidies, therefore, were introduced for barley, eggs, meat, poultry, and wheat in order to ensure quantity and price competitiveness for the export market. The government underwrote schemes for the improvement of livestock and poultry and aided land reclamation and improvement. Although it was only sensible for a country which by nature was an agricultural exporter to stimulate such exports, the abandonment of any pretense of self-sufficiency nettled old-line nationalists: "Ireland is again to become a fruitful mother of herds and flocks, a vast ranchland, a provider of the roast beef of old England."

Despite the necessity of a price freeze in 1951, the Irish Republic was reasonably well prepared for the end of Marshall Plan aid in June 1952. (The government was able to end rationing in July 1952.) Because southern Ireland maintained its neutrality and refused to sign the Mutual Security Pact of 1952 it was cut off from further American aid.

During the decade following the inauguration of the Marshall Plan the government of southern Ireland entered into more economic agreements with other nations than it had even contemplated in the first twenty years of independence. The Irish adhesion to the OEEC and the Irish-American Cooperation Agreement of 1948 are the best-known examples of the Republic's new economic internationalism, but these pacts should not overshadow a host of binational economic agreements between southern Ireland and European nations. Even a simple listing of the more important trade agreements indicates how deeply southern Ireland was now involved in the international trade economy: The Netherlands (1949 and 1951), France (1949 and 1951), Norway (1951), Germany (1951, 1952 and 1953), Spain (1947 and 1951), and Portugal (1952). The Republic of Ireland joined the International Monetary Fund in 1957.

Simultaneously, the Dublin government began a series of negotiations that made the United Kingdom its largest trading partner. (The decision to fly flags at half-mast from government buildings in Dublin on the death of King George VI was probably more a sign of respect for the United Kingdom's trade position than an expression of reverence for British royalty.) An Anglo-Irish trade agreement negotiated in 1948 accorded British goods preferential treatment on importation into the Republic in exchange for southern Irish agricultural and industrial goods enjoying duty-free entry into the British market. Significantly, when the agreement came up for renegotiation in the late 1950's Sean Lemass, who headed the Irish delegation, proposed that the two economies be completely integrated, that tariffs on British goods imported by the Irish Republic be totally abolished, and that southern Irish agricultural goods sold in Great Britain be given the same subsidies from the British Exchequer as United Kingdom produce received. The British rejected the proposal, however, and instead the 1948 agreement was simply extended to provide the same guaranteed prices for southern Irish cattle, sheep, and lambs fattened in Britain as were provided for British-bred stock. Although Britain later found it necessary to introduce a 15 percent tariff on industrial imports, this was only a brief setback, and in mid-December 1965 a comprehensive free trade agreement was forged. Under the terms of the pact almost all restrictions on trade between southern Ireland and Great Britain are to be gradually eliminated over a ten-year period. Thus, with each passing year, the two countries have moved closer to becoming a single economic unit.

Precisely how close the trading relationship of Ireland and Britain became is indicated by the fact that in 1965, a representative year, £173,441,000 of Ireland's £371,740,000 in imports came from Great Britain, and £127,450,000 of its £220,775,000 in exports were shipped to Britain.

In choosing to become part of the economic network of the British Isles, successive southern Irish governments have implicitly opted for a return to a status in many ways similar to that of a colony. For example, although the Republic mints its own money, it only in theory possesses an independent currency. For trade reasons the republic's pound is pegged at parity with the British pound. Not only does this facilitate trade but it means that southern Ireland is protected from speculations with its currency supply, since the parity relationship makes manipulation of its currency virtually impossible. In return for these advantages Ireland has given up control over major monetary decisions. When Britain devalues, Ireland devalues, and when Britain adopted the decimal system southern Ireland had no choice but to follow.

Another case: because there are virtually no restrictions on the movement of workers between Great Britain and southern Ireland, the southern Irish worker has greater employment opportunities than he would otherwise enjoy. But, simultaneously, the free market in labor means that basic industrial rates are set in Britain and that if Irish manufacturers pay much less than their British counterparts their labor pool will vanish. Any action of the United Kingdom government affecting British wages will also affect wages in the Republic. Similarly, the economic intimacy of the United Kingdom and Eire has great significance for southern Irish agriculture. Under the 1965 agreement large quantities of southern Irish beef and lamb are eligible for British domestic price supports. The farmer in southern Ireland benefits, but this means that agricultural prices within the country are determined to a considerable degree by the United Kingdom cabinet. Having noted that the Dublin government, in abandoning economic isolationism, turned the Irish Republic into an economic satellite of the United Kingdom, we must note that there was almost no alternative. Frozen out of the Common Market and desperately needing a trading partner in order to develop industry and agriculture, she had no choice but to adhere to the British economic empire.

And what of Irish-American economic relationships? As soon as the Marshall Plan ended, American influence on the Eire economy became peripheral. Granted, there were special agreements between America and the Irish Republic, such as the 1953 convention to prevent double taxation and the American investment guarantee plan of 1955, but these agreements were minor in comparison to the Anglo-Irish trade pacts. Granted, also, that American investors poured a good deal of money into southern Irish industry, but these sums were only a tithe of British and Irish investments in Eire industry. America's relative unimportance to the southern Irish economy is revealed most accurately in trade statistics. In 1965, when trade with America was at a then all-time high, imports of American goods into southern Ireland amounted to only £29,849,000 out of total imports of £371,740,000. Irish exports to America were valued at £8,817,000, total exports being £220,775,000. Thus, the Marshall Plan in Ireland had operated exactly according to scenario: having guaranteed by its actions in the late 1940's and early 1950's that southern Ireland would be able to enter the international economy, the United States then withdrew and allowed natural economic forces to operate. The result was that Eire gravitated into the European economic system and began to orbit as a small, nominally independent satellite with Great Britain as its major planet.

In discussing the change in southern Ireland's economic orientation from economic parochialism to economic internationalism, it is easy to overlook the crucial changes in the internal organization of its economy which made entry into the international market place possible. Simply stated, the Irish Republic in the late 1950's was transformed from a basically laissez-faire domestic economy to a managed economy. Like many aspects of the political and economic scene, the move to a planned economy was tinged with irony. Highly conservative politically, the government of southern Ireland nevertheless adopted comprehensive national economic planning before its socialist neighbor, the United Kingdom. There are no ideological overtones to the Republic's economic management, merely the desire to become richer faster. Because the idea of economic planning is repugnant to some, the government often refers to such activities as "development" in an attempt to take some of the menace out of the phrase. In any case, the southern Irish style of economic planning is distinctly democratic, albeit nonpolitical. Goals are set through consultation with industry, and targets are set for entire industries, not for individual firms. Punitive measures are not invoked for failure to meet targets. Government influence on most industries is through such positive incentives as subsidies and credit provisions rather than through imposition of government regulations.

The adoption by southern Ireland of long-range government economic planning came after a period of economic malaise. After the cessation of Marshall Plan aid, the country was able to stand on its own feet economically, but was unable to stride forward with any degree of confidence. Unlike most of the rest of Europe, southern Ireland's economy stagnated in the first half of the 1950's. From 1949 to 1955 the gross national product grew at an average rate of less than 2 percent per annum. From 1950 to 1955 industrial output rose an average of only 3 percent a year, while agriculture was under 2 percent in average annual growth. Matters came to a head in 1955. A consumption boom in the domestic market pressed prices upward, and at the same time trade in export of foodstuffs to Britain dropped. The result was a balance of payments crisis that threatened the stability of the economy of southern Ireland. After almost a year of doing nothing, the government took deflationary action in early 1956. As intended, the excess of imports over exports was reduced, but simultaneously production in the industrial sector fell (by roughly 5 percent between 1955 and 1956), with a consequent increase in unemployment and emigration.

Clearly something had to be done. The man who seemed to have the answer was T. K. Whitaker of the Department of Finance, the most powerful government department because of its financial supervision of other departments. As departmental secretary, Whitaker held the most prestigious post in the Civil Service. He approached the Minister for Finance in December 1957 with a proposal to involve the department in long-range economic planning. The minister and the cabinet proved receptive, and Whitaker was permitted to undertake a study which was presented to the government in May 1958 under the title "Economic Development." The government incorporated most of Whitaker's recommendations into its Programme for Economic Expansion, which was presented to the Dail in November 1958 and subsequently adopted.

Actually the plan was more of a rough outline than a precise blueprint and covered a five-year period, ending in 1963. The program set a goal of 2 percent annual increase in GNP, a conservative target by any standard. Although specific target figures were not presented except for state industries, the verbal descriptions of economic improvements were specific. A steady increase in agricultural output and export was prescribed, with emphasis upon increased productivity and land improvement. Fertilizer prices were to be subsidized as were high-quality stock-breeding efforts and related research. State funds were to finance research in marketing, transport, and utilization of agricultural byproducts. Simultaneously, rapid industrial development chiefly for export markets was prescribed. Foreign investment capital was to be encouraged through tax incentives. Manufacturers were to receive a tax remission on export profits and on expenditure for certain types of capital investment. A twenty-five-year tax exemption for industries in the Shannon Airport complex was suggested, and efforts to encourage the development of tourism were outlined.

Surprisingly, given the tenacious conservatism of southern Irish political opinion, the program was adopted with little opposition. Doubtless the economic stagnation of the 1950's and the crisis of the mid-decade made the public more amenable to the abandonment of laissez-faire ideology than it would otherwise have been. Certainly the possibility of southern Ireland's joining the Common Market and the obvious need to plan for that potentiality worked in favor of the Whitaker plan. By a feat of levitation, the government was able to raise the plan above party politics, presenting it as a national plan designed to meet national problems, a precedent which has held to the present time.

The first venture in planning was a great success. During the five-year period the gross national product grew at an average rate above 4 percent per annum, more than twice the original goal. Most encouraging was the response of the industrial sector, which grew at an average annual rate of more than 7 percent per year. Agricultural growth was somewhat under an average of 3 percent annually. Trade, especially exports, grew correspondingly.

While recognizing that the Republic's five-year plan was a success, we should also note that the plan had flaws and that its fulfillment was to some extent fortuitous: favorable external trade conditions boosted southern Irish trade to higher levels than would normally have been achieved. The chief flaw in the first plan was that it was not based on a set of comprehensive national accounts and, hence, most targets were either estimated or stated in verbal terms rather than in precise mathematical form. Further, the plan overestimated the part agriculture would play in economic growth and underestimated the potential of Irish industry. Also, the plan assumed that it would be necessary for the government to limit investment in social goods (education, housing, and so on), an assumption which did not prove true in the actual course of events.

Planners learned from their mistakes, and when the second program (covering the years 1964–69) was framed it included specific targets for each major economic sector based on a comprehensive set of national accounts. The planners corrected the overemphasis on agriculture which had flawed the first program, a sensible change in view of the fact that early in the first planning period southern Ireland had crossed an economic watershed by transforming itself from an agricultural country to an industrial one (in 1962 industry accounted for 30.0 percent of GNP, agriculture for 22.5 percent). Hence, the brunt of the burden for growth was placed on industry, the target for industrial expansion being 7 percent a year. The goal for agriculture was somewhat under 4 percent a year. The overall goal of the program was an average annual growth in GNP of 4.3 percent each year, which was slightly more than that actually achieved during the first program. Such an overall growth rate would have produced a 35 percent increase in GNP during the planning period, and probably would have reduced Irish emigration to 10,000 a year at most. Significantly, the second program, in contrast to its predecessor, emphasized the need for investment in human capital as well as in physical capital, and therefore suggested the raising of the school-leaving age and an increase in all levels of educational expenditure.

The good fortune which had helped to make the first plan such a success did not continue. The first year of the second plan went well enough, with most targets being exceeded easily, but then in 1965 a balance-of-payments problem similar to but milder than the crisis of 1955 interrupted the economic idyll. The problem was produced by a lag in export growth combined with rapidly rising consumer demand at home. The export lag was no fault of the Dublin government but rather a result of Great Britain's having imposed temporary import levies on many commodities because of the unfavorable British economic situation in 1964–65. The predictable result of an export lag at a time when consumer demand was high was a rise in imports, a drop in exports, and a burgeoning import excess (see Table A.10), which, in turn, threatened the nation's currency reserves. To meet this situation the government was forced to employ deflationary measures such as temporary wage and price ceilings and temporary import duties on consumer goods. The export problem was solved by the Anglo-Irish trade agreement of late 1965, but economic momentum was lost. A *Review of Progress, 1964–67* revealed that while GNP during the planning period was supposed to rise at an average annual rate of 4.3 percent, the actual rate thus far was 3.3 percent. Industry, projected at 7.0 percent, actually had grown only 5.8 percent and, most disappointing, agriculture, projected at 3.8 percent, had grown only an average of 0.8 percent a year. Hence it was with a distinct sense of relief that governmental economists were able to announce that the economy was once again buoyant in 1968, and that GNP had grown almost 5 percent in that year.

Nevertheless, when the third economic plan (for the years 1969–72) was published in March 1969, it was clear that the planners had been affected more by the pessimism of the 1964–67 period than by the optimism of 1968. One good indication of the government's disappointment was that the third plan was shoved ahead so that it covered the year 1969, a period which had originally been included in the second economic plan. Increasing governmental caution was also indicated by the fact that the third plan covered four years only, 1969–72. The overall annual growth rate for the four years was targeted at 4 percent, that for industry being a reasonably modest 6.5 percent per annum. Clearly, the planners were less confident than they had been when drawing up the second national plan. An average annual increment of 2 percent was prescribed for agriculture, a target so low that months of negotiation were necessary between the government and the National Farmers Association before the program could be published. In the actual event the planners' pessimism was more than justified because the troubles which erupted in Northern Ireland in 1969 seriously affected the southern economy, especially the vital tourist sector.

Although central economic planning has been reasonably successful in southern Ireland, the euphoria about "Whitakerism" which followed the first plan has dissipated, partly because of the technical failures of the second plan and partly because of growing doubts about the philosophic assumptions of the planning process. The most fundamental of these doubts concerns the excessively technocratic nature of the process, which works to the detriment of humane considerations. Planning for economic development is not married to planning for social development. Increasingly, Irishmen are coming to distrust those whose concerns are for economic growth irrespective of its societal implications. The technocratic character of planning has been exacerbated by its almost total insulation from political representation. Obviously it is important that a national plan not become embroiled in political controversy or become a piece of party propaganda, but the government of southern Ireland probably has been excessively fearful of these dangers and therefore has failed to consult political representatives upon important issues that really should involve humane social judgments rather than mathematical projections. There is some indication that planning methods could be improved if they were removed from the control of the Department of Finance, which is essentially a budgetary agency and ill-equipped to deal with nonfiscal considerations, and placed under a separate agency charged with combining social and economic planning.

Thus far we have been discussing the development of a managed economy in southern Ireland solely in terms of the development of economic planning. However, an understanding of the managed economy is impossible unless one also recognizes the important part played by state bodies. Many of the state bodies are simply nationalized industries, although they are never referred to by that menacing term. The creation of state bodies was not in any way associated with socialism, but Irish pragmatism in economics in many cases produced national companies that were indistinguishable from those prescribed under socialist theory. Indeed, in most cases the state bodies were established before socialism became the dominant political viewpoint elsewhere in the British Isles. The concept of state corporations is not new (some bodies were formed as early as the 1920's), but the magnitude and complexity of their recent operations and the ease with which these corporations can be manipulated by governmental regulations makes them a central instrument in the economic planning and control process.

A few of the state enterprises (most notably the post office) are run directly as government departments, with a minister in charge and civil servants as employees. Many more are statutory corporations, created by special act of the legislature. These enterprises are managed by a board appointed by the government. The employees are not civil servants. The most important corporations in this category are the Electric Supply Board (f. 1927), Bord na Mona (the Turf Development Board, f. 1934), and Coras Iompair Eireann (the transport corporation, incorporated in its present form in 1950). Another category of state-owned organizations consists of joint stock companies. These are chartered by registration under the Companies Act, not by special legislative enactment. The stock for these companies is vested in a government minister, usually the Minister for Finance. Overall direction of the organization is under state control, although the employees are not civil servants. Comhluct Suicre Eireann Teo (Irish Sugar Company, f. 1933) and Aer Rianta (the Irish airlines holding company, f. 1936, of which Aer Lingus now is a subsidiary) are examples. Other state organizations include those for developing a given industrial complex (for instance, the Shannon Duty Free Airport Industries), or for encouraging specific activities (such as the tourist trade) often by direct subsidy of private organizations. There are now more than fifty state bodies operating in the Irish economy.

Three examples may be cited to indicate the range and style of operation of the state corporations; these are Aer Lingus, the Shannon development scheme, and the Tourists Board. Aer Lingus was founded as a subsidiary of the holding company, Aer Rianta, in April 1937. It began with one biplane, one pilot, and a biscuit tin full of spare parts. Hindered by wartime restrictions, until 1945 the airline was an untrustworthy ferry service to Liverpool and Manchester. After the war, however, Aer Lingus acquired several DC-3's and a virtual monopoly on air service between southern Ireland and Great Britain as a result of an agreement made in 1946 between the Eire and United Kingdom governments, and Aer Lingus, British European Airways, and British Overseas Airways Corporation. Nevertheless, the company operated on a narrow profit margin because most of its routes were short: the average length of stages flown by the company was just over 200 miles in 1952. Hence, it was a major breakthrough when in 1958 Aer Lingus began to operate an Ireland-to-Boston or -New York run. Since 1950 the company has operated at a profit in most years. Like almost all large airlines, Aer Lingus is presently forced to make huge investments in the latest jet equipment, investments which are necessary if the line is to remain competitive, but worrisome because of the capital sums necessary to obtain a relatively

small return in profits. Also, there are serious conflicts developing about Aer Lingus's monopoly of the Dublin-New York run.
Yet, despite worries about the long-run profitability of air
travel, which Irish International Airlines shares with its American and European counterparts. Aer Lingus is presently one
of the most efficient and competitive of transatlantic carriers.

Although the development of long-range jet travel was a god-
send to Aer Lingus, the jets spelled potential disaster for Shannon airport. This fact brings us to a second example of state
bodies, the Shannon Free Airport Development Company.
When it became clear that most jets could overfly Shannon on
transatlantic flights, it was naturally feared that the previously
lucrative Shannon Airport complex would become moribund.
Therefore, an ingenious scheme was drawn up. A company was
founded to develop an industrial estate within the boundaries
of the duty-free zone. The company, underwritten by the
government of southern Ireland, was to seek out investors,
especially foreigners, and was empowered to offer them a
twenty-five-year period of tax-free profits on exports manufactured within the duty-free zone. Hence, tax concessions and
duty-free status were combined with ready access to air facilities. The plan was immediately successful, and by 1965 more
than £22 million a year was being exported by firms on the
estate, which employed almost 3,300 persons. In 1968 the value
of exports was above £32 million, which represented more than
one quarter of the total value of manufactured products exported from the nation. In that year over 6,600 persons were
employed on the estate.

Joining with Aer Lingus and with the Shannon group in
attempting to keep exports climbing is Bord Failte, the Irish
Tourist Board. From an economic viewpoint tourism is an export, for its effect is to bring foreign currency into the Irish
domestic economy in return for a "product" provided by native
Irishmen. Immediately after the Second World War Ireland
experienced a tourist boom, chiefly because English and continental travelers enjoyed visiting a country where rationing was
less strict than in their homelands and where the scenery was
unscarred by war damage. This boom soon came to an end,

and in an effort to promote a permanent tourist industry Bord Failte was established in 1950. State-controlled and state-financed, the Tourist Board is typical of the Irish state corporation in recruiting its employees mostly from the private sector under the same conditions as private industry. (Bord Failte employees are not civil servants.) Almost all the organization's income stems from the government. Originally, government grants to the board were limited to £45,000 a year, but this was raised to £125,000 in 1951, and by 1968 the board was able to spend £3.8 million in promoting Irish tourism. Of course much of this money is spent in advertising Ireland throughout the world, but funds are also spent in inspecting and classifying facilities. Loans and grants are provided for the development of amenities (these range from a £13,000 contribution to the restoration of Bunratty Castle to 20 percent grants toward the cost of new bedrooms for guest houses in the twelve western counties). The magnitude of Bord Failte's activities becomes clear when one compares the £3.8 million it spent in 1968 with the £3.3 million spent by Great Britain for tourist promotion and the £200,000 available to the Northern Ireland Tourist Board in the same year. As the budget of Bord Failte expanded, Irish tourist earnings skyrocketed. Receipts from tourism were £32 million in 1959; they were £92 million in 1968, an increase of nearly 300 percent over a ten-year period.

As the end of the Second World War approached, postwar planners among the Allies realized that an international trade network would have to be established if Europe's economic recovery was to be a reality. In 1946 the United Nations Economic and Social Council prepared a blueprint for an International Trade Organization, a body which actually never was established but whose suggested features were incorporated in the General Agreement on Tariffs and Trade of 1947. Eire, however, did not become a member of the GATT network. Indeed, despite the government's willingness to give up economic isolationism, it viewed most European alliances with suspicion. In particular, the decision of southern Ireland not to participate in the NATO treaty had long-range implications for the country's economic policy. The government refused to joint NATO partially because of Ireland's traditional neutrality, partially because of the continuing partition issue, and also because Sean MacBride, the Minister for External Affairs, was an Anglophobe. MacBride had been an IRA leader in the 1930's and viewed anything that would join England and Eire as allies as an abomination. In the coalition government of that period the advocates of NATO were not strong enough to budge MacBride. This fear of European military alliances had its parallel in Ireland's attitude toward European economic alliances, and when the idea of a European Economic Community was mooted the Irish showed scant interest. The proposals forged at the Messina Conference in 1955 were given slight attention by the Dublin government, and when the EEC was created by the Treaty of Rome in 1957 southern Ireland was out in the cold.

Ironically, the Republic's economic crisis of 1955–56 radically changed governmental and public attitudes on multilateral European trade alliances so that by the end of 1957 the desirability of joining the Common Market was generally accepted. Unhappily for the Irish, the admission of the United Kingdom was vetoed by General de Gaulle, with a complete breakdown of talks occurring at the end of 1958. Because the economy of southern Ireland was so closely tied to Britain's, it would have been economically suicidal for it to accept EEC membership on its own (EEC members impose a common tariff on nonmember countries, a policy which would have cut off Eire from Britain, its best customer). Therefore the southern Irish had no choice but to wait until the EEC member countries were willing to reconsider the United Kingdom application. When Britain took the lead in forming its own counterpart to the EEC, the European Free Trade Area (EFTA), Eire declined to join for the sensible reason that its goods already had near-free access to the British markets.

When negotiations began in mid-1960 between "the six" (EEC) and "the seven" (EFTA) about a possible merger, the government of southern Ireland could only sit hopefully on the sidelines. These negotiations failed, and Britain applied for Common Market membership on its own. As early as April 1960 the Taoiseach, Sean Lemass, had said in the Dail that "the best situation possible for us would be association with the Common Market, if Britain were also a member of it," so it was no surprise when a white paper issued in July 1961 made it clear that the government of the Irish Republic would be pressing for inclusion in the EEC if Britain succeeded in joining. Soon thereafter southern Irish and United Kingdom representatives met to coordinate their approach, the southern Irish decision to apply for admission being contingent on the United Kingdom's being accepted. Later in 1961 Eire went through application formalities without waiting for the United Kingdom to be accepted, although it was clear at that time that Ireland would not actually join unless Britain were also admitted.

Things did not go at all smoothly for the Irish. The EEC Council of ministers decided that it could not pronounce on their application because of insufficient data and therefore summoned representatives of southern Ireland to Brussels in January 1962 to elucidate their case. Sean Lemass represented the nation and was cogent and persuasive in his arguments. However, after the breakdown of the British negotiations in January 1963, the EEC council suspended action on the Irish application. The Irish reactivated their application in May 1967, but without immediate result. Finally, in the post-de Gaulle years the logjam broke, and in early 1972 the government successfully negotiated entry for 1 January 1973. The people of southern Ireland now were faced with the question of whether or not they actually wanted to join. Because adhesion to the EEC involved certain amendments to the nation's constitution, the people were given the choice of voting "yes" or "no" in a national referendum. The arguments of Fianna Fail and of Fine Gael were that southern Ireland should join because membership in the Common Market would provide higher prices for agricultural goods and additional foreign capital to develop industry. The opposition came chiefly from the Labour party and from militant nationalists who argued that the economic benefits were by no means certain and that the loss of national sovereignty was not to be countenanced. The people's vote was overwhelming: 1,041,890 "yes" and only 211,891 "no."

In all probability the economy as a whole will adapt reasonably well to free competition with European nations, because the Republic's three economic plans were framed under the assumption that the nation would eventually be entering the Common Market and therefore emphasized making southern Irish industry and agriculture competitive with its European counterparts. Having noted this point, it remains to be said that there are still popular counter-pressures to the ascetic planning necessary in the Common Market era.

For example, although no longer the leading sector in the economy, the agricultural interests continue to be the most powerful bloc in Eire politics. The Fianna Fail party is especially indebted to rural interests and is most reluctant to offend the agricultural bloc, as the maintenance of agricultural subsidies in the third economic plan clearly indicates. The result is that the inefficient farmer remains and that agricultural holdings are usually well below the size necessary for optimal efficiency in agricultural production. Only a small proportion of the farms exceed 100 acres and the most common size is fifteen to thirty acres. If Irish land were uniformly rich and if it were given over to intensive truck farming, farms as small as thirty acres could be economically efficient, but in the areas of average soil and mixed farming which predominate in Ireland most farmers are only one step removed from subsistence agriculture. The small size of the farms means that the mechanization of Irish agriculture has been slow and that the manpower involved is high relative to the ultimate crop yield. Granted there are strong social reasons for preferring smaller holdings and familial agriculture to larger, more impersonal operations, but because the entire economy is interrelated the lag in agricultural productivity hurts town and city dwellers who have little voice in the matter. If it were not for the slow growth rate of the agricultural sector, the growth rate of the entire economy would be satisfactory by European standards. But the weakness of the agricultural sector leads to balance-of-payments problems which tend to dislocate the entire economy. Nevertheless, a government statement of 1961 remains an accurate capsule of agricultural policy to this day: "It has always been our policy—it is indeed a directive principle of social policy prescribed in the constitution—to seek to establish as many families as possible in economic security on the land."

Related to the agricultural problem is the matter of differential regional development. To a considerable extent southern Ireland consists of two economies. One of these, centering on Dublin and extending through Leinster and much of Munster, is an advanced economy based on modern industry and on larger than average agricultural holdings and includes the best land in Ireland. The other economy is that of the west of Ireland, which suffers from minimal industrialization and an agricultural sector comprising mostly small holdings of marginal land. Despite brave attempts at industrialization (the Shannon Airport development being the most successful), in spite of development plans for Galway and Limerick Cities, and despite the tourist industry, the province of Connacht and the western portions of Munster will almost certainly remain agricultural for the foreseeable future: in the late sixties Connacht had only 8.3 percent of the nonagricultural establishment of the country, 5.0 percent of the output, and 5.0 of the jobs. Unless there is large-scale industrialization in the south and west (which seems highly unlikely) the young people of those areas will continue either to migrate to the eastern coastal cities in large numbers or to emigrate: in the period from 1966 to 1971 the net emigration rate for the province of Connacht was 10.6 per 1,000 of population, almost five times the rate of Leinster. Given that the flight from the rural areas produced nearly universal condemnation by Irish social critics, and that industrialization of the west and south will not occur overnight, if ever, what can be done to keep the people on the land? The only alternative open to the government is to subsidize small, inefficient farms, thus exacerbating the economic problems described in the preceding paragraph.

Southern Irish industry, while greatly improved in efficiency in the last decade, still suffers from flaws that may prove crippling under Common Market conditions. The most perplexing of these is one of social organization, not of economics per se. Briefly stated, southern Ireland's industrial relations, meaning labor–management relations, are chaotic. The number of trade unions is absurdly high. The nation has 125 separate unions. This compares with sixteen industrial trade unions in West Germany and thirty-nine in Sweden. Even Great Britain, which, next to the Irish Republic, tops the union chaos table, has a higher ratio of workers to unions, having more than 600 unions but for a proportionally larger industrial work force. Of the 125 Eire unions only fifty-six have more than 500 members, and forty have less than 100. Matters are made all the worse because the Irish Congress of Trade Unions has no real power over any of the individual trade unions. Each is an autonomous body, free to pursue the whims of its members without reference to other groups in the trade union movement or to the general welfare of the economy. Moreover, under southern Irish law collective bargain agreements reached between employers and unions are not legal contracts. Neither party can be taken to court for failure to honor the agreement. Therefore, it is common for unions to call strikes even while an agreement with an employer is supposedly still in effect. This makes planning on the part of the employer very difficult and greatly increases the man-hours lost in strike time. To make matters worse, the decisions of the labor courts are not compulsory, and it is common for such decisions to be loftily ignored. Not surprisingly, the Irish Republic loses more time proportionately in industrial strikes than any nation with a significant degree of industrialization. Until now her economy has not been penalized as much as it might by these troubles because most of its trade has been with Britain, a nation whose industrial relations also have been very poor. The situation in the Common Market, however, will be different.

It is clear that the wages paid the average southern Irish laborer per work day are lower than those of most European countries with which southern Ireland will have to compete now that it has entered the Common Market. It is equally true, however, that southern Irish productivity per worker is lower than that of its international competitors, so that the Irish Republic does not enjoy any appreciable advantage in respect of labor cost as compared with the European nations, or even with the United Kingdom. Hence, the relevant question: is southern Ireland's cost per unit of production rising faster or slower than that of its potential competitors? If it is rising faster, then the situation for her industrial exports will be a continually deteriorating one; if slower, then the situation will improve. The best available statistics (covering the years 1950 to 1962, which encompassed the period of southern Ireland's industrial spurt) indicate that successive wage rounds resulted in the Republic's losing competitively over time to France, Germany, Italy, and The Netherlands, and gaining only over Sweden and the United Kingdom. If this trend has continued (and in view of continuing wage rounds during the later 1960's and early 1970's, there is good reason to believe it has), the competitive prognosis for southern Irish industry under the Common Market is dim indeed.

The confusion in Irish labor relations, combined with a series of excessive wage rounds, leads us to the problem of returns on industrial investment in Eire. In southern Ireland a higher proportion of industrial income goes to employees than in any major European country or in the United Kingdom. If (as seems probable) the capital–output ratio is roughly equal between Eire and its potential competitor countries, then the rate of return on capital invested in its industry is lower than elsewhere. Almost certainly this differential holds vis-à-vis the United Kingdom, and probably for the continental countries as well. Hence, in a Common Market economy Ireland would have last call on money available for industrial investment. Only through government subsidies, grants, and tax remissions could this difficulty be overcome, and these are limited by EEC regulations.

The continuing spiral in wage settlements is seen by most economists as the chief, but by no means the only, cause of southern Ireland's high inflation rate. During the early sixties the increase in costs and prices in Eire was among the highest in Europe, but in the late sixties the situation became even worse. The year 1968 saw a 5.5 percent inflation in the consumer price

index, and 1969 about the same, while 1970 was a worrisome
8.2 percent and 1971 a very disconcerting 9 percent. The
adverse effect of such inflation upon the Republic's balance-of-
payments problem is too obvious to need elaboration. The situation becomes all the more disturbing when one discovers that
in recent years public expenditure in southern Ireland has been
rising at the rate of about 12 percent per year. Every single year
in the 1960's public spending grew proportionately more than
did the gross national product. Government expenditure (including the capital expenditure of state-sponsored bodies) rose
from under 30 percent of GNP in 1959 to over 41 percent in
1969. This hardly augurs well for the Republic in a situation
wherein her crucial balance of payments will depend largely
upon her ability to keep domestic prices rising more slowly than
do those of her Common Market competitors.

Conceivably, the government could improve Eire's international trading position by reducing inflation through cutting
governmental spending, but here it is caught in a bind: the
Irish Republic has a high level of endemic unemployment:
unemployment was nearly 9 percent of the insured working
population in early 1972, a figure shockingly high by European
standards. The best indication of the permanent nature of the
problem is found in the figures of net emigration. The average
rate of emigration per 1,000 population has been as follows:

1926–36	5.6
1936–46	6.3
1946–51	8.2
1951–56	13.4
1956–61	14.8
1961–66	5.7
1966–71	4.2

In theory, the southern Irish government has three alternatives.
First, it can encourage emigration. But this solution is unacceptable for political reasons—indeed, recent governments
have taken great pride in the drop in emigration. The fact
remains, however, that in the Republic's economy a reduction
in emigration means an increase in unemployment. Second, if

southern Irishmen are encouraged to stay at home, employment in the agricultural sector can be maximized by heavily subsidizing small, near-subsistence farms. This, however, has a debilitating effect on the entire economy. The government, therefore, has little choice but to follow the third alternative, that is, to provide social welfare programs, which, however, continue to increase more quickly than the economy as a whole. And that brings one full circle, back to the problem of inflation and its effect upon the balance-of-payments problem.

The balance-of-payments situation is a peculiarly crucial one for southern Ireland. Normally the combined total of imports and exports amounts to about four fifths of the value of the national product, a very high figure compared with most European countries. In the language of the economist, the Irish Republic is both a small economy and an open one. Just how vulnerable it is to the slightest change in the international or domestic situation affecting its trading relationship is revealed by the fact that the Dublin economists estimate that the troubles in Northern Ireland will reduce the tourist revenue in the south by 7 percent, and thus reduce annual growth in GNP by one eighth—from 4.0 percent to 3.5 percent.

Behind all these questions relating to the position of southern Ireland in the Common Market is a larger one: given her lack of natural resources *and* her adherence to certain social and legal patterns (fragmented unions and noncontractual collective bargaining arrangements) is it possible to meet both the imperatives of political nationalism (for an independent economy) and the demands of the populace for the modern high-consumption life? Eamon de Valera in the 1930's said "no"—and that it was better to be independent than well-off. Since then, southern Irish politicians have been tacitly admitting that the two goals were indeed incompatible, but that it is better to be comfortable than independent.

VIII   Religion and Values

That religion in southern Ireland means Christianity and that the Christian church means the Roman Catholic church may be seen in the statistical statement of Table A.3, in which the population is shown to be 95 percent Catholic. The non-Catholic percentage of the population has fallen regularly since 1926 and in all probability will continue to diminish. Emigration has been proportionately greatest among non-Catholics. The statistics, while compelling, do not indicate the level of devotion of the Catholic church's adherents. The average Irish Catholic is not a nominal churchman; he is regular in attendance, respectful of the clergy, and reverent toward papal authority. Without a doubt southern Ireland is the most devout of Christian nations and possibly the most religious country in the world.

When seeking an explanation for this religious devotion, the chief point to bear in mind is that in Ireland, unlike England, Scotland, and Wales, the Protestant Reformation made little impact among the great majority of the population. The genealogy of the Catholic church in Ireland is unbroken. During the years of English rule the English governors of Ireland and their Irish associates were Protestant, but the native Irish by and large remained Catholic. The Catholic people suffered severely for maintaining their religious beliefs for in the Catholic-Protestant wars of the seventeenth century the Protestants were victorious. The Protestants, who comprised less than a fifth of the population, followed their victory by framing a penal code whose aim was simple: to persecute the Catholic religion out of existence and to impoverish all who clung to it. Admittedly penal codes were common in seventeenth- and eighteenth-century Europe, but the Irish code was singular in

130

that it was directed by the religious minority against the majority of the populace. The experiences of the penal years were burned into the Irish folk memory. Under adversity a devotion to the Catholic church was forged which was equalled only by the people's hatred of Protestantism. During the second half of the eighteenth century the penal code was gradually repealed, but it was not until 1829 that the last major disability, the barring of Roman Catholics from sitting in Parliament, was removed. The achievement of this right (termed "Catholic Emancipation") was the result of the extraordinary political acumen of Daniel O'Connell. In organizing the Catholics to gain Emancipation, O'Connell transformed them from a bitter, fragmented, and irresolute body into a cohesive, self-respecting, and aggressive force. The very fact that the Irish Republic is a nation today is so inextricably bound together with the history of the Catholic faith that one cannot refer to her as a nation without implicitly referring as well to Irish Catholicism.

How is the Catholic church in Ireland organized? In an ecclesiastical pyramid is the simplest answer. At the apex of the structure are four archbishops, each of whom is in charge of a province. The ranking archbishop (but often not the most influential) is the Archbishop of Armagh, who is usually a cardinal and who is styled "Primate of All Ireland." The Province of Armagh, which may be thought of as being roughly coterminous with the historical province of Ulster, includes all of Northern Ireland plus some of the Republic as well. In 1956 there were approximately 968,000 souls in the charge of the Archbishop of Armagh. Under his immediate direction are nine bishops. The second ranking archbishopric (which is often filled by a man of greater practical influence than Armagh) is Dublin, which has four bishoprics and 988,000 constituents. The Archbishop of Dublin bears the title "Primate of Ireland." The two other archbishoprics are Tuam and Cashel. The former contains seven bishoprics and 440,000 persons in the west of Ireland. Cashel, which covers the southern counties, maintains seven bishops and includes 886,000 laymen. Taken together, the archbishops and bishops form a hierarchy which is probably the most powerful in the Christian world. The doc-

trinal opinions and social views of the clergy are kept within
very strict limits by the bishops.

There are 1,143 parishes in Ireland. Among the individual
dioceses the number of parishes ranges from eleven in Ross to
ninety-eight in the Archdiocese of Dublin. There were 2,514
Catholic places of worship in Ireland in the late 1950's. The
number of clergy serving these churches was 3,798 secular
(parish) clergy and 1,180 regular clergy in special orders (e.g.
the Order of Preachers). The ratio of priests of all sorts to laity
is one to 558, which despite popular misconceptions, is not particularly high. The ratio in Britain, for example, is one to 507.

It is imperative to realize that the Catholic church in the
Republic is a voluntary church. It is not established by law and
receives no direct financial aid from the state. Indeed, upon
examination it becomes clear that in some ways the Catholic
church in southern Ireland is treated less favorably than are
religious denominations in the United States. In particular,
church properties are subject both to local and central government taxation with only three exceptions: churches and
grounds, primary schools and grounds, and charitable institutions for the aid or education of the poor. Secondary schools
and institutions of higher education (such as seminaries) are
taxed. The income of the clergy, however, is treated very generously. Priests, brothers, and nuns pay taxes only if they receive a regular salary (for instance, if they are members of a
teaching order and are paid by the state for their educational
activities). The money priests receive in offerings from the
faithful (about 80 percent of the income of the Catholic
clergy) is tax-free. Hence, in contrast to the situation in the
United States, the church as an institution is taxed, while
the religious professionals receive wide tax exemptions. In the
United States, of course, the situation is precisely the opposite.

What political powers does the Catholic church have in the
Irish Republic? At first glance, the question seems to be unnecessary because the church rarely intervenes directly in
southern Irish elections and never gives its support to a specific
party. Politics, however, do not always have to be played

through the intermediary of established parties, and from one point of view one might even describe the church (by which in this section we mean the hierarchy) as a political party of its own, or at least a political lobby. From another viewpoint the synod of bishops may be regarded as a paragovernmental body which in practice has the power to veto whole classes of legislation prepared by members of the secular parliament. Later, we will give examples which illustrate how each of these interpretations is possible.

If one looks at southern Ireland's constitution, one is impressed by its inconsistencies. The constitution of 1937, for example, guarantees that the state will not endow any religion or impose any religious discrimination or interfere with liberty of religious conscience. The Catholic church remains, therefore, a voluntary rather than a state church. The church even lacks juridical personality under civil law. Thus, instead of owning property as a church, the Catholic church has to appoint its bishops and priests as trustees in much the same way that partners are appointed under the various companies acts. Yet, even though the constitution denies the Catholic church a juridical personality, in practice the church has a special position in the southern Irish polity which it has employed in three ways. The first has been to preserve and extend church control in areas of special interest. In particular, the church has almost complete control of southern Irish education at the primary and secondary levels. Its influence in this area is exercised in keeping rivals away from the field and in pressing the government for incremental funds. The second use of the church's position has been to induce the state to enact legislation embodying the moral precepts of the Catholic faith. The legislation on censorship, divorce, and contraception falls into this category. A third and considerably less publicized exercise of church influence is in efforts to prevent the introduction or passage of legislation which the hierarchy deems to be morally repugnant. The most publicized, yet least understood, action of the third sort was the notorious "Browne case" of 1950–51. This case is worth careful scrutiny for it indicates most clearly both the power and methods of the bishops when they enter the political arena.

The usual summation of the Browne case is roughly as follows: Dr. Noel Browne, naïve, energetic, idealistic Minister for Health, attempted to introduce a mother and child health scheme. The bishops disapproved because they believed that such a plan might lead to young women being taught non-Catholic practices relating to marital life and child-rearing. Thereupon the cabinet deserted Browne, and he was forced to resign.

In actual fact the case was much more complicated. The bishops opposed the legislation not merely because it was gynecological but because it was socialistic. Moreover, outside forces, in particular the Irish Medical Association, entered the picture and, not surprisingly, party intrigues were involved. Browne himself was not an innocent.

The chief actors in this church-state drama were five: first and most important was Dr. Noel Browne, an extraordinary man with a unique background. He had grown up in poverty, and both his parents had died of tuberculosis. His eldest sister tried to raise the parentless children in London but she too died of the disease. By great good fortune Browne was admitted to a private preparatory school where his sister had worked and was then educated free of charge by the Jesuits at fashionable and rigorous Beaumont. A patron paid his way through Trinity College Medical School. After practicing for a time in England, Browne returned to Ireland in 1944 and began work in the Newcastle Sanitorium in County Wicklow. Soon he was leading a national campaign against tuberculosis, and when Clann na Poblachta decided that an anti-tuberculosis program would be a good plank in its political platform, Browne was adopted as a candidate and elected to the Dail. In 1948 he became Minister for Health in the coalition government. The important points to be remembered about Browne are that he was a crusading zealot on medical matters, that he had no significant political experience before becoming a minister, and that although a devout Roman Catholic his educational background was considerably different from that of most of his political colleagues: he had much more education than most, and that education had been acquired abroad and in Trinity College, Dublin.

The second major figure was John Aloysius Costello, who became Taoiseach in February 1948 when the de Valera government fell after more than a decade and a half in office. A successful lawyer, Costello had been the Attorney General from 1926 to 1932 in the first government of the Irish Free State, and, though high in the ranks of the Fine Gael party during the thirties and forties, he always seemed to be more of a lawyer than a politician. When it became clear that the de Valera government could no longer command a majority, a coalition government was patched together from a gaggle of parties that had only two things in common: they were anti-de Valera and they wanted to be in office. The coalition was comprised as follows: Fine Gael 31, Clann na Talmhan (farmers) 7, Clann na Poblachta (republicans) 10, Labour 14, National Labour 5, Independents 8. The coalition was formed hastily, and the leaders of the various parties clearly mistrusted each other. Unfortunately, Costello was not a man trained to sail such a ship. He was by nature indecisive and retiring. At his most indolent he made Stanley Baldwin look decisive: "As one of his daughters remarked," the *Irish Digest* reported, "he is the sort of man who spends the evening perched on the edge of his favorite chair, in dreadful discomfort because his dog is occupying the centre of the seat and he doesn't like to disturb it."

The volatility of the political situation was increased by the presence of Sean MacBride, the head of Clann na Poblachta, as Minister for External Affairs and as the second most powerful man in the coalition ministry. MacBride's pedigree and education gave him the highest patriotic credentials, if they did not induce the most stable behavior. (As Minister for External Affairs MacBride spent so much time in Paris that he was popularly known as "the External Minister for Affairs.") He was the son of Sean MacBride, who was executed for his part in the 1916 rebellion and of Maude Gonne MacBride, the eccentric beauty who had inspired some of William Butler Yeats's poems. Born in 1904, he spent most of his teenage years fighting first the British and then the Free State government. In 1925 he became adjutant general in the Irish Republican Army and in 1936 commander-in-chief of the IRA. He resigned from the IRA a year later and took up the practice of law. When the Second World War ended he formed a new political party, Clann na Poblachta, which combined a New Deal-style program in social matters with old-fashioned republicanism in such matters as the partition of Ireland. It is worth noting that both MacBride and his political party were on record as favoring a mother and child health scheme in which no fees whatsoever would be charged.

The fourth and fifth major performers on the stage were institutions. One of these was the Irish Medical Association, which served as a combination guild, political lobby, and trade union for the southern Irish doctors. The IMA opposed any legislation that lowered the doctor's income, that interfered in any way with the doctor-patient relationship, or that smacked of socialized medicine. For comparative purposes the IMA attitudes in the later 1940's can be described as roughly the same as those of the American Medical Association today.

The other major group was the hierarchy of the Roman Catholic church. Politically the hierarchy at this time was highly conservative, being, in the words of one observer, "eighteen degrees to the right of the Spanish hierarchy." The hierarchy was wedded to laissez-faire economics and looked upon socialism as a moral evil. On moral questions the bishops were especially conservative, being hostile to any government program that might lead to a lowering of the standards of sexual conduct. The chief figure in the hierarchy was John Charles McQuaid, Archbishop of Dublin, who was deeply committed to protecting the moral welfare of the Catholic people and to preserving the privileges and position of the church as an institution.

It is not generally understood that the chain of events leading to the Browne scandal began not with the coalition government but with de Valera's ministry, and that the sequence was to a considerable degree a series of footnotes to a badly drafted Health Act enacted by Fianna Fail in 1947—a complicated measure which, among other things, provided for a mother and child health plan. This mother and child scheme (Part III of the Act, sections 21 to 28) gave local health authorities responsibility for making arrangements for safeguarding the health of a woman as respects motherhood, and for safeguarding the health of children up to age sixteen. Included in the responsibility for children was the duty to "provide for their education in matters relating to health." Expectant mothers were to be educated in medical matters relating to motherhood. The act, it is important to note, did not make it clear whether or not the mothers and children were to pay for the services and education or whether it was to be free to all. The only clause relevant to finance stated that the central government would pay up to one half of the expenses incurred by local authorities under the mother and child scheme. The most reasonable interpretation (one accepted by most politicians at the time) was that this meant a free-for-all scheme. The 1947 act did not name specific dates on which the various sections would become effective, thus making it incumbent upon those in office after the act was passed to develop arrangements and inaugurate the program.

Two groups attacked the health measure. Some political opponents of de Valera assailed the mother and child scheme as unconstitutional because it took from the parent the right and responsibility of educating children in matters of health. J. M. Dillon, an opposition deputy, tried to raise the constitutional issue during the debates on the bill, but the speaker of the house ruled that he could not do so. Hence, in early December 1947, after the bill had passed, a group led by Dillon began a court case asking that the mother and child sections of the Health Act be declared repugnant to the constitution. Interestingly, Dillon was soon to become a cabinet member in the new coalition government. John A. Costello was also involved in pressing the suit.

The second group which did not accept Part III of the 1947 Health Act was the Roman Catholic hierarchy. The bishops, it must be emphasized, operated secretly, and the Dillon-Costello forces were unaware of their activities. In October 1947 the hierarchy sent the then Taoiseach, de Valera, a letter in which they stated their disapproval, stating their objections to allowing a public authority to provide for the health of all children and expectant mothers and to its educating children and mothers in matters of health. The hierarchy pointed out that a public authority's claiming such powers was entirely and directly contrary to the teaching of the Catholic church and was in violation of the rights of the family, the church, and the medical profession. De Valera shrewdly delayed in answering the hierarchy and finally, in the middle of February, 1948, only two days before he left office, replied, stating that he had not written earlier because the Health Act was being questioned in court.

This left the Costello coalition, which came into office almost immediately thereafter, with a threefold problem: how and when to invoke the acceptable provisions of the Health Act, how to rewrite the constitutionally offensive portions, and how to mollify the Catholic bishops. Significantly—and this is of capital importance—Costello did not open conversations with the hierarchy, nor did he give his Minister for Health, Dr. Browne, a copy of the hierarchy's letter until more than two years later, long after the situation had exploded.

In late June 1948 Costello directed his cabinet's attention to the health situation, and Dr. Browne then brought forward the head of a bill to bring the mother and child section of the Health Act into operation. The plan involved the repeal of the portions of part III of de Valera's 1947 Act to which Dillon and Costello had objected. The cabinet gave Browne's tentative suggestions its approval and sanctioned a mother and child health scheme that would be free of cost to all who used it irrespective of their level of income. With the cabinet's directions in hand, Dr. Browne went to work.

The Costello cabinet was a loosely run affair, and by nature Browne was a lone crusader, so he forged his plan without more than passing consultation with his colleagues and the Taoiseach. He had in mind a twofold scheme which would provide the following free services to mothers before, during, and after childbirth: family practitioner care, special consultation and hospital treatment if needed, visits from a midwife to the home if required, and dental and eye treatment. For children up to sixteen years of age Browne wished to provide, also totally free of charge, medical care for all illnesses, special and hospital services, home visits by public health nurses, and dental and eye treatment. Browne envisaged a plan involving no means test, no contributions, and no interference with the doctor-patient relationship. Anyone who wished could use any or every one of the facilities offered, and even if all the facilities were used by a family, there would be no doctor's bill in respect of maternity or the health of children under sixteen.

In August 1948, in the course of his work, Browne wrote the Irish Medical Association telling them that the government had considered the opinion which the IMA had expressed earlier opposing a mother and child scheme without a financial means test and informing them that the government had rejected their proposal for the imposition of such a test. Following several months devoted to drafting the details of his scheme, Browne, in mid-1950, sent the Irish Medical Association a copy of his new proposals and began serious negotiations with that body. Proposals and counterproposals were made, with Browne clinging to his determination to introduce the mother and child scheme without a means test. Negotiations dragged on.

Now, it is fair to ask, did Costello and the cabinet know what Browne was doing? It is impossible to say. Costello stated that he never received from Browne a copy of the August 1948 letter which Browne sent to the IMA and that he finally had received a copy from a doctor outside the government. This is probably an accurate statement, since Browne in the later recriminations did not dispute the point. Browne, however, stated that he sent to each of his cabinet colleagues a copy of the draft proposals on the basis of which he began negotiating with the IMA in 1950. Costello never effectively disputed this point. That the cabinet knew by mid-1950 the nature of Browne's plan for a free-for-all mother and child service is indicated by the fact that the government consented to the inclusion of £400,000 in the budget of the Department of Health

for 1950–51 for a scheme without a means test. Further estimates for 1951–52 included £661,000 for the scheme. One
must conclude, therefore, that by April or May 1950 the full
cabinet knew what Browne was proposing and still was willing
to support his scheme.

But things turned sour. The IMA and the Irish Catholic
hierarchy moved hard against Browne in the late months of
1950. First to move effectively was the hierarchy. On 10 October 1950 the Bishop of Ferns, who was secretary to the Catholic
hierarchy, dropped a bombshell in the form of a letter to Taoiseach Costello. Because the letter vividly reflects the Catholic
bishops' social views during this period it deserves quotation
at length:

> In their opinion the powers taken by the State in the pro-
> posed Mother and Child Health service are in direct oppo-
> sition to the rights of the family and of the individual and
> are liable to very great abuse. Their character is such that no
> assurance that they would be used in moderation could justify
> their enactment. If adopted in law they would constitute a
> ready-made instrument for future totalitarian aggression.
>
> The right to provide for the health of children belongs to
> parents, not to the State. The State has the right to intervene
> only in a subsidiary capacity, to supplement, not to supplant.
>
> It may help indigent or neglectful parents; it may not de-
> prive 90% of parents of their rights because of 10% neces-
> sitous or negligent parents.
>
> It is not sound social policy to impose a State medical
> service on the whole community on the pretext of relieving
> the necessitous 10% from the so-called indignity of the
> means test.
>
> The right to provide for the physical education of children
> belongs to the family and not to the State. Experience has
> shown that physical or health education is closely interwoven
> with moral questions on which the Catholic Church has
> definite teaching.
>
> Education in regard to motherhood includes instructions
> in regard to sex relations, chastity and marriage. The State
> has no competence to give instructions in such matters. We
> regard with the gravest apprehension the proposal to give

to local medical officers the right to tell Catholic girls and women how they should behave in regard to this sphere of conduct at once so delicate and sacred.

Gynaecological care may be, and in some countries is, interpreted to include provision for birth limitation and abortion. We have no guarantee that State officials will respect Catholic principles in regard to these matters. Doctors trained in institutions in which we have no confidance may be appointed as medical officers under the proposed services, and may give gynaecological care not in accordance with Catholic principles.

The proposed service also destroys the confidential relationship between doctor and patient and regards all cases of illness as matters for public record and research without regard to the individual's right to privacy.

The elimination of private medical practitioners by a State-paid service has not been shown to be necessary or even advantageous to the patient, the public in general or the medical profession.

This documents speaks for itself, but three comments are in order. First, it is surprising to discover the tone of alienation from and suspicion of the Irish Republic which pervades the letter, for no government in the world was more intent upon governing according to Catholic principles than was the Eire government. Second, it is worth underscoring that the prelates, while ostensibly concerned here only with moral questions, enlarged the moral sphere to include political and economic matters as well. The hierarchy sanctified as morally desirable the laissez-faire approach to medicine which prevails in a purely capitalistic society. Third, the prelates' fears were to some extent based on misinformation. Browne did not contemplate an educational program with respect to motherhood which would in any way interfere with Catholic moral teaching. At most, he wished elementary hygienic practices to be taught.

The merits or demerits of the prelates' case were irrelevant, however. The real point was the power of the bishops. Dr. Browne acknowledged the bishops' power when, on being summoned in mid-October 1950 to appear before the Archbishop of Dublin, John Charles MacQuaid, he made immediate arrangements to appear the next day. MacQuaid, in the presence of the Bishops of Ferns and of Galway, read to Browne the hierarchy's letter to Costello, and a long discussion followed. What actually happened in the course of the discussion has never been determined precisely. Browne later claimed that he felt he had satisfied all of the bishops' objections and that everything was fine. Yet, his later actions indicate that he promised only to be certain that there was no potential friction in his arrangements between the church's activities and the educational activities of the health authorities. This left unmet the hierarchy's objections on moral grounds to having a mother and child scheme without a means test. Either Browne completely misunderstood the hierarchy's objection on the matter or, more likely in view of his later actions, he refused to admit the hierarchy's right to veto medical legislation simply because it smacked of socialism.

To be certain the hierarchy's point was understood, MacQuaid summoned the Taoiseach, and Costello responded to the archbishop's call with a speed equal to Browne's. On the twelfth of October, one day after the MacQuaid-Browne interview, MacQuaid told the Prime Minister that he was not satisfied with the previous day's conversation with Browne, and that Browne, while willing to consider the educational concerns of the hierarchy, had ignored the question of the means test. Before himself going to see the archbishop, Costello had told Browne that such a meeting would occur, and after seeing the archbishop the Taoiseach briefed Browne on the results. Browne stated later that the Taoiseach told him everything was all right, while Costello later stated that he informed Browne of the hierarchy's continued objections. Whatever the truth of either claim, it is clear that the hierarchy was not satisfied with the scheme, that Browne either was unable to see or refused to recognize these objections, and that Costello, who knew full well the bishops' objections, did not communicate them clearly and authoritatively to Browne. A strong prime minister in command of his cabinet would have broken through Browne's shell, but Costello was neither a strong personality nor fully in command.

Archbishop MacQuaid did not personally deliver the letter of 10 October 1950 until the seventh of November. On the ninth or tenth, Costello gave Browne a copy and asked for his suggestions for a reply. This transaction is a crucial point, admitted by both men. From the tenth of November onward Browne clearly knew that the hierarchy still had objections (if they had none, why would he need to reply?). His actions from that date, therefore, must be taken as an attempt to out-maneuver the bishops politically and also, if necessary, to out-maneuver those of his colleagues (especially Costello) who were willing to give in to the bishops' objections. This conclusion in no way impinges on the question of whether or not the bishops were meddling in something that was not properly their business, but does make the air of shocked surprise at the bishops' objection which Browne later feigned when the affair came out in the open ring decidedly false.

Sometime in November 1950 Browne handed Costello a draft reply to the archbishop's letter. In this reply, which was written for Costello's signature, Browne stated that it was presumed that the government plan of having no means test in the scheme would not be a factor in the hierarchy's objections. This, of course, was obviously not the case, and Costello did not send the letter. Whether or not Costello told Browne that he had not sent the reply to MacQuaid is uncertain—Browne later claimed that Costello did not, Costello that he had. In any case, after MacQuaid's return from Rome in November Costello was in regular communication with him, although Browne was not informed of these meetings. Clearly the latter months of 1950 and in early 1951 an alliance of the Taoiseach and the Archbishop of Dublin against the Minister of Health was developing.

While the hierarchy was kicking at Browne's one knee, the Irish Medical Association was attempting to dislocate the other. Matters came to a head in November 1950. For several months previously, Browne had been negotiating with the IMA. A plebiscite of the medical profession was taken, and the great majority voted to have nothing to do with the free-for-all scheme propounded by Browne. At this point Costello stepped in, not to shore up Browne's position but to undercut it. Costello forced Browne to meet the representatives of the IMA in a caucus attended by the Taoiseach himself and the deputy prime minister, Dr. O'Higgins. Shortly before the meeting Costello sat down and studied the 1947 Health Act, an exercise he had not performed for over three years. He came to the sudden conclusion that he had been wrong in the past in interpreting the act as requiring that the mother and child scheme be operated without a means test. Here was a political escape, for he now decided that there was nothing in statute law to keep him from mollifying both the IMA and the Catholic hierarchy by withdrawing the government's tacit approval of the free-for-all scheme. This he proceeded to do on 27 November, when he, O'Higgins, and Browne met the representatives of the IMA. Costello's new idea was that the government could still call the scheme a "free" one even if it had a means test, a bit of sophistry which fooled no one. In any case, Costello effectively let the medical profession know that he was not backing Browne. Browne was furious and, not surprisingly, accused the Taoiseach of having acted treacherously toward him.

Despite this setback, Browne continued to fight, hoping apparently to win the day by ignoring the opposition and presenting the free-for-all scheme to the public as an accomplished fact. The situation detonated in March 1951. On the eighth of March Costello received from Browne a printed brochure about the mother and child health scheme Browne was about to introduce. The scheme involved no means test. Costello was horrified. (Why, as Prime Minister, he had not kept events under his control is an interesting question.) Archbishop MacQuaid received a copy of the brochure on the same day that Costello did. MacQuaid immediately wrote to Costello, informing him that the scheme as publicly announced in Browne's brochure was not acceptable to the hierarchy. MacQuaid followed this by a letter of 8 March to Browne enunciating the same view. Browne claimed to be surprised by the hierarchy's opinion, although how he could have been is hard to understand. In any case, after being told by Costello that he would have to meet the hierarchy's objections he took the extraordinary step of asking the hierarchy for a definitive, official opinion on the scheme. This request was unheard of, for always previously the bishops had been able to exercise their influence secretly. Nevertheless, the bishops faced the issue squarely, and in a letter of 5 April the government was informed by MacQuaid that the hierarchy officially discountenanced Browne's mother and child health plan.

Meanwhile, during the month of March the Irish Medical Association was also bringing pressure on Costello about Browne's insistence on not including a means test in his scheme. Costello was now on record as opposing anything that even suggested socialized medicine and when, on 21 March, Costello received copies of a letter of instructions for the scheme which Browne was distributing to the IMA, Costello stepped in and quashed the mailing. The next day he wrote to Browne and told him that the program would not be acceptable to the government until Browne had modified it to meet the Catholic hierarchy's objections, by which Costello meant, at a minimum, the introduction of a means test. Browne was also told that he was not permitted to describe his scheme as government policy. The cabinet joined Costello in the retreat from the free-for-all scheme which it had mandated in 1948. On 6 April 1951, one day after the hierarchy pronounced definitely against the program, the cabinet voted that it would not approve a scheme which did not include a means test.

The coup de grace to Browne was given not by Costello, but by his party leader, Sean MacBride. Clan na Poblachta as a party was pledged to support a free-for-all mother and child health scheme, and thus MacBride was in a very dangerous position, because if his party followed Browne and adhered to its professed policy MacBride would be forced either to resign from the cabinet or to resign from his party. The ideal course would have been for MacBride to convince Browne voluntarily to give up the free-for-all idea, and then the party probably would have followed their joint lead in the matter. Accordingly, from December onward, MacBride tried to cajole Browne into abandoning the free-for-all approach, but with no success. When on 6 April the cabinet formally voted not to back a free-for-all scheme MacBride summoned a meeting of his party. This meeting was a remarkable session, beginning at three o'clock on Sunday afternoon, 8 April, and continuing until three or four o'clock the next morning. Browne was grilled incessantly. The final result was that the party did not formally abandon its support for a free-for-all scheme, but did pass a vote of loyalty to MacBride. But Browne still remained a threat to MacBride's control of the party; it appears that Browne was the more popular of the two men and that MacBride was resentfully jealous. Therefore, on Tuesday evening, 10 April, MacBride took the extraordinary step (he was not, after all, the Taoiseach) of asking Browne for his resignation from the cabinet. Browne, realizing that he and his program were about to crash, decided to go down in a pyrotechnic display that would illuminate the entire tawdry business. He resigned on 11 April. He supplied copies of the relevant documents to the press and precipitated a full dress debate in the Dail on his resignation and on his charges against the government.

The epilogue is interesting. The Browne incident lost the Costello coalition some very precious votes in the Dail, its control became unsure, and a general election was necessary. Ironically, the general election of May 1951 gave Browne and his few followers the balance of power between the parties, and Browne took his revenge and put de Valera's Fianna Fail back in power. Browne remained allied with de Valera until 1957 and then in 1958 founded his own party, the National Progressive Democratic party, which was a failure. Eventually in 1964 he joined the Labour party.

We have spent a considerable amount of time in discussing what was essentially a minor political intrigue. The reason for this is that the Browne case was the only instance in the history of independent southern Ireland when the curtains were drawn back and the public allowed to see the backstage maneuvering of politicians and bishops. It is, therefore, the only complete case study we have of the action of the Catholic church in southern Irish politics. Four interpretive points are in order. First, it must be reemphasized that the entire affair was a sordid, squalid bit of political intrigue. There were no heroes or villains, just people playing the political game. Costello was weak, indecisive, and eventually treacherous to Browne; Mac-Bride was disloyal to his party colleague and willing to sacrifice his own principles rather than leave high office; the Irish Medical Association acted as a monopoly guild seeking only its own economic self-interest and not the public good; Browne himself was by turn naïve and headstrong. Quite consciously, he tried to outmaneuver his opponents and committed the cardinal political sin of overestimating his own powers. And what about the hierarchy? The bishops were no worse (and no better) in the way they played the political game than were the others. They acted like any political interest group; they defined their self-interest and then played the political game to promote that interest.

A second point: every effort was made to keep the hierarchy's part in the affair silent. It was assumed, as part of normal cabinet procedure, that the hierarchy had the right to advise the government but that the bishops did not have to explain their intermeddling in politics to the electorate. "May I say," Costello told the Dail, "that all this matter was intended to be private and to be adjusted behind closed doors and was never intended to be the subject of public controversy." Or, he might have added, of public scrutiny. Third, an outside observer cannot help but be stunned by the extraordinary arrogance with which Archbishop MacQuaid treated the cabinet of the Eire government. The members of the ministry accepted this treatment as the natural order of things. According to Costello, who had no complaints against MacQuaid, "the Archbishop insisted in every interview he had with Deputy Dr. Browne and in every letter that was written that he dealt with me [Costello] as head of the Government and that it was only with the head of the government the hierarchy would deal and it was, in fact, as a matter of courtesy and kindness that the Archbishop of Dublin saw the Minister for Health on several occasions."

Fourth, it must be emphasized that every member of the cabinet (which was composed solely of Catholics) accepted the right of the hierarchy to veto legislation which was morally incompatible with Catholic teaching. Dr. Browne shared this acceptance. Sean MacBride summarized the situation as follows: "Those of us in the House who are Catholic are, as such, of course, bound to give obedience to the rulings of our Church and of our Hierarchy." In effect, the hierarchy of the church assumed a veto right over any legislation it believed to be morally repugnant.

Anyone reading the narrative of the Browne case cannot fail to be struck with how generously the moral sphere was defined by their lordships. It included not only matters relating to religion and education, but questions of political and constitutional theory. The bishops condemned as immoral any scheme of medical welfare for which no money was charged. Socialism, by clear implication, was an immoral creed, and the bishops would do their best to stem its onslaught. The classic (if slightly misleading) summation of the situation was published by Ireland's leading man of letters, Sean O'Faolain, in *The Bell* in June 1951. "Here in the Republic," he wrote, "as this crisis has revealed to us, we have two parliaments: a parliament at Maynooth [where the bishops meet] and a parliament in Dublin." He later added, "The Dail proposes: Maynooth disposes." While memorable because of its epigrammatic style, O'Faolain's likening of the hierarchy to a second parliament is misleading, because a parliament is an institution created to govern politically while the hierarchy is an institution created to govern religiously. Hence, Maynooth can have political influence but it can never have political power. The bishops possess a veto right not as a second parliament, but as a massively influential political lobby. The veto right of the bishops is dependent upon the ministry in power accepting their decision and upon the electorate consenting to this arrangement. Clearly, in 1951 the electorate and the cabinet were willing to accept the bishops' veto on legislative matters.

When we turn from the fifties to the seventies the question quickly becomes: do the bishops continue to claim a right to veto any Dail legislation of which they do not approve, and do the elected officials and the electorate still countenance this arrangement? Unfortunately, there is no way to know. The Browne case was a rare glimpse behind the religious-political curtains, and the chances of a similar case happening again soon are small. One plausible suggestion is that the hierarchy had its fingers burned so badly by the Browne affair that it no longer plays politics. An equally reasonable suggestion is that the bishops have reacted not by becoming timorous but by becoming more discreet and more efficient in their intrigues. Whether or not the electorate would still acquiesce to the hierarchy's veto if a controversial case came to light is a matter for speculation.

At this point it is appropriate to insert a brief parenthesis on the Protestant denominations, of which, for practical purposes, there are only three in the Republic: the Anglicans, the Presbyterians, and the Methodists. Each of these churches, like the Roman Catholic church, is organized on an all-Ireland basis. Unlike the Catholic church, each of the three has its greatest strength not in the Republic, but in Northern Ireland. In southern Ireland most of the constituents of each of these denominations are found in the towns and cities and especially in the Dublin area. The coastal strip for twenty miles south of Dublin is known as the "Protestant belt." The most important of the Protestant denominations is the Church of Ireland (Anglican) which, like the Catholic church, claims descent from the undivided western church of the pre-Reformation era. Until 1871 the Church of Ireland was the Irish state church, holding the same position in Ireland that the Church of England still holds in that country. The Church of Ireland is distinctly Protestant in its theology, but maintains a basic organizational structure similar to that of the Irish Catholic church. In the Church of Ireland the country is split into two provinces, Armagh and Dublin, each with its own archbishop. The province of Armagh contains eight bishoprics. Dublin six. In contrast to the Catholic church, the Anglican church in Ireland has a democratic component. Laymen are involved in the selection of local rectors and of bishops, and parish clergymen participate in the selection of the bishops who will be their religious superiors. In 1961 there were slightly more than 104,000 members of the Church of Ireland residing in the Republic. The other two Protestant denominations, the Presbyterians and the Methodists, are much less significant numerically than the Anglicans. The Presbyterians enrolled almost 19,000 members in the Republic in 1961, the Methodists between 6,000 and 7,000. Both of these denominations are organized on congregational rather than on episcopal lines.

Realizing that the Protestants are such a small minority in the Republic it is logical to ask how well they are treated. The answer is, reasonably well. There is no limitation on their religious or educational activities, and in the latter sphere the government bends over backward to be sure that Protestant children are adequately treated. From the very beginning of the Free State the Protestants were dealt with on generous terms, even though most of them had been unionists and as such had opposed the movement for Irish independence. The Protestants who remained in southern Ireland soon became accustomed to the new situation and at no time were they a threat to the new state. When Eamon de Valera came to power in 1932 the Protestants were frightened, but their fears were ill-grounded. Despite pressure from some of the Catholic bishops, de Valera maintained a benevolent position on the "minority problem," not only from personal conviction but also because any hopes of reuniting Northern Ireland with the south depended on the south's being able to demonstrate that Protestants could be fairly treated in a predominantly Catholic country. Most Protestants are genuinely appreciative of this toleration, but some say, bitterly, "They are treating us like household pets to try to show that if Ireland were united there would be no oppression of the northern Protestants."

Undeniably, Protestants still hold important positions in southern Irish society. They are better educated and wealthier than the majority of the population. Sixty-five of every 1,000 Protestants are directors, managers, or company secretaries. Only nine of each 1,000 Catholics hold similar positions. Eighty-three of every 1,000 Protestants hold professional or technical appointments in contrast to forty-three of every thousand Catholics.

Nevertheless, the Protestants are somewhat unhappy. Of course, any religious minority is apt to feel slightly uncomfortable when submerged in such a large majority, but there is more to the Protestant apprehension than that. The government of southern Ireland today is undeniably Catholic in tone. All major state occasions begin with Catholic religious exercises. It is difficult for Protestants, unless exceptionally wealthy, to have any influence on local affairs. Perhaps most disquieting to Protestants is the fact that the Catholic view of family life is enshrined in statute law. The sale of contraceptives is banned in southern Ireland as is the dissemination of information on methods of birth control not approved by the Roman Catholic church. There are no provisions for divorce, and the southern Irish courts have ruled that the written pledge of a Protestant in a mixed marriage to raise his children as Catholics is enforceable under Irish law. Granted, if both partners decide to ignore the pledge it is not binding, but if the Protestant partner goes back on the pledge without the consent of the spouse, the courts can intervene. In addition to these complaints, it is probable that most Protestants are less than enthusiastic about the Republic's censorship laws which operate according to Catholic dogmatic principles.

The result of these grievances and discomforts is that the Protestants emigrate in much higher proportions than do the Catholics. Protestant emigration was especially marked in the 1920's, but the rate continues to remain high. Thus, each year the Protestant proportion of the population dwindles, and the minority problems which lead to emigration are intensified. A demographer extrapolating from present population trends could point to the time, perhaps one hundred years hence, when the indigenous Protestants in the Irish Republic will have become a vanished species. It will be a great loss to the Republic if the last remnants of the old Anglo-Irish ascendancy class disappear, for, as William Butler Yeats remarked, they were not a petty people.

Generalization about southern Ireland's moral code are apt to be met by all manner of objections from rigid social scientists, especially in view of the absence of any sound empirical survey of morals and sexuality such as the Kinsey Reports provide for the United States. Having admitted the absence of such data, the fact remains that there *is* a moral code which the historian and the observer of the modern Irish Republic can describe with reasonable accuracy. This code, unlike that of most nations, is strikingly consistent throughout geographic and social groupings. There is one recognized moral code for the entire nation, and it is cohesive, self-consistent, and highly conservative.

Not surprisingly, the Republic's moral code is largely a function of the actions of the Irish Catholic church since 1850. The crucial date in the modern church's history was the appointment of Paul Cullen to the hierarchy in 1849. As archbishop first of Armagh and then of Dublin, Cullen worked efficiently and unrelentingly to stamp out irregularities and laxities in the clergy's moral teaching and in the laity's moral practices. In so doing he struck a sympathetic note in the Irish church, because ever since the founding of Maynooth Seminary in 1795 there had been strong elements of Jansenism in the training and outlook of the clergy. (Jansenism, for our purposes, may be thought of as the Roman Catholic equivalent of Puritanism.) The church's teachings on moral matters seem to have been frozen at about the turn of the present century, making possible Desmond Fennell's provocative, if overly simple, thesis "that what we call Irish Catholicism is simply the fusion of nineteenth-century Victorian culture with the thing that came from Rome [to Ireland] in the nineteenth century."

But, it might be asked, has not the church's teaching been liberalized in recent years? The answer is: not much. Major changes have been made in liturgical matters. For example, in June 1964 the bishops decided to use the vernacular in the liturgy; an Irish Theological Association has been formed to stimulate the clergy to an understanding of the new vistas in Catholic theology; a Biblical Association has been established and new systems of religious instruction have recently been developed. In 1970, Friday abstinence was abandoned. These changes, however, are devotional and theological. In the moral sphere the church's teachings remain almost totally unchanged since the late Victorian age (that is, if one discounts as insignificant such liberalizing measures as Bishop Browne's announcement in early 1969 that he was lifting his ban on Saturday night dancing in the diocese of Galway). Significantly, the laity has not pressed for major reforms in the moral code, nor has it ignored the code. In contrast to the fluctuation in morals and values characteristic of most Western nations in the twentieth century, the southern Irish moral schema remains a rock of stability, and, judging from the approval with which most Catholic Irishmen greeted Pope Paul's condemnation of artificial methods of birth control, the average layman accepts both the moral rigor and the conservatism with alacrity.

Important as the church is in shaping the moral system, the economic, social, and political components of southern Irish life have reinforced the church's influence. The Republic remains a nation characterized by a rural and parochial social system. Everyone in most towns knows everyone else's business, and even in Dublin anonymity is difficult to achieve. Further, the economic structure of southern Ireland has reinforced the ascetic elements in the ethical code. This is especially true of the landholding practices which developed after the Famine. Because the prevailing agricultural practice after the Famine was the consolidation of agricultural holdings, there was a continuing decrease in the size of the rural population. Voluntary limitation of sexual activity was a necessity, for a couple could get married only at a relatively advanced age when the parents of the groom were in their dotage and willing to pass on the farm to the son and his bride. Just as the social and economic facts of life have reinforced the moral code, so the southern Irish political system has strengthened it. As we illustrated in detail in the Browne case, the Dail operates within moral guidelines set by the Catholic bishops. Legislation on marriage, sexual conduct, and birth control is an embodiment in statute law of the church's teaching on these moral questions. It is hard to conceive of a culture in which religious precepts blend so efficiently with social, economic, and political configurations, thereby producing a tight, cohesive, and self-consistent moral system.

Turning now to the specific imperatives of the Irish moral system, it is well to begin with matters of family life, marriage, and sexual conduct. In the matter of sexual conduct it must be emphasized that by international standards the southern Irish marriage rate is low and the marriage age high, and that sex outside marriage is not approved conduct. In 1961, 48 percent of the women and 61 percent of the men in the Republic aged 15 to 49 were unmarried, by far the highest proportion in the Western world. (The respective figures for the United States were 22 percent and 31 percent.) In the early seventies the average age for grooms in the Republic was 25 to 29 and for brides from 20 to 24, a drop from earlier years, but still high by Western standards. Southern Ireland's illegitimacy rate has been low ever since reliable statistics were calculated late in the last century. Today, roughly one birth in fifty is illegitimate. This is less than one third of the British rate and is one of the lowest rates in the world. If anything, the southern Irish illegitimacy figures are probably very high for the amount of sexual activity involved, because contraception is less widely practiced than elsewhere in Europe. Therefore one can reasonably conclude that the southern Irish engage in nonmarital heterosexual activity much less than do other European peoples. When this conclusion is coupled with our knowledge of the low marriage rate, a second, derivative conclusion is unavoidable—that as far as heterosexual activity is concerned, the southern Irish are the most inhibited people in the Western world.

Even within marriage sexual expression appears to be limited, although the lack of definitive statistics makes this suggestion hard to document. There is room for a wide range of individual variation, but it is relevant that the church's view of sex is not seriously challenged. Stated simply, this view is that sex within marriage is for procreation, not recreation. According to the Bishop of Cork, "Parenthood is usually avoided for selfish and self-indulgent reasons. When, for any reason whatever, a married couple decide not to have children, the only way for them is the way of marital continence, of self restraint." Thus, within marriage fertility rates are extremely high. In

1963 one demographic authority noted that one out of every five mothers giving birth in the Republic already had produced five or more children! This fecundity makes up for the low rate of marriage, and southern Ireland therefore regularly has a natural increase in population (which until recently was offset by emigration).

The church's teaching on birth control has legal as well as moral weight; the publishing of information on artificial birth control (meaning anything other than the rhythm method) is prohibited by the Republic's censorship code, and the sale of contraceptives is illegal. It is true that individual doctors have freedom to prescribe birth control devices if pregnancy would medically or psychologically damage the mother, but until recently their services were open only to the well-to-do (in 1969 a low-cost family planning clinic was opened in Dublin to serve all social classes). Despite some unrest among educated urban families and a campaign by Senator Mary Robinson to repeal the restrictions, most Catholics still accept the church's teaching on birth control. Indeed, when Pope Paul promulgated his decree condemning artificial methods of birth control there seemed to be a general sigh of relief among southern Irishmen. Unlike the reaction in the United States, only one churchman of any influence, Dr. James Good of University College, Cork, publicly disagreed with the papal pronouncement, and he was quickly prohibited from exercising his priestly duties.

Not surprisingly, ignorance and fear in sexual matters—and indeed in everyday social relations with the opposite sex—are widespread. Most children are sexually segregated during their primary education, and almost all post-primary schools are single-sex institutions. Interestingly, this tendency toward sexual segregation continues even among groups of adults, all of whom are married; in many churches men and women sit on opposite sides of the church, and at social gatherings the men and the women divide into two groups and hardly speak to each other. Most unfortunate is the pathetic ignorance of teenagers and young adults about the most simple facts about sex. Sexual education, either in formal programs or by parents is almost nonexistent. This accounts for the columns appearing regularly in women's journals devoted to the most elementary sexual advice. The questions are usually extraordinarily naïve: a girl in County Clare wants to know if French kissing will make her pregnant; a Galway City girl thinks she has had intercourse —how can she tell? The saddest part of these columns are the letters from married women who still need basic information on how the human body functions and on what it is "proper" to do in marriage and how often. An American anthropologist concluded after extensive field studies in a small island off the Republic's west coast that it was "one of the most sexually naïve of the world's societies, past or present." Admittedly, this was an extreme case, encapsulating rural Irish sexual attitudes as they existed perhaps a generation ago, but the same observer found evidence of identical sexual attitudes and influences even among middle- and upper-class Dubliners.

As long as young Irish men and women remain at home, sexual fear and ignorance may make their lives somewhat unhappy, but that is not always calamitous. When, however, young people leave the Republic to work in England or overseas, ignorance becomes disastrous. The young people find themselves in societies where sexual expression is much less limited than at home and they do not know how to cope with the situation. The result is a high incidence of illegitimate births among young Irish girls. In London, for example, a study conducted in 1961 showed that, although Irish-born persons comprised only 5.4 percent of the persons living within the London County Council precinct, the Irish-born bore over 8 percent of the illegitimate children.

Because the avenues of heterosexual expression are so restricted in Ireland one might speculate that homosexuality would be relatively common. This seems not to be the case. Homosexual relations are vigorously denounced by the church and are generally abhorred. Indeed, the plain fact is that all sexual activities, heterosexual, homosexual, and auto-erotic, are severely discouraged except in the case of heterosexual activity within marriage for the purpose of procreation. This repression of the sexual drive is not, we must emphasize, something forced upon the southern Irish by outsiders. They accept the sexual code because they believe in it. Quite clearly there are signs that the code is being liberalized, but the changes are slow and should not be overemphasized. Southern Ireland is, and will certainly remain for a long time, the most sexually controlled society in the West, and probably in the entire world.

Marriage in this moral system is considered a lifetime obligation. Southern Irish statute law on marriage is, indeed, more rigorous than is Catholic canon law. Canon law allows marriages to be annulled under certain circumstances, but under Article 41 of the Eire constitution of 1937 the state is prohibited from granting dissolution of marriage, a stipulation which includes annulment as well as divorce.

Similarly, the Roman Catholic position on mixed marriages, with which the overwhelming majority of the Republic's populace agrees, finds reinforcement in civil law. The Council of Trent, in 1564, promulgated the well-known *Ne Temere* decree which required that a Catholic priest had to officiate to render a marriage valid in the eyes of the church. Because of the special difficulties of the Irish church, a concession of 1785 provided that although marriages made by Catholics outside the Roman Catholic church were sinful, they were recognized as valid by the church. This concession was withdrawn in 1908, and in 1918 the *Ne Temere* decree was rewritten as part of the canon law code. Under existing mixed-marriage rules both parties must sign a four-point pledge declaring (1) that there will be no interference with the Catholic party's religious practice, (2) that the Catholic party will endeavor to bring the non-Catholic into the church, (3) that all the offspring of the marriage will be baptized Catholic and brought up as Catholic, and (4) that the parties will not go through any non-Catholic marriage ceremony.

This written pledge has been interpreted by the southern Irish Supreme Court as having legal weight. The case establishing this precedent, the Tilson case, was raised when an Irish Protestant married a Catholic girl, signed the pledge, and then, when the couple quarreled, took three of the four children and began to raise them as Protestants. The mother brought suit, and the Supreme Court gave her custody of the children on the basis of the marriage pledge the couple had signed. This decision is not really startling, but it is illuminating. It is based on the generally accepted assumption that a child's religious welfare outweighs all other considerations. Under the Tilson precedent a Catholic parent guilty of child neglect or cruelty would receive custody instead of a Protestant parent with a responsible record in matters of child welfare. Similarly, the Republic's adoption acts of 1952 and 1964 prohibit the adoption of a child by the husband and wife of a "mixed marriage"—that is, when one is Catholic, the other not, presumably because this indicates a moral flaw in their union.

Censorship in Ireland, like the Republic's laws on family life, has been misunderstood. It is not imposed upon the people, but is viewed by them as necessary and desirable. When the British left southern Ireland there were a number of statutes on the books containing provisions for protection against indecency, but it was the southern Irish themselves who, in 1929, created their own thorough censorship regulations. Undeniably, the Catholic church was the chief force behind passage of the censorship measure, but the censorship campaign was as much a lay as a clerical movement. The bishops did not force censorship upon the people: the people wanted it, the politicians were strong Catholics, and the men in power in the 1920's had memories of ill-treatment by the press and by book publishers, and actively distrusted unregulated publishing activities. Under the 1929 act (which remained in force until 1946) a five-man board was appointed to recommend to the Minister for Justice the books and periodicals which should be banned. Not only were pornographic books and pictures to be prohibited, but no book or periodical was to be permitted which advocated the use of contraceptives. Below is a small selection of books by well-known authors which were banned as indecent under the 1929 censorship act:

Sherwood Anderson: *Horses and Men*
Giovanni Boccacio: *Pasquerella and Madonna Babetta*
Erskine Caldwell: *God's Little Acre*
Noel Coward: *To Step Aside*
James T. Farrell: *Studs Lonigan*
William Faulkner: *Sanctuary*
Sinclair Lewis: *Elmer Gantry*
Somerset Maugham: *Cakes and Ale*
Sean O'Faolain: *Midsummer Night Madness*
Bernard Shaw: *Adventures of the Black Girl in her
    Search for God.*

During the early 1940's considerable domestic criticism of
the Irish Republic's censorship procedures arose, with the result that in 1946 a new act was framed which remained in effect until 1967. The five-member board was retained, but now
the board assumed powers to ban books of its own right rather
than to make recommendations to the Minister for Justice. An
appeals board was established to which an author, editor, pub-
lisher, or any five members of the legislature, acting jointly,
might appeal within one year of a book's banning. In practice
the new procedures worked as follows: Someone—most often
one of the customs authorities, but occasionally a private citizen—would send the board a book or periodical he considered
indecent. One or more members of the board would then read
the book (or, more likely, the passages marked offensive by the
complainant or the board's staff), and if three of the board
members agreed, the book or periodical was banished from
southern Ireland. It is doubtful if most books examined were
read carefully: the board was composed of people fully employed in their own profession who, in the years 1946 to 1964,
were asked to rule on 11,410 books. Nevertheless, the censorship board felt no compunction in using its powers, for in that
same period 7,622 books were banned. (The appeals board
subsequently revoked sixty-eight of these bannings.) Among
these were the following:

Kingsley Amis: *Lucky Jim*
André Gide: *Fruits of the Earth*

Ernest Hemingway: *Across the River and into the Trees*
Thomas Mann: *The Confessions of Felix Krull*
Vladimir Nabokov: *Laughter in the Dark*
Jean Paul Sartre: *The Age of Reason*
Dylan Thomas: *Adventures in the Skin Trade*
Tennessee Williams: *The Roman Spring of Mrs. Stone.*

Significantly, most of the books banned under the 1946 act (and under its successor, the 1967 act) are those which most southern Irishmen would agree strike at their familial-sexual code. They are books which describe sexual experimentation or advocate contraception. A good example of the difficulties such a stance involves was revealed in 1949 when the report of the British government's Royal Commission on Population was banned because it recommended birth control as a necessary means of population limitation! (In this instance the appeal board reversed the censorship board's decision.) But while rigorous and exclusionist on matters threatening the rules of familial relationship and sexual conduct, the authorities do not censor to any significant extent religious writings which are anti-Catholic or political writings which are anti-government or revolutionary. This fact leads us to the important conclusion that the censorship system is a component of the moral system and cannot by any stretch of the imagination be described as theologically or politically oppressive.

The entire censorship system was considerably loosened in 1967 with the passage of a measure framed by Brian Lenihan, then Minister for Justice. As finally passed, the period for which a book could be banned without re-evaluation was reduced from eternity to twelve years. Thus, at one stroke all books banished before the mid-fifties were freed from the ban. Granted, a large number of the titles were eventually rebanned, but the new procedure had the advantage of allowing the censors to take into account changing community standards. Previously banned works that had become modern classics thus have become available to the southern Irish public. The Irish authorities now have a method of evaluating controversial books. They can ban the book and reevaluate it in twelve years' time, and if the book has gained a high critical reputation in the outside world, the Irish public can then be allowed to read it! This approach presupposes that the people of southern Ireland do not mind greatly having to wait a dozen years before reading an international bestseller.

Film censorship, although administered differently from book and periodical censorship, is based on similar principles. Material dealing with sexual experimentation is prohibited, but violence and sadism is allowed. In practice, the film censor seems to be prone to censor material because it is blasphemous or politically revolutionary, while the book censors are not. Soon after the Irish Free State government took office it established, in 1923, the office of film censor, a full-time, paid position. Under the 1923 act and the subsequent extending act of 1925, the censor views every film which is to be shown in Ireland and passes it as it stands, suggests revisions, or rejects it entirely. Most scenes having to do with sex are cut, with the result that the story line in movies shown in Eire jumps from the kissing stage to pregnancy in one swift sequence. Some films such as *La Dolce Vita, The Boys in the Band,* and *Myra Breckinridge* are banned totally. Others are drastically cut. Significantly, some films with anticapitalist overtones—such as Peter Sellers' *Dr. Strangelove*—have been allowed to be screened only after prolonged delay.

In contrast to the films and the printed word, the theater has no formal censorship apparatus. There remains on the books an act of the United Kingdom Parliament which allows police officers to close down obscene performances and to prosecute the producer. This course was followed in 1957 when a young producer staged *The Rose Tattoo* by Tennessee Williams. The producer eventually won his fight but at considerable personal expense. Actually, such state intervention is unnecessary. The theater presents little except nationalist drama, an art form which is designed to reinforce, not undermine, the Republic's cultural and moral system.

Significantly, the only medium which bids fair to alter southern Ireland's moral code is one which comes into the home—namely, television. One of the more perceptive observers of modern Ireland has listed the advent of television among the five principal events which influenced southern Irish life during the 1960's. Television broadcasting is a state monopoly. The Republic's service, Telefis Eireann, was opened on 1 July 1962. In inaugurating the station President de Valera presciently foresaw the great influence television would have:

> I must admit that sometimes when I think of television and the radio and their immense power I feel somewhat afraid. Like atomic energy it can be used for incalculable good, but it can also do irreparable harm... It can lead, through de-moralization to decadence and dissolution.

No one would suggest that Telefis Eireann has led to decadence, but despite close governmental control of the service, undeniably it has introduced foreign values into southern Irish society, values which do not always fit well into the moral system. About half the programs on Telefis Eireann originate within the Republic, but most of the rest consists of old American movies and American television series. Equally important, television viewers in the northern part of the Republic can receive BBC and independent television broadcasts from Belfast. Dublin residents can, with the proper equipment, receive BBC and ITV from Wales. A television rating survey has revealed that southern Irishmen watch these British and Northern Irish channels one third of their viewing time. The American programs and the British transmissions originate in societies where the definitions of permissible behavior, the relations of the individual to authority, the view of family life, and the pace of living all vary considerably from Irish standards.

Critics of southern Irish life state, accurately perhaps, that it is a nation of cultural isolation and of low intellectual horizons. For instance, Michael Sheehy, in his book, *Is Ireland Dying?* (1968), convincingly presents the thesis that modern Ireland mistrusts the writer and the intellectual, and that this distrust turns to hostility in the case of foreign writers and intellectuals. The result is that most of the best young Irish writers go into voluntary exile and that the intellectuals withdraw to their own small corner and take little part in the political and cultural life of southern Ireland. This undoubtedly is true, but to denounce the situation is to miss the point: Irishmen of their own volition have adopted a moral system which implies that a stable family life, a disciplined sex life, and a devout religious life are more important than a rich cultural life. Indeed, it might well be argued that if the nation tolerated a flourishing crop of perceptive writers and inquisitive, skeptical intellectuals, the first thing the writers and intellectuals would do would be to analyze, satirize, and attack the moral system. A rich cultural life is probably incompatible with the southern Irish moral system. Stating this fact is not in any way to imply a judgment upon the Irish. It is their society, not ours, and they of course have the right to their own modes of social and cultural organization. (The reader may be aware that in an effort to keep writers and artists at home and to attract new talents the government opened the seventies by making income from artistic pursuits tax-free; an admirable idea, but the plays, books, and films produced by these same artists still are banned!)

The southern Irish moral system, then, is a seamless web. It is a wonderfully thorough and efficient blend of religion, attitudes toward the family, sexual regulations, political and legal arrangements, and social configurations. Almost everything within this moral system fits with all the other components, and each part of the system reinforces every other part. The system is a rarity in the Western world, a code of belief, conduct, and government that is almost universally accepted within the nation. This means that southern Irishmen, unlike the inhabitants of the other English-speaking countries, do not merely inhabit a geographic region, but can be described accurately as a single nation; and not only politically but socially, morally, and culturally.

The great virtues of this moral system, its coherence and its universality, are also its vices. Because the system is so tightly organized there is little room for the individual who cannot accept it in its entirety. Whenever an individual comes into conflict with the moral and social code, he must either develop a means of escape or become emotionally ill. Unfortunately, the southern Irish system allows few means of escape. One traditional method, the one most approved, is for an individual to deal with his anxieties by immersing himself in compulsive religiosity. Because of the liturgical emphasis of the Irish Catholic church there is a great opportunity in religious practice for the neurotic individual to engage in compulsive and obsessive behavior. The classic case of such behavior was Matt Talbot, a man who, although he died in 1925, is held up to this day by priests as an example of saintliness. Talbot was a Dublin alcoholic who, in middle life, suddenly turned from alcohol to religion. He would arise every morning at 2:00 a.m. and pray on his knees until 4:30 in his room, then at 5:00 go to church for mass. He would next go to his job at 6:00 a.m. At noon hour, instead of taking lunch, he would spend most of his time in private prayer. At 5:30 in the afternoon he again went to church to visit the Blessed Sacrament before returning home for dinner. He spent the evening in prayer and spiritual reading up to his bedtime, 10:30. Each Sunday he spent a minimum of eight consecutive hours on his knees in prayer, rising only to receive communion. After Talbot's death it was discovered that he had been accustomed to wearing heavy chains under his clothes, presumably to prevent sexual sin, and had worn them so tightly that the chains had become embedded in his flesh. Men like Talbot whose histories belong in the pages of textbooks on abnormal psychology are rare, but the neurotic use of religion in Ireland is far from uncommon.

Although we would not draw any medical conclusions from the data ourselves, a psychiatrist might be interested to juxtapose the sexual suppression of the moral system and the strong Marian element in the Irish church. The imagery and devotional practice of the Irish church are highly feminine, and the central symbolic figure is the Blessed Virgin. The most interesting case of involvement with Mary as a cult object is the lay apostolic movement, the Legion of Mary. This group was founded in Dublin in 1921 by a group of men and women who were inspired by the *Treatise on the True Devotion to the Blessed Virgin* by St. Louis Grignon de Montfort. The group undertook a program of Marian devotion and social action.

The Legion expanded at an extraordinary rate, so that there are now chapters in 1,300 Catholic dioceses throughout the world and more than one million members. "The object of the Legion of Mary," according to its leaders, "is the sanctification of its members by prayer and active cooperation, under ecclesiastical guidance, in Mary's and the Church's work of crushing the head of the serpent and advancing the reign of Christ." The following excerpts from the Legion oath are revealing:

> . . . I know that thou [O'Holy Spirit], who has
>   come to regenerate the world in Jesus Christ
> Hast not willed to do so except through Mary;
> That without her we cannot know or love thee;
> That it is by her, and to whom she pleases, when she
>   pleases, and in the quantity and manner she pleases,
> That all thy gifts and virtues and graces are administered
>
> .   .   .   .
> I stand before thee as her soldier and her child,
> And I so declare my entire dependence on her.
> She is the mother of my soul.
> Her heart and mine are one;
> And from that single heart she speaks again those words
>   of old:
> "Behold the handmaid of the Lord;"
> And once again thou comest by her to do great things.
> Let thy power overshadow me, and come into my soul
>   with fire and love
> And make it one with Mary's love and Mary's will to
>   save the world.

Our visiting psychiatrist would also be interested to learn that each Legion member is sworn to absolute secrecy about Legion affairs and to discover that much of the Legion's work in Ireland consists of guarding communal moral standards—chiefly by badgering persons who are believed to be moral transgressors. Not surprisingly, much of this moral vigilante activity focuses on sexual matters. It is no accident that the Legion's first major activity in Dublin in the 1920's was trying to persuade individual prostitutes, through personal discussion, to give up their mode of earning a living.

Irishmen tolerate, although do not actively approve, other means of relieving the tensions often engendered by the system of morals. One of these means is gambling. Bookmaking is legal in Ireland, and the cities are studded with betting shops. The church turns a blind eye toward the turf accountants, and many a parish augments its funds with weekly bingo games. Probably much more dysfunctional than gambling is the high rate of alcohol consumption. Reliable statistics on alcoholism in southern Ireland are not available, but studies conducted in the United States show that persons of Irish descent have much the highest alcoholism rate of any ethnic group, and there is reason to believe that the incidence in the home country is also high; however, this is by no means certain.

There are two other ways an individual can relieve the tension produced by the all-embracing moral web, and both involve opting out of Ireland completely: he can emigrate or he can commit suicide. The former course is favored by the intellectual and writer classes. The latter course, most Irishmen would say, is rarely taken. Self-murder is a mortal sin, and few Catholics would risk damnation by disposing of themselves in this manner. Having said that, the fact that southern Ireland's suicide rate is the lowest in Europe tells as much about the manner in which the statistics are kept as about the incidence of suicide. According to one informed observer, "Unless a corpse is actually found dangling from a rope, some other verdict than suicide is usually sought and given."

And what about those individuals who feel suffocated by the moral schema but who can find no means of alleviating the pressure? The answer is found in the following statistic: in the Republic in 1961, 7.3 psychiatric beds were provided per 1,000 of population. This rate compares with 4.6 in England and Wales, 4.5 in Northern Ireland, 4.3 in Scotland, 4.3 in the United States, and 2.1 in France. Southern Ireland's rate is probably the highest in the world. The rate is not a result of the Republic's having a superior medical system (the British and Northern Irish medical arrangements are considerably better), but of the truly high incidence of serious mental illness. At any given time, about one Irishman in seventy above the age of twenty-four is in a mental hospital. As one might expect, given the sexual code, the incidence of serious illness, especially schizophrenic breakdowns, is highest among single persons. Mental illness is probably the Republic's most pressing health problem.

IX   Social Flux and Social Management

When the results of the 1966 southern Irish census were published there was considerable satisfaction in official circles: for the first time in more than a century Ireland's population had shown an increase. In population patterns, as in so many other matters, the Irish Republic is unique among advanced nations. In most matters the nation's social configuration does not conform to the template common to the European and English-speaking nations. Therefore, in viewing social developments in the Republic we are dealing with problems which are only partially international in nature; in large part they are uniquely Irish. We should not, therefore, be surprised to find that the Irish Republic's solutions to social problems are sometimes imitative of standard international solutions (e.g. unemployment insurance) and sometimes uniquely tailored to Ireland's peculiar situation.

To understand modern Irish social patterns one must first realize that Ireland was among the first of European nations to experience the population explosion of the eighteenth and nineteenth centuries. Indeed, the explosion was more pronounced in Ireland than elsewhere. But having been in the vanguard of European population patterns, the Irish nation suddenly veered off on a path of its own. The entire course of Irish social history was reversed by the Famine of 1847–48. Emigration became an established pattern, and every hamlet, indeed most Irish families, had one or two members in Britain, North America, or Australia. Even more important than emigration in shaping modern social patterns was the radical redefinition of family configurations. Having overextended himself in the pre-Famine potato culture, the Irish farmer now turned to growing grains and to pasturage. The land, therefore, could hold fewer people because a larger holding was required to support a family in the grain-pasturage economy than in the potato economy. Farms were necessarily handed down intact from father to son and not subdivided as had been the pre-Famine practice. Because the farm was not divided, all the children, save the son selected to receive the farm, had to leave the home and find employment in the towns and cities, or emigrate. The common practice was for the land to be transferred from father to son before the death of the parent. This ensured an orderly succession of title and at the same time guaranteed that the land would be worked by an able-bodied man even while the parents were in their declining years. The obvious problem was that most farmers wished to keep control of the land as long as possible, so that the inheriting son was often kept in a position of servitude until the parents were well beyond the age of three score and ten. Until he came into the farm on his own it was impossible for the chosen son to marry. Therefore, the extraordinary situation arose in which most men did not marry until well over the age of thirty, and marriage above age sixty was not at all uncommon. The social configuration of the Irish nation had changed almost overnight.

Because of the limitations on marriage and because of emigration, the Irish population declined steeply after the Famine. The decline gradually slowed until the late 1870's, but then a further sharp decline began once more, aggravated by the disastrous crop failures of 1879–80. This rapid decline continued for a decade, abating somewhat in the 1890's and in the first decade of the twentieth century. Census data for the years 1911 to 1926 revealed a further decline, probably stemming from the First World War and from the unsettled state of Ireland in the years of the troubles. After 1926 the population of southern Ireland stayed nearly stable, albeit with slight decennial declines.

However small, the regular decline of the southern Irish population was a continual embarrassment to the government. When, in 1953, the Reverend Dr. John A. O'Brien of Notre Dame University edited a collection of essays entitled *The Vanishing Irish,* which declared that southern Ireland was teetering perilously on the brink of near extinction, the Republic's government was so disturbed that it detailed its chief statistician to refute the dire predictions and gave his refutation wide publicity. Understandably, then, government officials breathed a relieved sigh when the 1966 census revealed, at last, a slight rise in the population. The data indicated that southern Ireland finally had overcome most of the social effects of the Great Famine. Certainly the nation had passed over a major social watershed; but, having noted this fact, it remains true that the Republic still is decades away from sharing the common European pattern of large regular increments in its population, and even farther away from having to worry about overpopulation.

In the past the incidence of emigration worried the southern Irish government as much as the more general problem of declining population. Net emigration (the excess of the number of emigrants over the number of immigrants) ranged from 5.6 to 8.2 per thousand in 1956–61. Obviously, the departure of a large number of persons, especially young people, from the society was deleterious. Successive governments brooded over the emigration problem because it indicated a national weakness; clergymen worried about the moral effects upon young Irishmen who emigrated to countries less Christian than Ireland; and innumerable ballad-writers made emigration a topic of often touching, often lugubrious songs. The most sensible new approach to emigration came with Sean Lemass's elevation as head of the government. Lemass was a hardheaded and realistic man who realized that emigration was usually predicated upon an economic judgment by the individual involved, not upon moral flaw. "We need to get young people more conscious of the growing opportunities within Ireland which the country's economic advance is opening up," he said, and his government did everything possible to make economic growth a reality. The result was that when the census data for 1961–66 were published it was discovered that emigration had dropped sharply (to 5.7 per thousand per annum) and that southern Ireland's rate of natural increase had outstripped the net emigration rate.

Whereas emigration to other nations now appears to be a problem well on its way to solution, another problem, that of internal migration, has arisen in its place. Southern Irishmen are moving to the cities in the twentieth century at a rate as fast, or faster, than Englishmen moved into cities in the nineteenth century. If one defines a town area as a population center of 1,500 persons or more, it appears that in 1901 only 28.3 percent of the population lived in town areas. By 1936 this proportion had risen to 35.5 percent, and by 1966 to 49.2 percent. Strikingly, most political leaders, when discussing the problems resulting from this internal migration, have emphasized not the problems of emergent city life, but the supposed calamity of rural depopulation. In part this tack is possible because the new urban life has grown up with relatively little stress so far as the cities themselves are concerned. The most fascinating aspect of urbanization in the Republic is that beneath the flux and confusion of emergent urban life there remains a stability and social cohesiveness that is distinctively rural in flavor. "It's just a big small town and everybody knows everyone else's business," is a common description of Dublin life. The Dubliner has yet to adopt the anonymous, compartmentalized life style which blights the inhabitants of most of the world's larger cities. When a countryman moves into the city he does not have to adopt a traumatically different set of values, or, because southern Ireland is such a small country, to lose touch with his rural roots. Perhaps most important, even in Dublin the Roman Catholic church has been able to command the allegiance and attendance of the populace with almost as much success as in the rural districts. Religion being the dominant element in framing the Irish scale of values, the transition from a rural to an urban society has been relatively easy. Thus, the most disruptive symptoms of urban confusion, such as rioting and frequent crimes of violence, are absent in Dublin and in the other southern Irish cities.

The growth of the small towns has been almost totally painless. Typically, a web of common interests, kinship, and acquaintance binds together the populace of the smaller towns and boroughs and the inhabitants of the surrounding countryside. When the son of a local farmer leaves school and decides to try his hand as a tradesman's apprentice, shopman, or clerk in the county civil service, he moves into a new domicile, but not into a new world. He still sees his family regularly, probably plays for the same sports clubs as before he moved into town, and the same parish priest probably keeps an eye on his behavior. Most small businesses in towns in the Republic are family-owned. A man may be underpaid or underemployed in these towns, but he is never anonymous.

It is possible to argue that the Irish Republic has solved, by its own unique methods, the two main problems which bedevil the modern world, namely, overpopulation and urban disorder. Unfortunately, these solutions cannot be exported: celibacy and emigration as a cure for overpopulation have obvious limitations, and the rich flowering of familialism and Roman Catholicism which prevents urban anomie seems possible only in Irish soil.

Although southern Ireland has not undergone the worst forms of social disorder experienced by other Western nations, its government is nonetheless faced with the necessity of moderating the random and unavoidable circumstances which make human lives painful. Problems of health, housing, unemployment, and old age affect the Republic as much as any other country. Present-day social welfare services in southern Ireland are divided among three government ministries. The most comprehensive of these is the Department of Social Welfare which was established in 1947. Old age and blind pension schemes, employment exchanges and unemployment insurance, children's allowances, and national health insurance are administered by this department. Also established in 1947 was the Department of Health, which assumed the medical functions that had previously been performed by the Department of Local Government and Public Health. Although chiefly concerned with non-welfare matters, the Department of Local Government has maintained an involvement in housing schemes.

In relation to United Kingdom and continental standards, southern Ireland's welfare measures are weak. This is not surprising, for by Western European standards, the Republic is not well off economically. National income per head is about half that of France, West Germany, and the United Kingdom, and roughly equal to that of Italy. Also, the doctrinaire conservatism of most southern Irish politicians has limited welfare development. The Republic's politicians espouse the gospel of private enterprise (even though they do not always follow these precepts). John A. Costello, who was Taoiseach when the Department of Social Welfare was created, stated, "The essence of the proposals [to establish the department] is to provide on a basis of social insurance for a greater co-ordination and improvement of existing social services . . . They involve no extension of state interference in the private lives of the people or in private enterprise." He emphasized that no suggestion of the welfare state was implied. A further impediment to the development of comprehensive social welfare programs has been the admirable, but inadequate, tradition of private charity, especially pious almsgiving. Quite naturally, some of the professionally religious dislike the expansion of government welfare services and are afraid of the diminution of their own powers consequent upon the expansion of state agencies.

Perhaps the least adequate of the Republic's social services is the health service, which, though less primitive than that of the United States, is much behind that of the United Kingdom. In Great Britain and Northern Ireland, almost 90 percent of national medical expenses is paid from public funds, while in the United States the percentage is only about 25 percent. Although no precise statistics exist for the Irish Republic, estimates place the country nearer the United Kingdom than the American end of the spectrum. The basic structure of the Republic's health service is defined by the Irish Poor Law Act of 1851. Under that act dispensaries were established by Poor Law Guardians to treat the poor without charge, dispensary doctors being free to take on fee-paying patients as well. When the Irish Free State was established the dispensary system was adopted wholesale and placed under the Department of Local Government and Public Health. The present Department of Health was created in 1947, the new title giving a neo-Beveridge veneer to what was really a minor piece of departmental reshuffling. Under the Medical Services Act of 1953 the dispensary system has been continued, with the administrative aid of the county and borough councils. To be eligible for physicians' and surgeons' services and for medicines without charge a person must have his name placed on the medical service register. A strict means test regulates admission to the register; about 30 percent of the Irish population—roughly the poorest third—are on the register. The remainder of the population has to pay full rate for all general practitioners' services and medicines. However, the Irish medical arrangements make 80–90 percent of the population eligible for low-cost hospitalization and services of specialists in cases of serious illness. Roughly half the total cost of the medical expenses which falls on the government is met from national revenues, the other half from local taxation.

When we turn from health services to government housing programs, we are turning from an area of antiquated and inadequate service to a well-organized (if not always adequately financed) program. The Ministry for Local Government in the Irish Free State was fortunate in inheriting from the United Kingdom an effective scheme of rural and urban housing for the underprivileged. Rural housing had begun under the Irish Labourers Acts of 1883 and 1885, urban housing under acts of 1875 and 1890. The Free State continued and expanded these programs, with the result that today over a quarter of all occupied houses have been built by the government. Chief responsibility for providing housing falls on twenty-seven county councils and upon fifty-three urban housing authorities. These bodies build houses which they rent or sell to local persons according to a complicated system of priorities. In addition, local authorities provide subsidies to individuals for the building of houses and flats. Most of the money for local activities is obtained by capital borrowing by the local authorities, who then recoup in rents and the sale of property. The Department of Local Government coordinates local activities, underwrites the larger portion of the loan charges incurred by local authorities, and also provides direct subvention of its own to home builders. In recent years more than one third of the houses built in Ireland have been built by local housing authorities (see Table A.12). In addition, the great majority of houses built by private parties are underwritten partially by some form of governmental subvention (for example, in 1966, 7,377 of the 8,266 houses built by private individuals earned some form of governmental grant for the builder). In toto, roughly four fifths of expenditure on housing comes from governmental sources.

The result of all this activity is that Eire's housing situation is above average by European standards. Table A.16 indicates that the Irish Republic has the second highest proportion of owner-occupied houses in Europe, and is in a median position, comparable with West Germany, in the average number of persons housed per room. Closer scrutiny of the table reveals, however, that the Irish Republic spends a relatively small proportion of the gross national product on housing and that the number of houses being built per thousand population is the lowest in Europe. How, then, can the Republic's program be so comparatively successful? The answer harks back to our discussion of population trends: the population of southern Ireland is growing more slowly than that of any other European country, and, in relation to the demand for housing, the government is therefore doing an excellent job. Granted, shortcomings exist in the housing network—the reliance on local authorities works in the country districts, but the Dublin City housing authorities are chronically underfinanced, and in 1969 there were 4,800 approved families on the Dublin corporation backlist. Nevertheless, in general the housing policy stands as the most successful of the government's social policies.

As established in Chapter VII, the Republic of Ireland suffers from a high level of chronic unemployment. In the recent past, unemployment has not fallen below 5 percent of the work force. In a full employment economy the size of Ireland's, only 2 percent should be unemployed. Therefore, some scheme is necessary to ameliorate the hardship of those who, for whatever reason, are without work. Like so many other of her social arrangements, the Republic's unemployment scheme is based on outdated United Kingdom precedents, in this case the National Insurance Act of 1911 as amended in 1920. All manual workers, irrespective of salary, and all other workers earning under £1,200 a year are required to contribute a regular amount—which is not graduated according to income—to a state fund. To the worker's contribution are added contributions from the employers and from the government. Benefits are paid out whenever an insured person is unable to work. The amount of the benefits is correlated with contributions made by the insuree in the past, but is not related to the level of past earnings. This insurance scheme covers all contingencies that lead to loss of employment, but the plan takes in only about one third of the working population. Farmers and other self-employed persons are not covered; nor are nonmanual workers who earn over £1,200 a year. Thus, the worst edge is taken off the curse of unemployment, but the scheme is far from comprehensive in its application.

The same mentality which draws a line between social classes in determining the coverage and benefits of unemployment insurance and health services is in evidence in the national pension schemes, of which there are essentially two. One provides old-age pensions for the very poor, the blind, and the widowed, without regard to whether or not the recipients have previously contributed to the pensions fund. These pensions, whose legal base is the Old Age Pensions Act of 1908, begin at age seventy. In 1961 a second tier was added to the scheme: workers are now given the opportunity to contribute to an old age pension scheme on a voluntary basis in much the same way they had previously contributed to private pension schemes. The minimum age for receipt of a pension under the contributory scheme is seventy years, which is the highest pension age of any Western European country.

The social welfare program that tells the most about the character of the southern Irish people is the program of family allowances, which are financed out of general taxation and are paid for each child born to an Irish family. The rate scale is graduated, not, as one might suppose, according to family income but according to family size. When a couple's first child is born, the parents receive the equivalent of about $1.30 a month; for the second they receive about $3.50, and for the third and each subsequent child about $5.00 monthly. In a country worried about the problem of population shrinkage, and one in which relatively few marriages occur, the subsidizing of large families is a sensible expedient and perhaps a demographic necessity.

Southern Ireland has one group of people who have not blended into the nation's social network. They are known colloquially as the "tinkers," officially as the "itinerants" and among themselves as "the travelers" or "the traveling people." This is a population of Gypsy habits, but not of Romany tongue or Gypsy blood. Almost all the tinkers are Irish by blood, the most common surnames being McDonagh, Connor, War, O'Brien, Maugham, O'Donoghue, Reilly, and Mongan, and their variants. By no means are all itinerants related to each other, but blood ties are extensive and strong, and there is an informal system of group control. A census of itinerants in 1961 found their numbers in the Republic to be 5,880, a population level that has held reasonably stable since the 1940's.

A minority of the tinkers, probably less than one third, travel for only part of the year or not at all, but the majority are constant migrants. Most, perhaps 60 percent, of itinerant families travel only within a local area, covering two or three counties in their journeys and no more. Only a small number travel any distance. The majority of the itinerants live in horse-drawn caravans which serve both as a means of transportation and as a place of abode. A considerable percentage, however, live in tents, relatively few having motor trailers or cars.

Only a few of the itinerants practice a recognized trade or craft, and those who do are usually tinsmiths, chimney sweeps, or flower makers. Some of the traveling people serve as seasonal agricultural workers or turf cutters. A few carry on a profitable and useful trade in scrap metal. Many are small traders. It is regular practice for itinerant children and mothers to be set to begging, either door to door or on town street corners. A good deal of petty thieving is done by itinerants.

The Republic's government has decided that the itinerants

constitute a social problem. For one thing, as the neutral observer cannot fail to observe, the squalor and filthiness of the itinerants' lodgings is a health hazard and the tents which a large number of the families inhabit are inadequate shelter for women and children. Almost every adult tinker is illiterate, and because the families do not stay in one place long enough for the children to attend school for a significant portion of time, the children remain illiterate. And despite the few tinkers who are able to support automobiles and motor caravans, most itinerant families are depressingly poor, living on the slim margin of subsistence. These problems are compounded by the fact that the average itinerant family has six to seven children (this is a phenomenally high marital fertility rate). Finally, the traveling people are resented and feared by those with whom they come in contact, partly for irrational reasons, partly because the itinerants do not have the same attitudes toward private property as the settled population.

The government has decided, therefore, that the itinerants must be induced to settle permanently and to merge with the rest of the population. This is probably a justified decision, because the itinerants, unlike the continental Gypsies, do not possess a distinctive culture; nor do they have a set of crafts of their own that would be destroyed by their melding with the larger population. The problem is, as the government admits, that most itinerants are satisfied with their present mode of life and do not intend to do anything to change it. A Commission on Itinerancy which reported in August 1963 recommended a carrot-and-stick approach to persuade the traveling people to settle. The positive inducements were to be financial assistance to those itinerants who settled in houses, and economic assistance to guarantee that family members did not need to return to the road to beg. In order to limit somewhat the tinkers' migrations the commission recommended that improved campsites be set up and that camping at other than approved sites be prohibited. Also, the commission suggested that legal steps be taken to prohibit begging. The law of criminal trespass, it was further suggested, should be amended to make it possible for farmers to keep itinerants off their property. It was hoped that the positive inducements to settlement when combined with limitations on mobility, trespassing, and begging would result in the traveling people's being absorbed into the general population. Thus far, however, the tinkers remain, undiminished and unbowed, and will probably remain so for the foreseeable future.

Educational institutions in the Irish Republic, as in all modern nations, serve both as social and as cultural agents. The schools standardize values throughout the culture and restrict the propensity of children to engage in antisocial behavior. Attitudes toward authority, toward work, and toward property all are shaped by educational institutions.

Having granted that southern Ireland's educational institutions are similar to those of the European and North American nations in serving as agents of social control, the important fact emerges that in most other aspects the Republic's educational system is markedly different from that of the rest of the English-speaking world. For example, in England and America it is assumed (although rarely stated publicly) that schooling is a responsibility of the state and that the government has a greater right than do either the child's parents or the religious authorities to determine how a child is to be schooled. In contrast, the Irish Republic's educational system seems to be based on the assumption that religious authorities have the principal responsibility for determining how children are schooled. Although obeisance is made to the principle of education as a parental prerogative, this is verbal only; in practice southern Irish parents have almost no influence on how their children are educated. In recent years the government's Department of Education has grown powerful enough to challenge the religious authorities on discreet issues, but the church maintains the upper hand.

When one strips aside the verbiage that obscures the operation of the educational systems of America and England one finds that they are founded on the fundamental assumption that equality of educational opportunity is a right. The individual in each country is presumed to be educable until proved otherwise. In contrast, in southern Ireland, whereas the child of parents of means almost automatically receives an academic schooling, the child of working-class parents is heavily handicapped in gaining an academic post-primary education. He must perform well on rigorous scholarship examinations to gain admission.

Yet another assumption underlying the English and the American educational systems does not hold for the Republic of Ireland. This is the assumption that the schools should unite religious and social groups. The Irish Republic's school system below the university level is religiously segregated. Almost all schools are managed by religious authorities, and in only a very small number of the Republic's schools (mostly vocational schools) will a Roman Catholic child encounter a child of a religious persuasion other than his own. This system of religious segregation, it must be underlined, is one with which the overwhelming majority of southern Irishmen are happy; it has not been imposed upon the Republic's society, but is, instead, a reflection of the attitudes which predominate in that society.

When the Irish Free State became independent in 1922 the newly formed government inherited three sets of schools: "national," "intermediate" (academic secondary schools), and "technical" (vocational training institutions). All save the technical schools were denominationally controlled, and there was no apparatus for coordinating the entire system. The Free State government dealt quickly with the coordination problem. In the provisional government formed immediately after independence, a Minister for Education was appointed. He assumed responsibility for national, intermediate, and vocational education. To the new Department of Education's credit it engaged in several major reforms in the 1920's. A scheme was devised whereby a child could pass smoothly from a primary school to the curriculum of the intermediate or technical school without having to jump a curricular gap. Also, the curriculum of the national schools was considerably revised (the details will be discussed in the next chapter because the modifications had to do chiefly with the position of the Irish language in the schools). In 1924 the former system of paying grants to intermediate schools according to their students' scores on examinations was abolished, and a new mode was introduced which was based on the number of students in the school who were following a course of studies approved by the Department of Education. This method gave intermediate school teachers much more freedom for creativity than they had previously possessed, but had the unfortunate side effect of making it desirable from the point of view of school finances to place intermediate schools near population centers. The result is that today a child in County Donegal has only one third the chance of receiving an intermediate school education as does a child in County Cork.

The new Irish Free State's most important step in improving primary education was the School Attendance Act of 1926. Previously, Ireland had possessed a compulsory attendance law, an obsolete statute of 1892. This act had proved unworkable because it left enforcement up to the discretion of local authorities in the towns, and no provision was made for enforcement in the rural areas. The 1926 Attendance Act required that all children attend school from ages six to fourteen and provided ample means of enforcement, ranging from tacit threatening by the police of parents not complying with the Act to court convictions and fines. As a result, whereas in the 1925–26 school year 73.5 percent of the school children on the rolls were in attendance on an average day, by 1933–34 the figure was 84.0 and is approaching 90 percent at the present time.

Vocational education was also greatly improved during the 1920's. In 1926 the department appointed a major commission to suggest new lines of development for vocational education. The commission reported in 1927, and as a result of its work a Vocational Education Act was passed in 1930. This act standardized and strengthened the local authorities who were responsible for vocational education. Under the act thirty-eight vocational education committees were appointed by the local rating authorities in the major towns and cities and in a number of rural areas. Most important, provisions were made for an increase in local rating powers for vocational education, and

vocational education committees were given permission to bor-
row for capital expenditure on the security of their own funds.
Moreover, the local rating authority was empowered to raise
loans for vocational education.

After the activity and progress of the 1920's the southern
Irish educational system entered a time of stagnation that lasted
through the thirties, forties, fifties, and well into the 1960's. All
that happened during these idle years was that reports of various commissions appeared, and even these were stale and
unimaginative. For instance, in 1935 an interdepartmental committee investigated whether or not school attendance should
be required of children fourteen to sixteen years of age. The
committee concluded that the Free State's compulsory attendance rules were as rigorous as those of other European countries
and that there was no need to raise the school-leaving age. In
1943 a Commission on Youth Unemployment chaired by John
Charles McQuaid, Catholic Archbishop of Dublin, decided
that, indeed, the leaving age should be raised to sixteen, but
the government ignored this conclusion. In 1950 a Council on
Education was established in imitation of the English government's Advisory Committee on Education. Unlike the English
original, however, southern Ireland's council was controlled by
educational conservatives. The council's first major report was
a survey of primary education published in 1954. This report
was a mixture of the inconsequential and the irresponsible. It
consisted almost entirely of minor suggestions for tinkering
with the national schools and not a single suggestion for major
structural improvement. The report's major conclusion was a
non-conclusion, namely, that full-time schooling to age fourteen was sufficient education for the nation's youth. The same
council produced a report on intermediate education in 1960
which included statements that would have been accepted in
nineteenth-century liberal England but that one is surprised to
find being made in the mid-twentieth century: "We would
advert to the frequently reiterated demand that our education
system should allow of free [intermediate] education for all.
Even a superficial examination of this demand will show that
in this unqualified form it is untenable." Why untenable? First,

because not all students would profit from the education and, second, because it would cost too much. "There are also objections on educational grounds," the report continued. "If [intermediate] education were universally available free for all, the incentives to profit by it would diminish and standards would inevitably fall."

The Irish Republic, then, entered the 1960's with an obsolete educational system that was not at all improved over that of the 1930's. Fortunately, the economic changes that began in the late 1950's finally affected educational opinion. The key event in energizing Irish education was the appointment in 1961 of Dr. Michael Hillery as Minister for Education, hitherto an obscure and relatively unimportant post in the cabinet. Hillery changed that. His most important action was to appoint in October 1962 a team to survey Eire's educational system. This survey team, which reported in 1965, approached education from a totally new angle. Whereas most previous policy studies of Irish education had been dominated by religious and philosophical considerations, the Hillery-appointed group viewed education from the economic and societal angle; the title of the committee report, *Investment in Education,* indicates this new perspective. The team's method of reporting was statistical and analytic. The data presented made it clear that among thirteen- and fourteen-year-olds, for instance, southern Ireland had the lowest percentage in Europe of children in full-time education. The same statistical approach, however, also made it clear that although the Republic of Ireland had a lower school-leaving age than England or Northern Ireland, a higher proportion of older children stayed on at school than in either of those two countries. This even-handed statistical approach raised the report above the level of religio-politico squabbling that had so hurt southern Irish education in the past. Although it made no formal recommendations on educational policy, the Hillery-appointed team's report forced certain conclusions. Chief among these was that the economy needed more highly trained manpower if economic growth were to continue, and that the government would have to be prepared to pay a substantially increased bill for educational services in general if the economy were not to stultify. Further, post-primary educational opportunities would have to be equalized between various socio-economic and regional groups.*

While his survey team forged an economic rationale for an expansionist educational policy, Hillery himself articulated specific policy proposals. For example, in 1964 the Department of Education began making grants to assist intermediate schools in erecting school buildings, thereby indirectly increasing the provision of school places in academic secondary schools. Another Hillery policy was his committing the department and the government to raising the school-leaving age to fifteen by 1970. (It was later postponed to 1972.) One of Hillery's successors as Minister for Education (Hillery became Minister for Industry and Commerce in 1965), the dynamic Donagh O'Malley, carried on Hillery's reforms by inaugurating grants toward school fees in postprimary schools, with the eventual goal the availability of free postprimary education for all.

Education in the Irish Republic has clearly made major strides in the past decade. What questions or problems remain? At the heart of any consideration of further improvement of the system is the question of whether or not its basic structure is viable. The national schools and the academic intermediate schools, which include the great bulk of children being educated, are not state schools. The schools are owned by the religious authorities. The teachers are not civil servants but are employees of the school managers. The primary and intermediate school systems, therefore, are not state systems but are state-aided systems. Although governmental authorities have recently taken a stronger hand in educational matters than they have in the past, the question remains as to whether or not the aided system can be adapted successfully to an era when educational policy is increasingly recognized as a vital component of national economic and social policy.

Although the religious arrangements in the Republic's schools

*During the fifties it became general usage to call the intermediate schools "secondary schools." For the sake of continuity the former usage, intermediate schools, is here retained to refer to academic postprimary education.

seem satisfactory to most Irishmen, the outside observer cannot help but be troubled by the continuance of religious segregation in the schools. Denominational segregation has not been diminished by the energetic reforms of the last decade. The assumption remains that education can occur only when Protestants and Catholics are separated. The policy of religious segregation does not, we must emphasize, imply that Protestants are badly treated. Quite the contrary. The government goes to considerable lengths to make certain that "minority rights" in religious matters are protected. Since the mid-1930's the government has made special grants toward busing Protestant school children to Protestant national schools too distant for them to reach on foot. In practice the government has set the number of children needed for a school to earn a government grant considerably lower for Protestant than for Catholic schools. The issue therefore is not the protection of minority rights, but the fundamental question of whether a nation's educational system should accentuate or moderate the differences that exist between constituent national groups.

There are two groups which are presently excluded from any significant influence over southern Ireland's educational system. These are the parents and the teachers. In the case of the former, Article 42 of Eire's 1937 constitution recites the theory that the primary and natural educator of the child is the parent and that parents are free to provide in their homes or in schools for the education of children as they see fit. This is an admirable principle, but when one looks at actual practice the picture is entirely different. The church and state control everything. The secular curriculum of primary and intermediate schools is set by civil servants in Dublin. On the local level, appointing and discharging of teachers is entirely in the hands of the school manager, who is usually the parish priest. With the special exception of vocational schools there is no provision for local committees of citizens, or local government bodies to oversee, inspect, or even influence the schools. Because religious rather than local governmental authorities control each local school, the individual parent who objects to some aspect of the school's administration is placed in the invidious position of challenging the church, a position few parents are willing to assume in a devoutly Catholic country. Parents are most apt to become aware of their impotence when one of two perennially painful questions arises. The first of these is the excessive enthusiasm of some school managers for the Irish language. For example, in 1967 in Toomore, County Mayo, parents had to threaten a school strike in order to force the manager and principal teacher to conduct the work of the school in English rather than in the Irish language. The other area of parental anxiety is the use of corporal punishment on children. Southern Irish schools are internationally notorious for the physical punishment meted out to children, but even in the case of harsh child beatings by a teacher there is very little a parent can do short of taking the teacher to court (a derisory one shilling in damages was awarded recently to the parents of a child who had been severely beaten by a member of the Christian Brothers). In the long run it is questionable if citizens of the Republic will bear increasing tax burdens for expansion of an educational system over which they have little influence and less control.

Teachers have their unions and professional associations but they are almost as unsuccessful as the parents in establishing a right to influence the educational system except in their individual capacities as teachers. Although there are restrictions on removing teachers without due cause, the Department of Education has been reluctant to cross clerical authorities who have dismissed school teachers. Thus, one of Ireland's better young novelists, John McGahern, was dismissed after his novel *The Dark* appeared in 1965. The novel was a somber study of the interworking of religious zeal, ambition, sex, and guilt in the life of an Irish adolescent candidate for the priesthood. The book was banned, McGahern fired from his teaching post, and effectively blacklisted. Certainly the servile attitude demanded from teachers by the school governors does little to make the teaching profession an attractive one.

Among the Catholic schools a situation exists unique among modern nations: a system that discriminates between clerical and lay teachers in most secondary schools and in some primary schools. In 1964–65 there were 571 recognized intermediate schools in Ireland. Of these, 512 were church-controlled, 468 of the number being Roman Catholic. There were 1,726 lay persons teaching in the Catholic schools and 2,438 religious teachers (religious includes sisters, brothers, and priests). In addition, 615 of the 4,404 Catholic national schools were controlled by religious orders. Now, in the case of the Catholic intermediate schools and the Catholic national schools conducted by orders, a recent study revealed three unusual practices. First, that certain orders discriminate strongly against hiring lay teachers, whatever their qualifications. The Redemptorist Fathers hire no lay teachers whatsoever, and the Franciscans hire only a few. Second, and more important, there is in almost all secondary schools and in those primary schools controlled by religious congregations an absolute boundary on the professional career of a lay teacher. Lay personnel are limited to classroom teaching and are almost never promoted to administrative posts. In effect, a lay teacher in a Catholic secondary school is not eligible for a headship or vice-headship. The third, and most brutal, fact is that the lay teacher is under the constant threat of "displacement." This means that as an individual he can be removed and have his position taken whenever a religious teacher becomes available (the heads prefer religious teachers partly on theological grounds, partly because the religious draw much lower compensation). Collectively the results are clear. The proportion of laymen to total teaching staff in southern Ireland's secondary schools has declined since independence. The emigration rate among lay teachers has been high.

Three.   The Future Imperfect: Issues of the Seventies

X Continuing Southern Nationalism

The present and future problems pressing hardest upon the Irish people, north and south, are in part problems of international policy. An overriding issue for the Republic as a state is the resolution of the tension between the traditions of Irish nationalism and the international orientation characteristic of modern European nations. The Northern Ireland question is a separate issue. Each government involved, those of the United Kingdom, the Irish Republic, and Northern Ireland (whatever its present constitutional position), claims that this issue is essentially a domestic matter: the Republic that it should be settled by Irishmen without British interference, the Northern Ireland and United Kingdom authorities that it is their joint business and only an indirect concern of southern Ireland's government.

Chapters X through XII focus on issues that almost certainly will dominate Irish history in the 1970's. If the material sounds familiar, that is no accident. Hark back for a moment to the watershed years of 1920–23 and recall what happened then: southern Ireland achieved independence, but soon the southern nationalists were violently at odds with one another. In the same period, north and south were separated. In essence, the problems of the 1970's were created by the mistakes of the early twenties.

Let us look first at "conventional" or "official" nationalism, the outlook which prevails among the average citizen of the Irish Republic. In order to gain perspective one should first enumerate the characteristics of Irish nationalism—in, say, 1915—and then note the changes which time has wrought. In the first instance, republican nationalism in 1915 was a minority creed. The majority of the Irish people were indifferent or only mildly favorable to political nationalism and unaware of cultural nationalism. The relatively small band of Irishmen who embraced nationalism in its various forms partially made up for the smallness of their numbers with the intensity of their beliefs. A second characteristic of Irish nationalism in 1915 was its essential negativism. It was vitriolically anti-British, but lacked constructive ideological content. There was a socialist faction which, unlike other segments, had a positive ideologically based formula for life in the new Ireland, but this socialist group was destined to be short-lived, for its only effective leader, James Connolly, was to die in the 1916 Rising. Third, Irish nationalists were to varying degrees historically oriented in their thinking. They all looked back to a golden age—some to the era before 1800 and others before 1170— when Ireland was allegedly well-governed and apparently self-governing. This focusing upon Irish precedents as models for action rather than upon other nations' experiences meant that Irish nationalism was essentially inward-looking, parochial rather than international in orientation. A fourth characteristic was that within the nationalist camp there was a scattering of intellectuals, some professors and scholars, but especially poets and prose artists, who added a dignity and high style to Irish nationalism rarely attained by a nationalist movement. A final point: most nationalists were at best in a tense relationship with the Roman Catholic church, and many were in open conflict with it. The church had helped destroy Parnell, the prepotent constitutionalist leader, and the bishops tried to deny the sacraments to the revolutionary nationalists. (However, there were always sympathetic priests—especially Franciscans— willing to turn a blind eye or deaf ear.)

Now let us change our vantage point to the early 1970's and see how nationalism in the Republic has changed. In the first instance we note immediately that nationalism is no longer a creed, or set of creeds, professed with great intensity by a minority. Instead, it is a part of the conventional culture shared by nearly everyone, but rarely with any great passion.

What once was the belief of a minority has now become institutionalized by official government rituals and widespread propaganda. The nation is dotted with an ever-increasing number of plaques and monuments to the nationalists of the pre-1922 years. Streets, bus depots and train stations have been renamed in honor of nationalist heroes, and the state television service regularly carries programs extolling their lives and activities. Perhaps most important, nationalism has become part of the official culture transmitted to children in their schools. School texts tell of the glories of the Irish past and describe the course of history solely from an Irish nationalist's point of view. By the age of thirteen or fourteen the average child has had his outlook on the world shaped according to the official nationalist line. (Before self-righteously denouncing the Irish for "brainwashing" their children, the American reader would do well to remember that in most American schools at least one hour a day is set aside for political indoctrination under the title of American history, modern problems, civics, or whatever.)

As we have seen, Irish nationalism in the earlier years of the century was essentially without ideological content, and this characteristic has changed only slightly. Whereas early twentieth-century nationalism was bitterly anti-British, but not pro-anything, conventional nationalism in the Republic today is flaccid, still affirming no ideology and only sporadically willing to shake a fist at the United Kingdom. This colorless quality is the natural consequence of the popularization of nationalism, combined with the fact that a successful revolution was followed by a divisive civil war. Except on rare occasions, anti-British feeling is no longer a major public emotion, but no great pride in things Irish and no ideology of Irish life has risen to fill the emotional void. Only faint echoes of the old negativism still persist, such as the strongly anti-Communist bias of conventional nationalist culture. For many the Communist imperialist has replaced the British imperialist as the source of all evil. This anti-Communist tone has been strongest in clerical circles, and the anti-Communist line has been used by the church to discredit the more radical nationalists, especially the IRA. For example, in 1956 Cardinal D'Alton denounced the activities of Communist agents among Irish nationalists, and especially those who demanded a "Worker's Republic" and who believed in the abolition of private property. Similarly, when in 1956 Conor Cruise O'Brien, then of the Department of External Affairs, announced that he favored the recognition of Red China, he met widespread clerical negativism and, later, the Bishop of Galway called for a purge of the Department of External Affairs.

The enthusiasm for history remains unabated. Indeed, because of the program of nationalist education in the Republic's schools it is probable that more people know the narrative of Irish history up to 1922 (where the texts tactfully stop) than ever before. The actions of former nationalists still have power to inspire young people. To this faith in history has been added a new romantic element, namely, the glorification of western Ireland. The far west, especially Connemara, has become mythologized as a repository of much of Ireland's greatness and as the home of a people who reveal the basic nobility and durability of an Ireland unbesmirched by British culture. For many, trips to the west are not merely annual holidays but are pilgrimages. Thousands of young people travel there each year to perfect their grasp of the Irish language and to participate in the virtuous life. The government spends millions annually in special programs to shore up the financial position of those who live in the west, and although these programs make little economic sense they are a nationalistic necessity.

Perhaps the greatest contrast between the situation in 1915 and that of the present day is the relationship of the intellectual and literary classes to nationalism. Whereas previously the professors and the writers were central to Irish nationalism, contemporary writers are alienated from official nationalism. There are too many limits on the freedom of thought of the scholar and on the freedom of expression of the writer for either to be completely at ease in the contemporary Republic. Few writers on the modern Republic can overlook the contrast between the poets' glorious vision in 1916, for example, and the grim realities of the twenties and thirties. There are, to be sure, writers who celebrate uncritically the glories of southern Irish life, but these are minor talents at best. Irish nationalism once could claim such poets as Yeats and Æ; today it draws the devotion of retired civil servants and unpublishable schoolmasters.

While losing the writers from its van, the official nationalist tradition has gained the adhesion of the Catholic authorities. Whereas the revolutionary nationalists were once at odds with the church, those days are past. Only the relatively small band of IRA men remind one of the days when the interests of churchmen and of the nationalists collided.

By far the most controversial component of official nationalism in the Irish Republic is the commitment to the revival of the Irish language. The language question is so shrouded in charge and countercharge that a stint of demythologizing is necessary before we can obtain an unobscured view of the present situation. The first piece of clarification necessary has to do with vocabulary. The form of Gaelic spoken in Ireland is generally known as "Irish." This nomenclature is appropriate, but it leads to an unfortunate state of affairs wherein anyone who has scruples about the revival of the Irish language is labeled as "anti-Irish," a term which impugns his patriotism. One hears the question: "How can a man be an Irish citizen and be anti-Irish?"—a statement that is grammatically correct but, rhetorically speaking, grossly unfair. Similarly, one must guard against the assumption that the Irish language, which is denominated the "first national language," is actually the language of government and commerce in the Republic of Ireland. In reality, the second official language, English, is the predominant tongue, with Irish in most instances reserved for state occasions.

Just as it is easy for the vocabulary of the language enthusiasts to obscure the picture, so the taunts of their opponents can cloud the issue. It is easy enough to point to anomalies and absurdities. The chief of these is that the Republic of Ireland is a nation which has refused to recognize the native language

(English) as the national language. Or, one can point to the folly of spending large amounts of time in translating the classics, such as Dante's *Divine Comedy,* into Irish when almost every literate person in the population could, if he wished, read them in existing English translations. Equally amusing is the common ploy of placing in newspapers official notification in Irish that one is applying for planning permission to develop a property. This satisfies official requirements, and no one is apt to notice if the builder is planning a public monstrosity. Less amusing is the Electricity Supply Board's policy of placing warning signs in Irish on its high-voltage facilities despite the fact that only a minority of people can decipher the warning. But these anomalies, real as they are, should not be the focus of one's attention when looking at the language question. The real focus should be statistics of language use and the effect language teaching has had, for better or worse, upon the Republic's educational system.

The most prevalent and misleading myth about the Irish language is that it was somehow taken from the people as the result of an English conspiracy. This view is nonsense. The Irish people gave up the Irish language of their own volition. Monoglot peasants made sure that their children learned English. Why? For the obvious reason that it paid to learn English. English was, and is, the language of trade. Politics was, and still is, conducted chiefly in the English language. The fact is that the English government did not need to conspire to take the language from the people; once Ireland lost its independence, the decline of the language was inevitable, for then it was in the English-speaking world, not the Irish-speaking world, that fortune and power were to be obtained.

Even long before the Great Famine, the Irish language had ceased to be the native language of the Irish people (in 1851 only 23.3 percent of the people in the entire nation could speak Irish). Accurate statistics for the geographic area that is now the Republic of Ireland are available only for the years 1851 and thereafter (see Table 1), but an extrapolation of the trend indicated in the data reveals that Irish may have ceased to be the native language as early as 1800.

Table 1

Year	Number who could speak Irish	Percentage of population which could speak Irish
1851	1,524,286	23.3
1861	1,077,087	24.5
1871	804,547	19.8
1881	924,781	23.9
1891	664,387	19.2
1901	619,710	19.2

It is often claimed that two groups—the Roman Catholic clergy and the Commissioners of National Education—were responsible for the decline of the Irish language, the former only rarely conducting their ministry in Irish, the latter leaving little or no room for the language in the national schools. While granting that the priests used English and that the national system of education was the vehicle through which children learned English and abandoned Irish, the fact is that neither the priests nor the education commissioners were notably hostile to the Irish language. Indeed, neither group seems to have thought much about it at all. And why did they not have to deal consciously with the issue? Because their attitudes meshed with those of the peasantry, the majority of whom wished to learn and use English, not Irish. Only in the 1870's was the issue of the Irish language brought forcibly to the attention of those who administered Irish primary and intermediate education. As a result, in 1878 the Commissioners of Intermediate Education began paying grants to students who passed an examination in "Celtic." Similarly, in 1879 the Commissioners of National Education began to pay grants to children who were taught Irish as an extra subject in primary schools. In 1900 a "revised program" in the national schools allowed Irish to be taught as an optional subject during school hours provided this did not interfere with other instruction. Perhaps the most important change in educational policy toward the Irish language made before independence came in 1904 with the publication of the first bilingual education program. This program permitted the teaching in national schools in Irish-speaking and bilingual districts to be conducted in both Irish and English. Special fees were payable to teachers who followed this program, the aim of which was not to strengthen Irish but rather to accelerate the acquisition of English by Irish-speaking children. By 1922 Irish was included in the curriculum of 1900 schools, and the bilingual program was followed in another 240.

None of these moves by educators was motivated by a desire to revive the Irish language. The impetus for revival came from a band of language enthusiasts. The roots of the Irish language revival movement go back well before the Famine, but the effective origin must be dated as either 1876 or 1893. In the former year the Society for the Preservation of the Irish Language was formed. It was this group that pressured the Intermediate Education Commissioners into accepting the Irish language as a subject for which schools could earn grants. The society's other activities were scholarship and translation. In the latter category were the translations into Irish by John MacHale, Archbishop of Tuam, of the writings of Homer and of Thomas Moore's *Irish Melodies*. In 1893 the most important organization in the history of the language revival, the Gaelic League, was established. The league was an amalgam of nationalist politicians, off-duty Fenians, poets, and scholars. It advocated not only the revival of the Irish language but the pushing back of English cultural influences. By 1904 the league had 593 branches and had members in every significant Irish town. Members of the league taught and attended classes in Irish, studied Irish folklore and mythology, and learned Irish dancing. The league also served as an educational lobby, and it was partially due to its efforts that the bilingual program was introduced into the Irish national schools.

Significantly, as the power of the language enthusiasts grew they followed the path taken by so many evangelical sects: they moved from voluntary piety to the institutionalization of their beliefs. In 1913 the national convention of the Gaelic League passed a resolution demanding that Irish be taught to all pupils in Irish national schools. This was to be compulsory irrespective of whether or not the children's home language was Irish, or whether or not their parents wanted them to learn the language. In 1920 the demand for institutionalization escalated to the point that the league called for Irish to be the principal language in all Irish schools for all school exercises (prayers, calling the roll, and so on). The league demanded that Irish be taught for at least an hour each day. Then, in 1922 the league received significant reinforcement when a conference organized by the Irish National Teachers Organization called for the compulsory use of Irish as the medium of instruction for history, geography, and music in all Irish schools. Moreover, it was suggested that the two years of infant classes be entirely in Irish.

The metamorphosis from voluntary enthusiasm to institutionalized compulsion was completed in the early years of the Irish Free State. One of the first acts of the new government was to issue a public order effective from 17 March 1922 (hardly, one notes, a randomly selected date) that the Irish language should be taught or used as the medium of instruction at least one hour a day in schools where a teacher was competent to teach it. From 1922 to 1926 was the era of the "First National Program." Special summer courses in Irish were set up for teachers, and attendance was obligatory for anyone under forty-five years of age. A "Second National Program" conference was convened in March 1926 when it became apparent that the first program, especially the requirement that the first two years of school be conducted in Irish, was unenforceable and highly unpopular. The conference report, which to this day remains the basis of primary education in the Republic, reaffirmed the importance of the Irish language, and a minimum of one hour a day in Irish was prescribed for all children in national schools, with Irish used additionally as a medium of instruction whenever possible.

While these changes were being wrought in primary education, the government was reworking the intermediate system. The prescribed curriculum, still basically unchanged to the present, required that each secondary school had to include instruction in Irish if it were to receive a government grant.

The highwater mark in the campaign to institutionalize the

learning of Irish came in 1943 when the Dail passed a bill that would have made parents who sent their children abroad for schooling (meaning Protestants who had their children educated in Great Britain or Northern Ireland) liable to prosecution for failing to have their children taught Irish. To his great credit Douglas Hyde, then President of Ireland and the founder and first president of the Gaelic League, refused to sign the bill, and the Supreme Court eventually declared it unconstitutional.

At present, classes in Irish are obligatory for all primary school students and must also be available in intermediate schools. Secondary schools are given a grant for each child who studies Irish, with the provision that the fees of any child who declines to study Irish are to be raised £10 a year. No child can receive his secondary school-leaving certificates unless he passes the examination in Irish.

The Irish revival was institutionalized in the schools in the first instance, but other government devices also formalized the movement. Without passing an Irish proficiency examination one cannot enter the Republic's civil service, or the legal profession, or the University Colleges at Dublin, Cork, or Galway. A government grant is made to the parents of each child whose first language is Irish (in practice this means a special subvention is made to families in the west of Ireland). The government helps underwrite Irish language summer schools and gives study grants to students. Street signs in Irish cities are in two languages, and increasingly—to almost everyone's confusion—bus routes are specified in Irish rather than in English. The state television and radio service tries to produce as many programs in Irish as possible, although by so doing it usually loses most of its audience. The government-controlled Abbey Theatre requires its actors to be fluent in Irish and gives healthy subventions for the production of plays in the language.

There is, then, an Irish language industry. What has been the result of this large-scale linguistic endeavor? The combined effect of these activities has been to arrest the decline, in absolute numbers and in the percentage, of the people who can speak the Irish language (see Table 2). While the number of persons

Table 2

Year	Number of Irish speakers	Percentage of total population
1926	543,511	18.3
1936	540,802	23.7
1946	588,725	21.2
1961	716,420	27.2

Table 3

Year	Population of Gaeltacht
1926	479,391
1936	452,392
1946	426,013
1956	387,279
1961	366,154

able to speak Irish has risen, the number of persons in the Gaeltacht—defined as areas where at least 25 percent of the population speak Irish as a first language—has declined (Table 3). We can conclude, then, that the official Irish language policy has been successful in reviving Irish as a second language, but unsuccessful in staying its decline as a primary language. Irish, therefore, is increasingly an artificial language, its acquisition a useful accomplishment by people whose native language is English and who will, in the natural course of events, raise their own children with English as their native tongue.

The success of the Irish language preservation movement has not been without expense. The financial costs are obvious, if impossible to calculate precisely. Much less obvious and much more important are the educational costs. A fascinating study by Father John Macnamara, published in 1966, indicates clearly what the intangible costs are of the Irish language campaign in the schools. First, Father Macnamara's study revealed that, on the average, 42 percent of the teaching time in the Republic's primary schools is spent in teaching the Irish language. Further, in many schools, even in English-speaking districts, arithmetic and the English language are taught through the

medium of the Irish language. The result is a severe retardation effect in English language skills and in arithmetic skills as
compared to British school children who follow a similar academic regimen through the English language. Hence, even
after corrections are made for socioeconomic differences, the
average Irish child aged 12–13 is seventeen months behind his
British peer in his English language skills. The comparative
retardation in arithmetical skills is eleven months. This is a
high price to pay for acquiring a second language, and can be
explained only by reference to national pride. In Easter week,
1966, de Valera wrote the following words: "Language is a
chief characteristic of nationhood—the embodiment as it were
of the nation's personality and the closest bond between its
people. No nation with a language of its own would unwillingly
abandon it."

Ever since the civil war there has been a rival to the official
nationalism of the governing parties. A convenient shorthand
phrase for the alternative is the "IRA," although through the
years a wide variety of groups, political fronts, and splinter sects
have presented militant alternatives to the essentially pacific
character of conventional nationalism.

The IRA's genealogy harks back to the men of Easter Week,
but the "new IRA" with which we are here concerned was
formed in the years immediately after the Anglo-Irish treaty
by men who opposed acceptance of the treaty. Up to 1925 the
IRA recognized Eamon de Valera as president of the Irish
Republic, but thereafter it became a wholly underground military organization with only tangential contacts with men of
politics. The IRA position was orthodox Fenianism, which rejected the continued ties with Britain and especially the British
"occupation" of Northern Ireland. Ever since the 1920's, a
Marxist wing of the IRA has preached not only an all-Ireland
republic, but a worker's republic as well. In recent years this
group has become dominant in one of the two wings of the
modern IRA. During the 1920's the IRA spent its time denouncing as traitors the majority of Irishmen who were satis-

fied with the Free State, and in inflicting occasional acts of terror uponthe IRA's opponents. Although for a time Eamon de Valera used the IRA as his unofficial strong-arm ally, the IRA program of bombing, burning, and political murder finally forced him to declare it an illegal organization in June 1936. Under government harassment the IRA went further underground, and a body of members (perhaps 200) took their republican instincts to Spain, where they fought against Franco. From the late 1930's to the early 1950's the IRA was weak, partly because the actions of the de Valera and the Costello administrations, in modifying the government along republican lines, undercut the position of the IRA, and partly because of internecine warfare in the organization's own ranks. During the early fifties the IRA came to life again. It had reinvigorated leaders and a new cause—a renewed Ulster campaign. New organizational groupings appeared: the IRA's political arm was Sinn Fein, its new Ulster campaign group "Saor Uladh," literally "Free Ulster." During the mid-1950's policemen in Northern Ireland were shot, customs houses burned, and post boxes blown up. This Ulster campaign elicited a crushing response. The Northern Ireland government, under the special powers act, moved unhesitatingly against the IRA. The Roman Catholic hierarchy condemned in January 1956 the organization and its campaign, and reaffirmed that a member of the church could not join any unlawful society which plotted against the lawful civil authorities. The government of southern Ireland cooperated closely with northern authorities in crushing the IRA and, in fact, arrested twelve men, including the leaders of the IRA executive, in Dublin in July 1957. (One of the cases was appealed by the IRA defendant to the European Court of Human Rights, where it was decided unanimously in the government's favor.) The combined result of the actions of the church, the Northern Ireland government, and the government of the Republic was that by 1962 the IRA was decimated and forced to call a cease-fire.

During most of the 1960's the IRA was more a comic than a terrorist organization. Its members cut down an occasional telephone pole, painted slogans on the macadamized road in rural areas, and surreptitiously sold the IRA newspaper. The greatest achievement for which the group could plausibly take credit was the blowing up of Nelson's Pillar, and credit for that was not universally accorded (one school of Dublin thought still maintains that the statue of the notorious English adulterer was destroyed by the Legion of Mary in an effort to protect public morality). But suddenly the fortunes of war changed. The civil rights movement in Northern Ireland was organized, and by mid-1968 violence between Catholics and Protestants was a continual possibility. When, in 1969, the northern violence erupted, the IRA was able to begin a major recruiting campaign and to send men and guns to aid the northern Catholics. Even so, its effective armed strength was estimated by informed sources at no more than three hundred men.

Simultaneously, the IRA came to life in the south. So far, its southern activities seldom have been overtly directed at the Dublin government, but consist chiefly of attacks on foreigners living in Ireland. In June and July 1969, for example, five houses in Louth and Meath that belonged to Englishmen were burned. At roughly the same time an American-owned lobster boat was burned in Galway Bay in order, "to protect the Irish shell-fishing industry against exploitation by foreign interests." Other American companies located in the Shannon area have been the subject of unsuccessful IRA attacks. German industrialists and landowners also have been assaulted.

The key event in recent IRA history was the split in its ranks in late 1969, a division which appears to be both violent and permanent. The background is as follows. During the 1960's the dominant outlook of the IRA was changed from traditional and completely negativistic nationalism to a strong left-wing ideology, the catalyst for this change being the leadership of republican intellectuals combined with a general feeling that something had to change if the frustrations of the preceding decade were not to be repeated. In moving to the left, the IRA majority was leaving its traditional rural nationalist base— which was bitterly anti-British and equally anti-Communist— and moving toward a program more congenial to the urban worker. Further, the new leaders decided in 1969 to run candidates for the Dail and for the Northern Ireland and United Kingdom parliaments. This violated the long-standing canon of the IRA that the existing governments of the north and south should not be recognized even implicitly. To make matters worse in the eyes of the traditional IRA men, when Protestant mobs attacked the Catholic areas of Belfast in 1969, the IRA proved remarkably weak and almost completely incapable of defending the Catholics.

Out of this complex situation came the IRA split of late 1969. The "Provisional IRA" was established to rival the "Official IRA." The Officials are leftist and Dublin-dominated, although they are strong in parts of Belfast. In doctrine they are nonsectarian in the sense that they believe that the enemy is the British Army and that Protestant and Catholic workers eventually have to be united in a class war against, first, the foreign imperialists and then the ruling classes. This means that they are somewhat discriminating in their choice of targets, shooting at British soldiers but refusing to make random attacks on civilians.

The Provisionals, on the other hand, are nonideological. The locus of their power is in the north, and they are especially strong in Derry and in parts of Belfast. In contrast to the Officials, they are violently anti-Protestant and are given to seemingly random bombing campaigns directed at everything from cinemas to military lorries to ladies' lavatories. Although the two rival IRA factions have directed most of their energies at their self-defined enemies, there is considerable evidence that between attacks they have waged gang battles against each other.

The problems the activities of the two IRA's imply for the authorities in Northern Ireland are obvious. What is not so obvious is that they also provide the Republic's government with major problems. The relationship of official nationalism (as represented by the government in Dublin) and militant nationalism (as articulated by the two IRA groups) is a two-way phenomenon. In times of relative prosperity and international calm, militants tend to lose their fervor, to abandon their cause as unrealistic, and to accept the government's version of nationalism. In times of crisis, such as the present situation in the north, the flow is reversed and the militants gain adherents. The conversion from official to militant nationalism is easy, because the government has used the schools and the media to inculcate an acceptance of the very same symbols employed by the militants: the brave men of 1916, the glories of the Irish past, the unique virtues of the Irish language, and so on. It is no difficult task to make the transition from responding to these symbols as the government wishes (as an affirmation of its own legitimacy) to reacting in a militant manner (as a repudiation of the government's passivity).

Paradoxically, therefore, any event which escalates the violence in Northern Ireland threatens the southern regime as much as it does that of the north. A significant increment in IRA activity in the north brings British pressure upon the Dublin government to impede the flow of arms and men to the north. There are compelling diplomatic reasons for the Republic's government to respond affirmatively to such demands, but despite these and despite the southern government's dislike of the two IRA's (which, after all, refuses to recognize its legitimacy), the Dublin government cannot move too strongly for fear of provoking backlash which will bring it down. Similarly, an increase in British military activity (such as the "Derry massacre" of 1972) brings great popular pressure to bear upon the Dublin administration to aid the nationalists in the north. If the Republic's government is seen to move too slowly, then it invites electoral defeat; if too strongly, then it will anger its largest trading partner, Great Britain. The tightrope is a wobbly one, but the Dublin government has not yet toppled off.

XI   Once Again an Ulster Question

When the Ulster situation burst onto the front pages in mid-1969 it was because a condition of unstable equilibrium had been destroyed. Throughout most of the 1950's and 1960's the myriad conflicting forces in Northern Irish society had somehow balanced each other. Violence had disappeared, it seemed, as a part of Ulster life and, gradually, hostile social groups were learning to live with each other peacefully, if not happily. The resulting equilibrium was a very delicate one, and any significant change in the balance of power within Ulster society would very quickly destroy the balance. Hence, Northern Ireland had to be a conservative society—changes, reforms, and innovations had to be introduced gradually—if it was to avoid social conflict. When in 1968 the activities of the civil rights movement coincided with the reformist activities of the then Prime Minister, Captain Terence O'Neill, the balance within Ulster society was disturbed, and a reaction followed which resulted finally in the explosions which began in 1969 and continue to the present. Rather than immediately becoming engaged in the drama of violent events it is better to step back and look at the conditions which produced the violence. Three matters warrant scrutiny: the nature of the Ulster economy, the configuration of its government, and the patterns of communal division.

The economy of Northern Ireland differs from that of the Irish Republic in two ways. First, no pretense is made that the Ulster economy is an integral unit of its own. Northern Ireland clearly is a regional component of the economic system which encompasses the entire United Kingdom. The monetary and fiscal system of Northern Ireland is integrated with that of Great Britain, and goods move between Great Britain and Ulster without impediments. The second difference between

Ulster and the rest of Ireland is that Ulster became industrial-
ized during the nineteenth century in concert with Great Britain
while the rest of Ireland did not.

The foundation of Ulster's industrialization was laid in the
eighteenth century with the development of a vigorous linen
industry. In the last quarter of the century a strong cotton industry emerged based on power-driven machinery. The first
cotton spinning mill in Ulster, water-powered, was built in
1784, and the first steam-powered cotton factory was built in
1789. The Ulster cotton industry, which was centered in the
Belfast area, grew rapidly in the buoyant economic climate
engendered by the Anglo-French war. The decline in the demand for cotton consequent upon the end of the war in 1815
almost destroyed the industry, but it sputtered along, and Ulster
textile manufacturing was saved in 1828 by an invention which
adapted cotton-spinning techniques to the production of linen.
The market for linen was firm, and within less than ten years
linen manufactured by machines had become Ulster's leading
industrial product. By 1835 the port of Belfast was the leading
Irish port in value of trade, and over half the total Belfast
exports were linen. By 1841 Belfast had almost 71,000 inhabitants, which made it equal in population to Cork and second
only to Dublin. Belfast's population in 1800 had been roughly
20,000. In a forty-year period Belfast, under the influence of
textile industrialization, had jumped from being the fifth largest
town in Ireland to the twelfth largest city in the British Isles.

The next stage of industrialization in Northern Ireland occurred after mid-century and was a result of the development
of the shipbuilding industry in Belfast. The crucial event in
this process was the forming of the partnership of Harland and
Wolff in 1858. The partnership was a brilliant blend of engineering genius with successful selling techniques. Other firms
followed in the wake of this resourceful partnership, and up
through the First World War shipbuilding was a prosperous
heavy industry. By 1900 Belfast had a population of almost
350,000. Clearly, by then Belfast belonged to the world of the
British industrial revolution, not to the world of the Irish
agricultural economy.

Despite its industrialization, Northern Ireland is an economically vulnerable society. One reason for this vulnerability is that there are almost no industries which produce raw material or fuel for industry. The lack of natural resources places Northern Ireland industry at a disadvantage vis-à-vis regions where such material or fuels are located close by and thus can be cheaply attained. Also, the dependence upon outside suppliers of raw material and fuels means that Ulster industries are apt to be affected by problems in economic areas over which Ulster businessmen and governmental authorities have no control. Ulster's susceptibility to economic ills is compounded by the concentration of its working population in three major activities, namely, heavy engineering (shipbuilding, and so on), textiles, and agriculture. The heavy reliance on a limited number of industries increases the region's vulnerability to economic fluctuations. The concentration in heavy industry and textiles is especially unsettling because the engineering and shipbuilding industries produce durable capital goods, whose product-life is usually very long. The demand for such products tends to be highly unstable, since in times of recession a firm can usually put off for a considerable time buying industrial equipment if its resources are limited; this is in contrast to raw materials which a manufacturing firm must buy to stay in business and for which the demand, therefore, is relatively stable. The result is that the fluctuations in the Ulster heavy manufacturing industry tend to exceed the general fluctuations in the United Kingdom economy. In times of low industrial profitability (a characteristic of the United Kingdom in recent years) the demand for heavy goods falls, and the recession in Northern Ireland's heavy engineering field drags the whole Ulster economy down with it. The textile industry suffers from similar problems, although for entirely different reasons. Linen goods in particular are troublesome because linen is a semiluxury consumption item which is manufactured chiefly for export. When consumers are pinched financially it is the sort of article they will cease buying. Hence, the linen industry is highly susceptible to changes in foreign economies. All these factors make it difficult for governmental authorities to keep Northern Ireland's economy healthy for any considerable length of time.

The result of Northern Ireland's economic weakness is indicated by its having in mid-1969, for example, 7.3 percent of the labor force unemployed in comparison with only 2.5 percent unemployment in Great Britain. In view of this economic situation, one might think that Ulster residents would stream into the Republic of Ireland. Such is not the case, for depressed as it is, Northern Ireland is a good deal better off economically than the Republic. Even with unemployment, average incomes per head in the north are 35 to 40 percent higher than in the south. In manufacturing industries, average earnings are about 15 percent higher in the north. Agricultural productivity per unit of land in the north is almost triple that of the Republic. These economic facts explain why unemployed Northern Irishmen emigrate not to southern Ireland but to England.

The economic advantages of the Ulsterman over his southern counterpart become even more obvious if one examines the provision of social welfare services. The social services in the south, which we described earlier, are minimal. In contrast, Northern Ireland is part of the British welfare state. Ulster benefits in unemployment compensation, medical services, and pensions are set at parity with Britain. Thus, an unemployed Ulsterman with a wife and two children receives £12.50 a week in benefits, while a man in a similar situation in the twenty-six counties receives £10.20. Although the Republic's population is almost double Northern Ireland's, the 1970–71 education budget in the north was £82 million, that in the south £84 million. In the same period, health and local welfare service expenditures were £69 million in the south and £73 million in the north. Even after taking into account the higher tax rates in the north, the economic position of the Northern Irishman is considerably better than that of his counterpart in the south, a fact which affects the thinking of many Ulster residents about the possible reunification of Ireland.

At present the government of Northern Ireland is suspended prior to being reshaped, but because it operated until 1972, its arrangements are of more than historical interest. The entire governmental structure of Northern Ireland was predicated upon three sets of arrangements: the boundary settlement, the administrative and legislative framework of the Government of Ireland Act 1920, and its financial relations with Great Britain.

The first matter, the border, was a question settled definitively but unpleasantly in the 1920's. The border was of capital importance to the Ulster unionists; it determined the economic and human resources under their command, and the extent of those resources determined whether or not Northern Ireland could survive separation from the remainder of Ireland. The Government of Ireland Act of 1920 had defined the six counties that were to constitute Northern Ireland, but in 1920 it was still unclear whether or not the United Kingdom cabinet intended partition to be permanent. In late 1921, during the course of the negotiations of the Anglo-Irish treaty (negotiated between the Irish nationalists and the United Kingdom government), the British suggested that provisions be made in the treaty for a "boundary commission" to revise the Northern Ireland boundaries in accordance with the wishes of the inhabitants should the Ulster unionists remain adamant in their refusal to join the south. In essence, this proposal was an attempt to bring pressure to bear on Ulster's unionist leaders to consider seriously reunion with their southern neighbors. The Counties of Tyrone and Fermanagh had nationalist majorities, and there were strong nationalist enclaves in Londonderry, Down, and Armagh. If the wishes of the inhabitants of these areas were respected, Northern Ireland would lose them and probably acquire only a small portion of Donegal, which had unionist leanings. As finally enacted, the Anglo-Irish treaty of 1921 contained a provision that if the Parliament of Northern Ireland decided not to join the newly created Irish Free State, a boundary commission would be appointed consisting of three persons, one chosen by the Free State government, one by the Northern Ireland government, and one by the British government, the last being chairman. This commission was to determine "in accordance with the wishes of the inhabitants, so far as may be compatible with economic and geographic conditions, the boundaries between Northern Ireland and the rest of Ireland."

The boundary commission was convened in 1924. The British appointed Judge Feetham of South Africa. Feetham was a judge of the Supreme Court in South Africa and had excellent experience in dominion affairs. The Irish Free State appointed Professor Eoin MacNeill, its Minister for Education, who had long been an able and literate spokesman for the nationalist cause. Faced with the possibility of losing some of its territory, the Northern Ireland government refused to appoint a member. The British cabinet, under Ramsay MacDonald, responded by appointing Mr. Joseph R. Fisher, a Protestant Ulsterman, to represent the interest of the north (Fisher was an old friend and political ally of James Craig). This appointment by the British government was given legislative sanction by a special act passed by the Westminster parliament in October 1924.

The commission met regularly up through the autumn of 1925. It conducted investigations of local opinion and economic conditions all over Northern Ireland and was apparently ready to report in November 1925. In that month, however, the London *Morning Post* published a map purporting to give the decision of the commission. The map showed only minor changes in the existing frontier, including, to the Free State's outrage, an area of eastern Donegal being transferred to Northern Ireland. Professor MacNeill resigned from the commission, making lame explanations as to why he had continued so long when the commission was moving toward a conclusion he deemed unacceptable. Once the Free State representative had resigned, the commission was dismantled, its investigation being totally disregarded and classified as secret (the report was made available to the public only in 1968!). Nevertheless, all three governments signed an agreement late in 1925 which ratified the existing boundaries. From this tangle one conclusion became clear: the north had won. No changes were made in the boundary of the six counties, and Northern Ireland remained an economic and governmental unit of viable size.

Turning next to the structure of government as it existed before the spring of 1972, the basic principle underpinning the Northern Ireland regime was the principle of devolution. Northern Ireland was not a sovereign state and had powers and responsibilities only in matters specifically defined and delegated by the government at Westminster. The division of powers between the Stormont (the seat, near Belfast, of the northern administration) and Westminster governments was between matters of local concern and those of concern to regions other than Ulster. The British Parliament legislates on matters affecting the entire United Kingdom, including Ulster. The arrangement for Ulster representation in London was unchanged by the suspension of the Stormont Parliament. Northern Ireland has twelve M.P.'s who are elected under the same rules which prevail in Great Britain, namely, universal adult suffrage on the one man, one vote principle.

The old Stormont Parliament was a scaled-down version of the United Kingdom Parliament. It was bicameral, the lower house, or Commons, consisting of fifty-two members. These M.P.'s were elected on the same basic franchise as prevails in Great Britain, namely, universal adult suffrage. (Before the passage of the Electoral Law Amendment Act of 1968 there was an additional vote for owners of businesses valued for tax purposes at £10 or over.) The upper house of the northern parliament, the Senate, was not directly elected. It consisted of twenty-four members (plus the Lords Mayor of Belfast and Londonderry *ex officio*) who were chosen by the members of the Stormont House of Commons. In practice the upper house had few powers, membership serving chiefly as a reward to Unionist party stalwarts.

Technically, the cabinet which headed the Ulster legislative and executive branches was an executive committee of the United Kingdom Privy Council, but this was a theoretical complication. In actual operation, the Ulster cabinet was a regional replica of the British cabinet. Before being suspended, there were ten cabinet members, eight of whom were department heads: Agriculture, Commerce, Development, Education, Finance, Health and Social Services, Home Affairs, and Community Relations. In addition, the Prime Minister and the Leader of the Senate served without departmental affiliation. The Attorney-General and other junior departmental ministers were not members of the cabinet. With the exception of the Leader of the Senate, cabinet members usually were members of the Commons. When one notes that there were ten members

of the Commons in the cabinet, plus eight parliamentary secretaries (one for each department), plus the Attorney-General,
the junior ministers, and the Speaker, it becomes clear that
more than one quarter of the membership of the Parliament
of Northern Ireland was in receipt of official salaries.

We have now described two of the three legs of the tripod
on which the Northern Ireland government rested—the
boundary situation, and the formal constitution of government.
The third leg was the financial relationship of Northern Ireland and Great Britain. This relationship was (and still is) extremely complicated, and its details are not open to public
scrutiny, but the most important fact is this: the government
of Northern Ireland receives a sizable subsidy from the United
Kingdom government so that the citizens of Northern Ireland
pay less for the same social and governmental services than do
the British. The best estimates are that the British Exchequer
provides a subsidy of at least £80 per year for every inhabitant
of Northern Ireland. This is not what was originally intended.
The 1920 Government of Ireland Act was written during a
time of economic optimism, and it was believed that Northern
Ireland would be able to bear its proportionate share of the
United Kingdom's financial burdens, but by the mid-1920's it
was clear that Northern Ireland was unable to do so. Northern
Ireland remains today an economically depressed area when
compared to the rest of the United Kingdom, and therefore the
burdens on its social and welfare services (which are kept at par
with Great Britain's) are relatively high and its tax revenues
comparatively low. Because Northern Ireland received a subsidy from Britain, the former government of Northern Ireland
has had restricted financial freedom. As Northern Ireland's
benefactor, the United Kingdom Exchequer has carefully scru-
tinized all Ulster expenditures, and any hint of prodigality on
the part of the Ulstermen has brought the threat of reduced
British subsidies.

A useful place to begin a discussion of the religious situation
in Northern Ireland is with the population data given in Table

A.3. The revealing figures are the Roman Catholic census data. The Catholic population has stayed remarkably stable both in absolute numbers and as a proportion of the population since the government of Northern Ireland was founded. In 1926 there were 420,428 Catholics, representing 33.5 percent of the population. The Catholic population in 1961 was 497,547, comprising 34.9 percent of the total population. Although the total population of Northern Ireland has been almost static during the years since the Ulster government was formed, Northern Ireland has the highest rate of natural population increase of any country in the British Isles. Obviously, heavy emigration has occurred. Further, the Roman Catholics in Northern Ireland have the highest rate of natural increase of any of Ulster's religious denominations, yet their numbers stay relatively stable; hence, it is clear that the Catholics have the highest emigration rate. The forces which lead Catholics to emigrate in relatively large numbers will become clear in the course of this chapter. For the moment, the signal point is that the religious composition of Northern Ireland is very stable and is unlikely to change significantly in the near future.

Northern Irish social life consists of two entirely separate social systems, Protestant and Catholic. Even outside of formal organizations, Catholics and Protestants have generally differing social patterns. Whereas Protestants usually do not attend amusements on Sunday, Catholics customarily use Sunday as a day for recreation once their religious duty is done. Even sports are sectarian. Rugby-football, cricket, and girls' field hockey are predominantly Protestant games, while the various Gaelic games are almost exclusively Catholic. Association football (soccer), tennis, and golf are ecumenical sports (!).

These differences in social style are accentuated by economic differences between the two communities. By and large, the Catholics are poorer and less well educated. One of the results of this implicit social segregation of the two faiths is that mixed marriages occur only infrequently. Both faiths strongly discourage mixed marriages; in any case, the existence of two complete, separate social systems greatly reduces the chance for such marriages.

Social toxins permeate each community. The Protestant community often worries about being swamped in numbers as a result of the high Catholic birth rate. Many Protestants view the Catholic civil rights campaign as part of a master plan to attack Protestant civil liberties, and eventually to overthrow the government. Even if a Catholic majority were to maintain the Union with England, Protestants argue, it would make laws hostile to the Protestant faith.

If Ulster Protestantism is characterized by a siege mentality, Northern Irish Catholicism bears the imprint of a ghetto mentality. Social and political life is often seen as a hostile conspiracy. The Protestant ascendancy is frequently blamed for social and economic problems that have nothing to do either with religion or with the Protestant authorities, but with the fundamental economic problems of Northern Ireland. Negativism, bitterness, and useless aggressiveness are endemic in the Catholic community.

The volatility of the Northern Irish denominational situation was made clear in the very first years of the Ulster government. In 1922, 232 persons were killed in sectarian rioting and almost 1,000 were wounded. During the depression years strife was endemic. An attack on an Orange procession by a band of Catholics began widespread riots in 1931, while the cauldron was kept boiling in 1932 by Protestants attacking Catholic pilgrims on their journey to a Eucharistic conference in Dublin. In 1934 there were assorted incidents, and in 1935 the worst rioting since 1922 erupted in Belfast with eleven persons killed, the Catholics suffering most heavily. World War II temporarily reduced the chances of violence within Northern Ireland by calling forth most of the region's surplus energy and manpower, but Protestant suspicion of the Catholics grew. The Catholics were associated in the Protestant mind with Eire, which was neutral and was widely believed to be sympathetic to Germany. Moreover, the Irish Catholic church refused to be identified in any way with support for the Allies. There were weighty reasons for this neutrality on the part of the Catholic hierarchy, but it was not surprising that many Protestants viewed the Catholics as potential traitors in their midst. Relations between the communities deteriorated throughout the 1940's but seem to have grown no worse during most of the 1950's. In the late 1950's, friction between religious groups diminished and relations between Northern Ireland and Eire became more cordial. But by mid-1965 there were signs of a backlash. Prime Minister O'Neill came under fire from his colleagues in the unionist party for being too generous to the Catholics. Then came the civil rights movement, student unrest, the emergence of the revolutionary left, and the fall of O'Neill. By mid-1969 Ulster was back where it had been in 1922. Riots, arson, and murder were again the order of the day.

No one should be surprised to learn that politics in Ulster follow denominational lines. Protestants have almost always voted unionist, and Catholics almost always have voted nationalist, or some variant thereof, a split which is not merely political.* For the majority of Protestants the question of the Union replaces all matters of ideology, and although the Unionist party at Westminster aligns itself with the British Conservative party, this is as much a matter of convenience as of principle. In actual fact the Northern Ireland government worked equally easily with labour and with conservative cabinets and it accepted the welfare state without hesitation. Not only do constitutional questions override ideological considerations in Ulster politics, but constitutional matters greatly overshadow considerations of social class. Protestant workingmen vote overwhelmingly for the Unionist party and Catholic workers for the nationalist. Only in the largest urban areas does the class-oriented labour party have any drawing power. The frozen nature of Ulster politics is indicated by there having been only five prime ministers in the region's political history and all of them Unionist.

For most of its existence the Unionist party has been a highly disciplined, efficient electoral machine. It has a ward organization which covers the entire six counties. At the local level the

*A note on vocabulary: in the special lexicon of Ulster life, "nationalist" has become a generally accepted synonym for "Catholic" and is so used late in this chapter. Similarly, "unionist" is often used as a synonym for "Protestant."

Unionist strength stems chiefly from the Orange Order. The order's influence is prodigious. A responsible scholarly estimate indicates that in the mid-fifties two thirds of the adult male Protestant population in Northern Ireland belonged to the order. The Grand Lodge of the order chooses 122 delegates of the 712 members of the Unionist Council. At the local level the order's influence is considerably greater, and except in urban areas it is almost impossible to be adopted as a unionist candidate for any office without approval of the local lodge. Almost all members of the Stormont government were members of the order.

In contrast to the unionists, the representatives of the minority have been badly organized. This is hardly surprising, because Northern Ireland politics have pivoted upon the question of the Union, and the stable demographic patterns discussed earlier guaranteed that the nationalists could gain control neither of Stormont nor of Ulster representation at Westminster. Party discipline could not be maintained while it was clear that an individual politician had little to lose by becoming a maverick (there were no spoils of office for him no matter how loyally he toed the party line). Further, the opposition was debilitated by two divisive questions: should the representatives of the minority implicitly recognize the legitimacy of the Northern Ireland regime by taking their seats in the Stormont Parliament, and, if so, was the party's job to press for the reunification of Ireland or the bettering of the minority position under the existing northern government? Only recently have the opposition politicians formed new groupings which give promise of a release from the sterility of their political past.

Now, let us go to an arbitrary date shortly before the recent troubles began—say, 1 January 1969—and examine the degree of social, political, and economic discrimination in Ulster life. Given the degree of estrangement between the Protestant and Catholic communities, it was inevitable that members of both groups discriminated whenever possible against their opposites. Both communities, it must be emphasized, practiced extensive discrimination, but because the Protestants controlled most of the instruments of power, the deepest grievances were on the Catholic side.

Turning first to electoral discrimination, it is important to distinguish between the various levels of government in Northern Ireland, or one loses sight of what the real problem was. For instance, it is easy to note that while Catholics comprised roughly one third of the population in 1969, the nationalists held only two of the twelve Ulster seats in the United Kingdom Parliament and hence to conclude that this is evidence of wholesale discrimination. Actually, this pattern was the result of the existence of a system of single-seat constituencies rather than of any electoral maneuvering by the Protestant government. There was no plural voting in elections for the United Kingdom Parliament, and there was no evidence of gerrymandering. Indeed, the two largest constituencies for Westminster elections were South Antrim and North Down, both Protestant areas; this was just the opposite of what the situation would be if gerrymandering had taken place.

Electoral arrangements for the Stormont Parliament were not as scrupulously fair as were the elections for the United Kingdom Parliament, but the degree of discrimination was not consequential. Thirty-nine of the fifty-two seats in the Stormont Parliament were held by unionists, a percentage larger than the Protestant proportion of the population; but, again, one should realize that the existence of single-seat constituencies exaggerated the influence of the majority party. This was an imperfection in the machinery of electoral politics, not a matter of Protestant conspiracy. Of course one could argue that manipulation of constituency boundaries discriminated against the Catholics, but in actual fact the nationalist-held constituencies tended to have smaller populations than did unionist constituencies. Thus the nationalist representation, not the unionist, was magnified.

Where the real electoral discrimination came was at the local level. There were sixty-eight principal local government units in Northern Ireland, each of them controlled by an elected council. Three facets of the local electoral system stand out.

The first of these was that the franchise system was doubly discriminatory against Catholics. Not all adults had the right to vote—only those who were the occupiers of a house. The occupiers' children of adult age and any servant or subtenant were excluded from voting. Thus, whereas the electorate for the Stormont Parliament in 1968 was roughly 942,000, that for local government elections was only about 694,000. A larger proportion of Catholics than Protestants were in the excluded categories. Moreover, there were plural votes for businesses as well, a practice which redounded to the Protestants' benefit (there were in 1968 about 13,000 plural votes cast in local government elections). Further, local electoral boundaries in Northern Ireland were drawn under the principle that the valuation of property in a given area was as important as the number of people in the district. Hence, constituency boundaries could be drawn in local governmental areas without the necessity of equalizing the number of persons in each ward. The classic case of gerrymandering to thwart the desires of the Catholics was in Londonderry. In that city there were three wards containing an electoral population of roughly 14,300 Catholics and 8,700 Protestants. Yet the unionist party controlled the city council. This was accomplished by lumping together the Catholics in one of the city's three major wards and leaving small Protestant majorities in the other two wards. Similarly, the unionists controlled thirty-eight of the fifty seats on the Fermanagh Council Council even though the county had a Catholic majority.

The electoral law's requirement that one be an occupier of a house in order to vote led to discrimination in the allocation of locally provided public housing units. The law meant that if a town council, of whatever persuasion, filled its housing units with those of the opposite party it was automatically creating votes for its opponents. This led both unionists and nationalists to discriminate heavily against the religious opposition in housing in areas under their control, the only difference between the two groups being that the unionists controlled more local government bodies.

At this point it should be made clear that the other im-

portant social services besides local housing were managed by
Stormont or United Kingdom authorities who did not discriminate against Catholics. Indeed, the services of the welfare
state—health services, national assistance, old-age pensions, and
family allowances—have been of greater benefit to the Catholic
community than to the Protestant. The reasons that Catholics
have benefited more than Protestants from social service arrangements are that Catholics as a group are poorer, more often
unemployed, and generally have larger families than Protestants.

What about discrimination in employment? Comprehensive
statistics on the private sector are not available, but it appears
that in medium- and small-sized firms (especially local retail
operations) discrimination has been severe. This discrimination
has taken place either at the point of entry (by refusing to
allow any, or only a few, persons of the opposite faith to begin
employment) or within a given firm (by favoring one group
in advancement policies). The available information indicates
that both Catholic and Protestant businessmen have discriminated, the only difference being that Protestants have controlled
more of Northern Ireland's economic resources, and therefore
Catholics have been proportionately disadvantaged. This is not
to say that there were not firms which did not discriminate; the
large, internationally owned corporations tended to be outside
the closed circles of Ulster affairs, and were thus able to appoint
and promote individuals according to nonreligious criteria.

As one might expect, employment patterns in local government revealed severe religious discrimination. In 1969, for
example, although the majority of the Fermanagh population
was nationalist, unionists controlled the County Council with
the secondary result that only thirty-two of the 370 persons
employed by the council were Roman Catholic. Similar figures
held for most unionist-dominated local government units, and
in the few Catholic-controlled areas (Newry, for example) discrimination against Protestants was equally strong. In 1969
only twenty-three of the 319 persons in administrative grades
in the Northern Ireland civil service (the highest rank) were
Roman Catholics. There seems to have been no discrimination
in the branches of the British Civil Service which are located

in Northern Ireland. Almost precisely one third of the Inland Revenue staff was Catholic, and Catholics had more than half of the post office appointments (indeed, from these figures one could well argue that anti-Protestant discrimination might be occurring in the United Kingdom service branches).

The salient characteristics of the Ulster employment situation were, first, that Protestants were overrepresented in the upper-income brackets and in the professions, and second, that Roman Catholics were more apt to be without work than were Protestants. The higher Catholic unemployment rate was, we speculate, the most important reason Catholic emigration exceeded Protestant emigration. It is this differential in the emigration rate that has kept the Catholic–Protestant ratio in the population stable over the past four decades.

In the 1960's approximately three quarters of the population in the academically selective secondary schools and in the university-level institutions in Northern Ireland was Protestant. When the government of Northern Ireland came into existence it inherited two denominational systems of education, primary and intermediate, as well as the less important nondenominational technical school system. Immediately, a single ministry superseded the primary and secondary boards, and in September 1921 the government appointed a committee to make recommendations for reform. The authorities of the Roman Catholic church refused to give evidence, and its adherents refused to serve as members. Nevertheless, the education act of 1923 which stemmed from the committee's investigations was religiously neutral. The act set up Local Educational Authorities on the English model attached to each county and county borough council and reorganized primary education (intermediate education was not dealt with until the 1940's). The act provided that there would be three types of primary schools. The most favored of these would be schools completely financed and controlled by the Local Educational Authorities. In these schools the education was to be completely secular and no religious material was to be allowed. The government hoped that most denominational authorities on both sides would transfer their schools to the local authorities and concentrate on providing supplementary religious instruction outside of school hours. The least favored primary schools would be those which remained denominational. They would be completely controlled, as before, by denominational authorities and would have 100 percent of teachers' salaries paid by the government, but they would receive no aid for construction or maintenance costs. Religious instruction could go on as before in these schools. A third, median, category of schools was to be the "four and two schools." In each of these schools control would be vested in four people named by the manager (himself and three other priests if he wished) and in two persons named by the Local Educational Authority. Denominational control and teaching would be maintained, and, in return for giving the secular authorities minority representation on the governing board, the school would receive in addition to teachers' salaries financial aid toward maintenance costs and, at the discretion of the local authorities, some help toward capital costs as well.

This 1923 education act was an impressive piece of statesmanship and its failure was no fault of its framers. Both the Catholic authorities and the Protestant extremists feverishly attacked the measure. The Catholic authorities objected on theological grounds to an arrangement that would separate religious from secular instruction. Jealousy of their own prerogatives made them refuse to cede any of their authority over education to civil officials. They also refused to sanction the mixing of Catholic children with Protestant children in schools. The public explanation of this refusal was that such mixing might endanger the faith of the Catholic children. All these reasons explain why the Catholic church would not transfer its schools to local civic authorities, but they do not explain why so few priests chose to join the "four and two" scheme. By so doing they would not have subjected their children to any of the theologically condemned dangers of the secular schools, nor would they have lost control of the schools. The reason for the abstention seems to lie in the almost pathological fear of the state which the Roman Catholic church in Ireland (both south and north) exhibited during this period as well as in a more reasonable fear that the representatives of the Local Educational Authorities in Northern Ireland would not be sympathetic in their dealings with the Catholic schools. In any case, the refusal to join the "four and two" scheme meant the Catholic primary schools received less money than they would have and that Catholic pupils suffered thereby.

Short-sighted and self-serving as the Catholic attitude was, that of the right-wing Protestants was worse. The Protestants were as steeped in religious bigotry as the Catholics and had no more desire for the religious integration of children than did their opponents. Further, the Protestants vigorously objected to the banishment of Bible teaching from the schools under state control. Unlike the Catholic authorities, however, the militant Protestants did not fear the state. Hence, whereas the Catholics refused to enter into the state school arrangements, the Protestants pressed vigorously for the modification of those arrangements to their own tastes. In the face of efficient, well-organized Protestant pressures the unionist government gave in. In 1925 the government passed an amending act allowing Bible reading to be given at the end of the school day, with attendance voluntary, and allowing the religious denomination of a candidate to be taken into account in the hiring of teachers. Under these arrangements more than 440 Protestant schools were transferred to local government control within four years' time. But the militant Protestants were still not satisfied, and in 1930 they wrung another set of concessions from the government. These were first, that the former managers of denominational schools that transferred to the government receive majority influence on the school management committee which was charged with nominating three candidates for each teaching vacancy in the local school, one of whom had to be chosen by the Local Educational Authority; second, religious instruction approved by the former managers of the transferred school was to be allowed during school hours; and third, any teacher found not acceptable to the school on religious grounds could be transferred at will. Under these terms almost every Protestant primary school in the country was transferred to local control, while the Catholic church refused to transfer its schools. Much to his credit, Sir James Craig, the Northern

Ireland Prime Minister, made certain that the 1930 act contained a significant, if not balancing, concession to the Catholics, namely, that in the future denominational primary schools would receive a 50 percent grant toward building and equipment costs (a figure which was raised to 65 percent in 1947 and to 80 percent in 1968).

The result is that there are now two systems of primary education in Northern Ireland. One is an ostensibly state-controlled but actually a Protestant system financed totally by government funds, the other is a Catholic system in which the state pays all teachers salaries and most, but not all, capital or maintenance costs (the total grant averages about 90 percent of all costs). The injustice of this situation seems obvious. But one comment is in order: there is nothing which prevents the Catholic authorities from taking as full advantage of the government's revenues as have the Protestants. The arrangements for the transfer of schools to the local authorities left the former denominational managers with the right to determine the religious instruction to be given in the schools and to control the appointment of teachers. The statutory mechanisms are as amenable to Catholic as to Protestant manipulation. Certainly in transferring title of its schools to the Local Educational Authorities the church would be entering an alliance with the state which it had previously abhorred; certainly it would have been necessary for the local parish priest to negotiate on occasion with the Local Educational Authority in a way which has not been necessary in the past. But the benefit to Roman Catholic school children would have more than compensated for the inconvenience suffered.

A final topic related to the issue of religious discrimination in Northern Ireland was the organization of the police. The Royal Ulster Constabulary was created in June 1922 as the northern successor to the Royal Irish Constabulary which had enforced the law throughout all of Ireland. The regular police force, which in 1969 numbered about 3,000, was directly responsible to the Minister of Home Affairs in the Stormont cabinet. The Ulster police did not have the confidence of the bulk of the Catholic population. This was hardly surprising, because in spite of the past history of widespread Catholic participation in the old Royal Irish Constabulary, Catholics rarely joined the new police force; the force, after all, was spearheading the fight against the Irish Republican Army and other nationalist extremist groups, almost all of whose members were Catholic. Even though one third of the places in the constabulary were reserved for Catholics, only 12 percent of the force was Catholic. Inevitably the Catholics were distrustful of a force dominated by their religious opponents.

The greatest police problem, however, was not with the regulars but with an auxiliary force known as the "B Specials." In November 1920 the government of Northern Ireland began forming a defense force against the nationalists. The force consisted of three classes of special constables. Class A comprised those who were willing to perform full-time duty, Class B those who were able to give part-time service, and Class C was a reserve. By 1925 conditions were sufficiently peaceful to allow the demobilizing of Classes A and C and the reduction of Class B. The Class B special constables remained intact, however, as the Ulster Special Constabulary (the "B Specials"), and when IRA activities began again in the 1930's, they were pressed into service. During World War II the B Specials constituted the Home Guard, and their number grew to almost 43,000. After the war their number was fixed at a level of approximately 10,000. In the years 1951 and 1954–56 the Specials were used to offset a large-scale IRA campaign against the Northern Ireland government. This militia was entirely Protestant, Catholics having refused to join a body whose chief purpose was to fight the extreme nationalists. The resulting situation was naturally embittering to the Catholics. Membership in the B Specials gave a Protestant extremist the license to harass his Catholic opponents under the guise of protecting the public order. The existence of the B Specials, more than anything else, discredited the Ulster police.

Catholic hostility to the police was intensified because after 1922 Northern Ireland was under various "Special Powers Acts," and "Emergency Powers Acts." These statutes give the government power to suspend under certain circumstances normal civil liberties and to ignore normal legal rights such as habeas corpus.

The initial occurrence in the sequence of events which led to the violence of recent years was the election in 1963 of Captain Terence O'Neill as Prime Minister of Northern Ireland. There was nothing in O'Neill's background to suggest that he would unwittingly set off sectarian clashes. He seemed an ordinary unionist politician, if a cut above the standard in education and background. He was a direct descendant of Sir Arthur Chichester, who was in charge of the plantation of Ulster under James I, and was related to a number of influential politicians in modern Ulster. He was educated at Eton and then served in the Irish Guards. After the Second World War he entered the Northern Ireland Parliament, serving from 1946 to 1948 on the back bench and then from 1948 to 1956 in a series of junior ministries. In 1956 he received his first senior appointment as Minister of Home Affairs and was soon thereafter transferred to the Ministry of Finance, a position he held until 1963. In that year he became, somewhat to the surprise of most observers, Northern Ireland's fourth prime minister. Seemingly another loyal, trustworthy, colorless unionist party stalwart had become head of the government.

When O'Neill took over as prime minister, Northern Ireland was in a state of unstable equilibrium. On the surface, community relations were improving and overt sectarian strife was not in evidence. But this tranquillity, it later became clear, was not attributable to the fact that community relationships were noticeably improving but that the opposing forces were quite evenly balanced and there was no specific issue to set off hostilities. O'Neill entered the picture and began making moves which would improve conditions for the Roman Catholics. Undoubtedly he was chiefly motivated by idealism, but also by long-term political expediency, since he foresaw a coming increase in the electoral strength of the Catholic population.

O'Neill's recognition of the necessity of alleviating many Catholic grievances was not coupled with an understanding of the fears of the average Protestant. His meeting with Sean Lemass, then Taoiseach of southern Ireland, in January 1965 raised Protestant anxieties about his commitment to the Union with England. O'Neill's refusal to ban the 1966 celebration of the fiftieth anniversary of the 1916 Easter Rising led to a permanent estrangement of the Protestant right wing. As time passed O'Neill's support within the unionist party declined, and to compensate for this loss he appealed over the head of the party to the electorate. (In September 1966 an attempt to overthrow him was made at a unionist party meeting; it failed chiefly because there was no acceptable alternative leader.)

Given the delicate balance of forces within Northern Ireland it probably would have been impossible for anyone to improve the Catholics' condition without setting off a reaction among Protestant conservatives. Certainly that is what occurred when on 22 November 1968 O'Neill announced a five-point reform plan under which his government undertook to (1) develop arrangements whereby the allocation of public housing would be carried out on a nondiscriminatory basis, the primary criterion for allocation being the need of the applicant; (2) establish procedures for investigating and alleviating citizens' grievances; (3) introduce an economic development plan for Londonderry; (4) reform local electoral procedures, specifically by 1971, to revise the local government structure and abolish the business vote in local elections; (5) allow the Special Powers Acts to lapse as soon as possible without hazard to the public safety. Unfortunately, the reform program only intensified the right-wing Protestant backlash against O'Neill. Also, while the Catholics were pleased with the reforms, O'Neill's suggestions created what has been called in the American context a "revolution of rising expectations." That is, even though the Catholics' position was being bettered, the improvement stimulated demands for even greater governmental reforms, with the result that instead of being pacified by the reforms, many Catholic leaders were energized.

If Captain O'Neill was primarily responsible for the changing governmental position on Catholic grievances, the Civil Rights Association was the chief agency for changing popular opinion among the Catholic population. In 1964 a Campaign for Social Justice in Northern Ireland was founded to protest against anti-Catholic discrimination mainly, in housing. Next, in February 1967 the Northern Ireland Civil Rights Association was founded to press the Catholic cause in more general terms. In viewing the Civil Rights Association's early history it is necessary to understand three points. The first is that the association was not publicly concerned with the basic constitutional arrangements under which Northern Ireland was governed. The association's leaders seemed at that time to accept the Union with Britain because it was a tie which the majority of the people in Northern Ireland wished to maintain. Hence, one should not equate the original Civil Rights Association with the nationalist movements of the past. The association's goal was to give Catholics full membership in the political, economic, and social system of Northern Ireland as a constituent of the United Kingdom. Second, although members of the Irish Republican Army had an interest in the Civil Rights Association from its beginning, their position was a subordinate one. The men of the IRA did not assume positions of public leadership, although they accepted the association's activities as likely to be contributory in the long run to their own cause. Third, although the association worked to overcome discrimination against Roman Catholics, it was a secular organization over which the authorities of the Catholic church had no direct influence. The Civil Rights Association, therefore, was something totally new to Ulster, an attempt to build a mass movement on the principle of social justice, independent of the old nationalist propaganda machine and independent of the clerical authorities.

To return to the narrative, the specific sequence leading to the first significant outbreak of violence began in June 1968 when the local authorities in Caledon, County Tyrone, evicted a Catholic tenant from a council house and allocated it to an unmarried Protestant girl. On the 20th of June, Austin Currie, a nationalist M.P. (N.I.), occupied the house in order to publicize this and similar injustices to Catholics in the allocation of local government housing units. Next, the Civil Rights Association staged a march from Coalisland to Dungannon on 24 August to dramatize the situation. This was the association's first mass demonstration. About 2,500 persons took part. Then the association agreed to join a march instigated by left-wing activists in Londonderry to call attention to the Catholic grievances in that community. The march, set for 5 October, was to follow the path through Derry traditionally taken by Orange processions. Fearing violence, the Minister for Home Affairs, William Craig, prohibited the procession. The organizers decided to stage the march anyway. Clashes occurred between police and demonstrators. It was later judged that the police had used unnecessary force. Following the conflict between police and civil rights demonstrators, hooligan elements in the Londonderry population who had nothing to do with the movement rioted, with attendant looting and damage to property.

In direct response to the police brutality in Derry a group was founded, based in Queen's University but not restricted to university students, called "People's Democracy." The organization had no specific membership requirements or constitution and was soon to lapse into obscurity. But for the moment it was vibrant, its program an amalgam of various radical viewpoints. Demands ranged from one man, one vote to worker control of all branches of industry. More important than the group's specific demands were its methods: unlike the Civil Rights Association the People's Democracy did not bind itself to nonviolent methods. At first the group had wide support among the Queen's University student body but this support waned as the People's Democracy became increasingly radical. The core members of People's Democracy decided that they should join the Civil Rights Association. Whether or not this was an attempt to take over control of the association is unclear, but the effects were unmistakable: the Civil Rights Association was moved toward greater activism. It became at once more radical in its demands and at the same time more aggressive in prosecuting Catholic grievances. It moved from demanding Catholic equality to demanding Catholic power. At the same time the Civil Rights Association was becoming more militant, the moderates in the association were becoming uneasy and some were leaving the organization altogether.

Recall at this point that November 1968 was the time when Prime Minister O'Neill introduced his five proposals. These proposals were the working-out of ideas he had prior to the rioting, but it was natural that they would be interpreted by Protestants and Catholics alike as a response to the October disruptions. To the Protestant right wing, therefore, the proposed reforms seemed like a surrender in the face of violence. To the Catholic militants the reforms seemed to validate their activist policy. These conclusions were reinforced by O'Neill's dismissal of William Craig as the Minister for Home Affairs in December 1968. Craig was responsible for the maintenance of civil order and had come to view the civil rights movement as a front for revolutionary republican activities.

Meanwhile in Londonderry, after the 5 October riots, a moderate group was trying to stabilize civil rights activities. This was the Derry Citizens' Action Committee headed by John Hume. (The reader will note that for all practical purposes "Derry" and Londonderry are synonyms.) Ivan Cooper was a leading member of the executive committee. Both these men were among the original leaders of the Civil Rights Association and in creating the new Derry organization they were committed to pressing Catholic grievances, but only by nonviolent means. Sit-downs and marches were conducted during the last quarter of 1968, but always with discipline and without either creating or provoking violence. If this group had been able to maintain complete control of civil rights activities in Derry, peace would probably have been preserved. The People's Democracy, however, decided to organize a Belfast-to-Londonderry march for early January 1969. The Derry Citizens' Action Committee objected (as did Edward McAteer, leader of the nationalist party) because the march would almost certainly lead to violence. The People's Democracy persisted, and finally the Civil Rights Association gave its support to the march, although this support was only nominal.

The Belfast-Derry march, which lasted from the first to the fourth of January 1969, inflamed sectarian passions. The marchers were met by a hostile crowd at Burntollet Bridge, and the police did not protect the marchers. More than a dozen persons were injured and several were taken to the hospital. But the real trouble came in Derry itself. Counter-demonstrators met the marchers, and there were clashes between the opposing groups. A number of Derry citizens joined the marchers and replied in kind to the stone-throwing and other aggressive acts of the counter-demonstrators. These clashes set off further serious riots in Londonderry. By the fourth of January violence had already become the keynote for Northern Ireland in 1969.

In February 1969 Prime Minister O'Neill, realizing that Derry was a powder keg, appointed the Londonderry Commission which he had promised in his reform program of the previous year. This body superseded the former unionist-controlled city council, whose corruption and discrimination had been a major Catholic grievance. Urgent steps were taken to expedite a major housing program for Derry. Nevertheless, in mid-April further riots stemming from civil rights activities were only narrowly averted.

With each incident the members of the unionist party were becoming less and less happy with Prime Minister O'Neill's apparent inability to maintain civil order and increasingly suspicious of his apparent truckling to Catholic pressures. The only reason O'Neill was kept in office was that there was no alternative leader. O'Neill's chief rival, Brian Faulkner, did not command enough support to upset him. But then Major James Chichester-Clark became a viable rival by the simple expedient of resigning from the cabinet. His ostensible reason for resigning was that O'Neill's one-man one-vote policy, announced on 23 April 1969, was pushing reform too fast, a reason which would appeal to the hard-line dissidents in the unionist party. On 28 April O'Neill resigned, and on 1 May 1969 the unionist M.P.'s met and by a vote of 17 to 16 moved Chichester-Clark into the prime ministership.

But a new prime minister did not bring Northern Ireland

peace. The beginning of a summer of turmoil was signaled by the twelfth of July parades of the Orange Order. These traditional parades are highly inflammatory to the Catholic population since the marchers are affirming their Protestant solidarity against the alleged Catholic threat. Usually the Catholics have the good judgment to stay at home, but in Derry the Orange parade was followed by street fighting and by looting and arson by Catholic hooligans. On subsequent days pitched battles between the police and Catholics took place, and fighting also erupted between the police and Protestant mobs which were trying to attack the Catholic sector of Derry. Similar flare-ups occurred in several smaller towns in Ulster. But the real trouble was not unleashed until the second of August when Protestant and Catholic mobs clashed in Belfast. These clashes re-occurred night after night, while barricades were thrown up for protection by each side. The police were unable to control the rioting and arson and appeared to have been anything but impartial in their efforts to restore order. Sectarian violence, which had dwindled momentarily in Derry, was rekindled on 12 August when the Apprentice Boys of Derry, a Protestant fraternal order, held their annual parade. Finally, the United Kingdom government, realizing that the Stormont government had lost control of the situation, sent in troops. The troops arrived on 14–15 August and were concentrated chiefly in Belfast and Londonderry. The very day the troops arrived the rioting claimed its first fatality.

Significantly, the arrival of British troops was considered a victory by the Catholics, for the British were believed to be more impartial in protecting lives and property than were the Protestant-dominated Royal Ulster Constabulary and the B Specials. Moreover, the necessity of British intervention was a judgment of incompetence against the Ulster government, so in this instance pragmatic considerations overcame the traditional nationalist opposition to having British troops on Irish soil; the British soldiers were hailed as allies by the Catholics. The British, however, were not immediately able to restore order. Severe rioting continued in Londonderry and Belfast.

By the end of the first week in September the death toll was up to nine, and only in the second half of October were the troops able to quiet the province.

The introduction of British troops signaled the beginning of the intervention by the London government in the internal affairs of Ulster on an unprecedented scale. In mid-August Major Chichester-Clark was summoned to 10 Downing Street by Prime Minister Wilson. A seven-point declaration was issued jointly by the two men on 19 August. Predictably, the declaration reaffirmed the commitment of the British government to maintain Northern Ireland as part of the United Kingdom and affirmed the right of Northern Ireland to jurisdiction in its own domestic affairs. The real message followed: "The United Kingdom government have ultimate responsibility for the protection of those who live in Northern Ireland." The declaration affirmed that "every citizen of Northern Ireland is entitled to the same equality of treatment and freedom from discrimination as obtains in the rest of the United Kingdom, irrespective of political views or religion. In their further meetings the two Governments will be guided by these mutually accepted principles." Beyond the words of this declaration was a simple relationship: the United Kingdom government had told the Northern Ireland government to put its house in order and to alleviate Catholic grievances, or London would take command. Officials of the Ulster government bravely maintained that there had been no diminution of the powers of the Northern Ireland government, but the claim rang hollow.

As if to underline the superior-subordinate relationship of Great Britain and Ulster, James Callaghan, Home Secretary in the London government and the man with direct responsibility for Ulster affairs in the United Kingdom cabinet, visited Northern Ireland from 27–29 August. His welcome in most Catholic areas was close to triumphal. More important, two meetings of the Northern Ireland cabinet were conducted with Callaghan present, and from those meetings emerged a statement by the Ulster government affirming the necessity of maintaining "the momentum of reform." It was agreed by the Northern Ireland ministers that effective action was needed in the following five fields: (1) equal opportunity for all public employment without regard to religious or political considerations; (2) protection against incitement of hatred and intimidation for all citizens; (3) guaranteed fairness in public housing, with need the only criterion; (4) effective procedures for investigating grievances against public bodies; and (5) fair electoral laws. To emphasize the importance of these goals the prime minister of Northern Ireland stated that he would appoint a governmental minister with special responsibilities for communal affairs. Now it should be noted that this forward-looking program was being presented by Major Chichester-Clark, who a scant five months before had overthrown Captain O'Neill as prime minister because O'Neill was proceeding too quickly along reforming lines. Clearly the United Kingdom government was dictating the Northern Ireland cabinet's new policy. To keep the Ulstermen to their pledges, arrangements were made for joint working parties composed of officials of the Northern Ireland and United Kingdom governments to examine the Ulster government's actions in the major reform areas.

The first test of whether the Northern Ireland government would keep to the new reform line came in September when the "Cameron Report" was submitted to it. This was a report of a tribunal headed by a Scottish judge, Lord Cameron, which had been appointed in March 1969 by the then prime minister, Terence O'Neill, to investigate the disturbances of late 1968 and early 1969. The Cameron Report presented not only a detailed chronology of the events but dealt in considerable detail with the Catholic grievances which were predisposing causes of the disorders. Significantly, the Ulster cabinet, instead of rebutting the criticism in the Cameron Report, responded by a commentary which reaffirmed its commitment to the new reform policy.

More important, serious (albeit ultimately unsuccessful) attempts were being made to gain the respect of the Catholic minority for the police system. In October 1969, the Northern Ireland government, under strong pressure from London, named an experienced British police officer as the Inspector

General of the Royal Ulster Constabulary. His taking office roughly coincided with the appearance on 10 October of the "Hunt Committee Report" on the police in Northern Ireland. This committee, which had been appointed in late August 1969, recommended that the B Specials be disbanded and replaced by an unarmed force less disruptive to community relations. The regular Royal Ulster Constabulary, it was suggested, should be relieved of all duties of a military nature (that is, anti-IRA activity) and should be limited to normal police responsibilities as soon as possible. The Royal Ulster Constabulary should become an unarmed force. Vigorous efforts to recruit Catholics were recommended.

Predictably, the effort to make the police structure acceptable to the Catholics brought about a violent reaction among Belfast Protestants. The Hunt Committee Report was introduced on Friday 10 October 1969. Toward evening of Saturday the 11th, a band of some 3,000 Protestants in the Shankill Road district attempted to vent their rage upon the Catholics in the Unity Flats apartment complex. Rifles, pistols, and automatic weapons were used, as well as petrol bombs, stones, and bottles. The British Army responded swiftly: by Monday morning two Protestants were shot dead, eighty were in court on riot charges, and the area was combed for illegal arms.

Naturally the Protestant militants were furious at the series of "betrayals" by the London and Stormont governments. But were the Catholics correspondingly gratified? On the surface it appears they should have been, for by early 1970 they had been granted all of their demands: in November 1969 a permanent ombudsman had been appointed to protect any citizen with a valid grievance; in December 1969 a commission was established to investigate complaints against local governmental authorities; the Londonderry City Council, long a unionist bastion, had been abolished; the hated B specials were dissolved; one-man one-vote legislation was passed, effective in the local elections of 1972; a Community Relations Board was created and a Minister of Community Relations was appointed; and the government promised that the allocation of housing was to be taken from local hospitals and placed in the hands of a new

Central Housing Authority which operated on a nondiscriminatory points system developed in England (the act became law in February 1971). Thus, within three short years, 1968-70, the aims of the Civil Rights Association had been obtained.

Seemingly as a harbinger of better days, the old fragmented unproductive gaggle of nationalist political sects came together in the autumn of 1970 to form the Social Democratic and Labor Party ("SDLP"). This party gained the allegiance of most leading Catholic politicians and, although it refused to become an official opposition, promised to promote efficiently the Catholic interest in Northern Ireland politics. Some optimists thought that the era of two-party politics was, at last, dawning in Ulster.

Yet, within the Catholic communities of Londonderry and Belfast there was continuing unrest and violence. This violence was a result of incitement by traditional IRA nationalists as well as a product of young revolutionary radicals of the sort common in most Western nations. But much of the violence seems to have been recreational rather than ideological. Sniping, petrol bombs, and gelignite were used against British troops, who were under strict orders not to retaliate. Finally, in early July 1970 the British Army did in the Catholic Falls Road area what it had done in October 1969 in the Protestant Shankill: soldiers began firing on mobs who fired upon them. This action on the army's part was imperative if any vestige of civil order was to be maintained, but it had the most unhappy result of redefining the issue for many Ulster Catholics from that of civil rights back to the classic nationalist issue of British troops versus Irish Catholics.

Still, the first half of 1971 was sometimes hopeful. The resignation in March of Chichester-Clark under Protestant dissatisfaction with his alleged failure to move effectively against rioters and terrorists was not disruptive, for he was replaced as Prime Minister by Brian Faulkner, generally accepted at the time as the most able unionist politician. In June, Faulkner made the extraordinary offer (for a unionist politician) of seats for the SDLP opposition on three new functional policy committees, for social, environment, and industrial services. Two of these bodies were to be chaired by opposition M.P.'s. Potentially, a major break-point in Northern Irish history had been reached. On 7 July interparty talks were held at Stormont, and it was clear that the opposition was seriously interested in the proposal. But then, on 8 July, two rioters were shot dead by the British Army in Derry under questionable circumstances (the question was whether they were merely rioting or intent on killing British soldiers). Thereupon the SDLP, afraid of being out flanked by the IRA, veered sharply and announced that it would withdraw completely from Stormont unless a full inquiry were conducted at once under conditions acceptable to the SDLP. Soon the opposition, now withdrawn from Stormont, was meeting in various "alternative assemblies." Almost overnight the Catholic representatives had gone from being prospective partners in governing Ulster to self-defined political exiles.

If Faulkner's constructive initiative offered both communities their best brief hope, the introduction of internment of suspected IRA terrorists without trial on 9 August 1971 was disastrous for everyone. Admittedly there were compelling short-run arguments for internment, the chief being that the terrorist intimidation of juries made it almost impossible to gain a conviction. But in October 1971 Northern Ireland's criminal code was brought into line with the rest of the United Kingdom, a jury verdict of ten of twelve, rather than the previous unanimity, now being required for conviction. This was a remedy which wisely might have been tried before the more drastic one of internment without trial. Internment can only be seen as a political move to quiet the unionist ranks, but it set the game back to square one. Four weeks of sectarian rioting followed the beginning of internment, during which, according to one authority, "Belfast underwent a social upheaval akin to that suffered by many English cities during the Blitz." In this case, at least 10,000 people left their homes and hundreds of houses were either burned out or badly damaged. The sectarian riots drew ever more sharply the lines of residential segregation, for in areas of integrated housing both working-class Protestants and Catholics destroyed the homes of their religious opponents or intimidated their occupants into leaving. Of the approximately ten thousand who were forced to move, 40 percent were Protestant and about 60 percent Catholic. Large areas of Derry and somewhat smaller areas of Belfast were sealed behind barricades and ruled by IRA men. The two branches of the IRA, and especially the Provisionals (or, as they are colloquially known, "The Provos"), began a massive bombing campaign notable both for its audacity and its savagery. The year 1971 ended with the deaths of forty-three United Kingdom soldiers, five Ulster Defence Regiment members, eleven Royal Ulster Constabulary men, thirty civilians (presumably by IRA bombs), plus ten civilians by United Kingdom army "mistakes" and seventy-four by other causes; 1,692 bombs were exploded, and there were 427 armed robberies, most, seemingly, for political purposes.

The daily rioting and attacks upon the British troops ended in a tragic event—the killing of thirteen civilians in Derry on 30 January 1972—often called "Bloody Sunday." The date and place could have been different, but, given the continual rioting, the event was a high probability. Subsequent investigation showed that the troops, in responding to anti-internment march-cum-riot, were not completely justified in their actions. As in the previous autumn's shootings in Derry, there was no question that those shot had been aggressively confronting the troops, but not, it seems, with murderous intent. Admittedly the soldiers were fired on by snipers, but their response was indiscriminate.

The march which led to the Derry shootings had been organized by the Northern Ireland Civil Rights Association, revitalized by internment after having become moribund in the winter of 1970. It was, however, a new organization within the old shell. The Official IRA previously had been content to manipulate the association indirectly. Now, during 1971 and early 1972, the Officials began to squeeze out the independents from the leadership of the association and turned that organization into an Official IRA satellite. Meanwhile, the SDLP, in response to internment and the Derry shootings, assumed a bitterly belligerent stance which precluded its working with even those Protestants of the most liberal persuasion. Thus, the situation was more sharply polarized than it had been for decades. On one side was the Protestant establishment, backed by the United Kingdom Army, on the other the two IRAs, the Civil Rights Association, and the SDLP, all acting as extreme sectarians.

In March 1972 a Dublin weekly paper made the telling point that, according to United Kingdom War Office records, the Allied agents in France and their French assistants used 3,000 pounds of explosives in acts of sabotage during World War II, but that in the seven months since internment British military sources estimated that more than 8,000 pounds of explosives had been used in terrorist bombing attacks in Northern Ireland. Finally, the London government decided that things had to be brought under control. In March 1972 Prime Minister Heath made three proposals to the Northern Ireland government: that internment be phased out, that full responsibility for law and order be transferred to Westminster, and that periodic plebiscites on the border issue be conducted—this last was tied to a promise that there would be no change in the border without majority consent of Northern Ireland's people. Apparently Prime Minister Faulkner was willing to accept the first and third demands but not the second. Heath insisted, Faulkner's government resigned, and on 24 March Heath announced that the Stormont government was being "temporarily" suspended and that Northern Ireland was to be directly governed from London.

Catholic opinion was generally approving of the British move, while Protestants were confused; some talked of the necessity for a unilateral declaration of independence, while at the other extreme many accepted the British move as a step toward the desirable goal of total integration into the United Kingdom. The British officials were sufficiently conciliatory that on 22 June the Provos followed the Officials' example of 29 May and declared a cease-fire. A few halcyon days were all the respite from violence Ulster enjoyed, however, because the Provisionals abandoned the cease-fire on 9 July and began a bombing campaign remarkable—even by terrorist standards—

for its brutality. On one memorable day, "Bloody Friday," 21 July, twenty-two bombs went off within two hours, killing nine and injuring 130. Why the Provos broke the cease-fire is hard to say but it is probable that purely domestic considerations within their organization made it necessary: if the national leaders had not called off the cease-fire, the Belfast units probably would have done so on their own. But there were tactical reasons as well, for, as we shall see, only by provoking either the British Army or the Protestant vigilantes into excessive reprisals could they maintain their position as defenders of the Catholic population and continue forcing events along what they believed was the path toward a united Ireland.

If the aim of the Provisionals was to strike a spark to the Protestant tinder, they came perilously close. The Protestants generally had been enraged by the black vision of Bloody Friday—the sight, literally, of pieces of human bodies being shoveled into plastic bags as the only means of dealing with the tattered fragments—and among the Protestant working class there had emerged a massive paramilitary force, the Ulster Defence Association. The UDA had been founded in Armagh in mid-1970 but it did not become important until the days following the suspension of Stormont, when it emerged as a Belfast-based cadre whose ostensible purpose was the protection of Protestant areas against IRA attacks. Soon the UDA had a fully articulated command and unit structure and a body of adherents who seemed all the more frightening for their being tightly disciplined. The UDA pressed the new London-controlled administration for firmer measures against the IRA, set up their own "no go" areas to match the Catholic areas from which troops and police had been withdrawn, and threatened action of their own against the IRA should the government not move. In such anti-IRA action, many observers feared the UDA men would not be overly careful in discriminating between the ordinary Catholic and the IRA man.

Faced with increasing terrorist activities and the threat of a violent Protestant reaction, the government had to move. It smashed the barricades which long had sealed parts of the Catholic areas of Derry and Belfast and which thereby had

formed sanctuaries for the terrorists. The troops met no significant resistance, and for the moment a sharp reduction in
terrorist activity took place. Certainly this government military
action alone would not be enough to restore peace to Northern
Ireland, but there were glimmerings of hope. Perhaps the
politicians, the elected representatives of all sides, were to have
their day at last.

There are almost as many scenarios for the future of Northern Ireland as there are interested groups. Let us look first at
the Catholic side and then the Protestant, and finally the
British.

Two groups who might be expected to have well-articulated
plans, the Irish-Americans and the Dublin government, have
none. The lack of sustained interest in Ulster among Irish-
Americans actually is not so surprising, for most are now two
generations away from direct experience of Irish life, and as a
group those of Irish descent are securely assimilated into the
American establishment. Further, most Irish-Americans stem
from the west or the south and have little acquaintance with
the tradition of Ulster bitterness. The fund-raising visits to
America by various Northern Irish leaders, most notably Berna-
dette Devlin, have been remarkable chiefly for their lack of
general success. The Irish-Americans, to the extent that they
can be any longer identified as a distinct group, are politically
conservative and have not reacted warmly to the militant
socialism of the Ulster Catholic leaders. The vestigial commitment to a United Ireland evinced by many Irish-Americans
largely has been offset by their distaste for revolutionary violence. Small ad hoc groups, such as the National Association
for Irish Freedom, Northern Aid, and the American Committee
for Ulster Justice, have pressed the issue but with scant success.
IRA-front groups have raised money for guns, but in amounts
smaller than their forebears raised for similar purposes during
the nineteenth century. A fascinating throwback to the forties
and fifties, when a "free Ireland from Britain" resolution was
passed annually by Congress, was the introduction of the Ken-

nedy–Ribicoff Senate resolution and the Carey House resolution on Northern Ireland in early 1972 and the later hearings on Northern Ireland held in February and March by the House Foreign Affairs Subcommittee on Europe. Neither set of events received more than passing attention in the press or among Irish-American leaders. For the American Irish, the era of old-time ethnic politics is long past, and hardly anyone applauds now for the old songs.

If the lack of interest on the part of Irish-Americans is understandable, the failure of the Eire government to develop any coherent plans for Ulster's future is not. Granted, the constitution of 1937 declares that Ireland as a governmental unit should comprise the entire island, but in actual practice few steps have been taken toward unification. The Dublin government's response to Northern Ireland's troubles has been almost entirely reactive, a policy of reacting to the events rather than of trying to shape them. (The nature of that response, which is primarily by diplomatic means, is discussed in the next chapter on southern Ireland's international relations.) If Ireland is to be reunified, many laws must be changed which Protestants believe violate their civil liberties: the impossibility of dissolving an unsuccessful marriage, the rigid censorship code, and, in the case of mixed marriages, the enforcement of church-required marital promises by the civil courts. Further, in the socio-economic sphere, a great deal of concrete planning would be necessary if the southern government were serious about merging the two societies. Per capita income is more than one third higher in the north than in the south. Also, northerners, both Catholic and Protestant, are accustomed to the full range of services offered under the welfare state and are unlikely to accept a diminution in their social security as a consequence of reunification. (To bring social welfare schemes up to northern standards the southern government would have to increase its health and welfare expenditures 100 percent. The mechanisms of the welfare state serve to redistribute wealth, with the result that the economic structure of Northern Island is much more egalitarian than that of the south: whereas in Northern Ireland 5 percent of the population owns 47 percent of the personal wealth, in the Republic 5 percent owns 72 percent. Most Northerners, whether Catholic or Protestant, are apt to be unenthusiastic about joining an economic system which would increase the economic inequality in their province.

This leads to the question of whether or not the cost and inconvenience of reorienting attitudes and institutions that would be necessitated by the reunification of Ireland is one which the populace of the Republic is willing to pay. Undeniably, the southerners have a strong sympathy for the northern Catholic minority, and there is direct support in many quarters for the IRA in the north. But the statement of Conor Cruise O'Brien, Labour's shadow Foreign Affairs Minister in August 1971 rings true: "No one in the South," he said, "wants the sudden incursion into their state of one million frantically-opposed Protestants." The Fine Gael shadow Minister for Foreign Affairs, Richie Ryan, echoed O'Brien's words: "The people here don't really understand the situation but they are certainly afraid of what would be involved if a united Ireland came about tomorrow." That these statements represent a widely held viewpoint is indicated by the opinion poll conducted in the Irish Republic in March 1971, shortly before internment. Sixty-eight percent favored a political settlement which for the moment maintained the status of Northern Ireland within the United Kingdom, while giving Catholics a greater share in the government. (Eight-five percent opposed the IRA's violent methods, and 55 percent opposed the withdrawal of British troops from Northern Ireland in the existing circumstances.) Thus, in noting that the Republic's government has merely reiterated the principles of reunification and has done very little in the way of actual planning for a united Ireland, one is simply noting that the politicians have done what they are supposed to do in a democracy, which is to represent the will of the majority of the people.

The plans of the Provisional IRA, unlike the Republic's government, are nothing if not concrete. They have two rival scenarios which seem to alternate in accordance with immediate circumstances. The first of these, the "older" plan, runs roughly as follows: (1) employ the tactic of continual attack upon both the British Army and the Protestant population (the Provos, in contrast to the official IRA are avowedly sectarian and see the Protestant working class as part of the enemy bloc); (2) make Northern Ireland ungovernable so that the Westminster government is compelled to invoke direct rule; (3) make direct rule impossible so that finally the British withdraw —a relatively easy step, because it is assumed that a large body of Protestants will also oppose direct rule and for their own reasons make the work of the government difficult; (4) at that point wait for the Protestants to cave in. Most of them will accept life in the reunited Ireland and the rest will emigrate. This scenario was devised well before the imposition of direct rule in March 1972 and is impressive because it was the Provos who forced London to move. The remainder of the script, however, is based on two assumptions which may well be invalid: that the Protestants will refuse to acquiesce to direct rule and that if the British Army should leave, the Protestants would quietly give in.

At times the older scenario seems not to work, and then a simpler Provo plan comes into operation. Its purpose is to provoke the long-awaited "Protestant backlash" and thus incite a Protestant-Catholic bloodbath of such proportions that the British Army cannot staunch the flow. This, it is believed, will finally force the Republic's army to move into the north, the old struggle of Catholic-Republican versus Protestant-Briton will be engaged and out of the holocaust a united Ireland will emerge.

In contrast to the Provos, the scenario of the Official IRA seems almost irenic. The Officials refuse to accept the Provos' prescription of sectarian war. They believe the enemy is not the Protestants but the ruling class. Thus, the Officials are ideologically committed to promoting a unity among the working class and then, and only then, moving in total force against the rulers. To maintain this vision of a revolution by ecumenical (!) revolutionaries requires great patience. "Once the Irish church is dead, the Protestant Irish tenants in the province of Ulster will unite with the Catholic tenants in the three other provinces of Ireland and join their movement" was Karl Marx's prediction. Like many of his prophecies it well may be right, but it seems a long time in the future. For the time being the Officials have no option but to watch, not shape events. They were opposed to the suspension of the Stormont Parliament on the grounds that it removed power from an accessible local body to an inaccessible national one. They would have preferred the radical reform of Stormont, for their capture of the Civil Rights Association fitted them well to move within a political framework. The suspension of Stormont left them without a short-run policy, and outrage among the Catholics of Derry at their shooting of a Catholic boy home on leave from the British Army in Germany forced them to suspend military activities, effective 29 May 1972. Thus, although their long-range plan remains clear, their immediate future is problematic.

As for the elected leaders of the nationalist community, most of whom are associated with the SDLP, they want politics again to become possible. The suspension of Stormont was greeted approvingly by the SDLP, since this had become one of their fundamental demands. As a gesture of good will the party urged those who had been engaged in the campaign of non-cooperation with the local government bodies (a movement which had become widespread among Catholics in response to internment) again to cooperate. The SDLP states that its other fundamental demand, an end to internment, must be met before the party can engage in politics, but a succinct version of the SDLP scenario is as follows: (1) an end to internment; (2) SDLP then free in conscience to re-enter electoral politics; (3) the British government becomes convinced, preferably nonviolently, that a united Ireland is the only viable solution, and this unification is negotiated between London, Dublin, and the two religious communities in Ulster; (4) as a transitional measure some kind of representative government for the north of Ireland (not necessarily the same six county area which presently constitutes Northern Ireland) be formed in which the SDLP can play a decisive influence.

When one turns to the Protestant community it is more difficult to discover precise plans for the future, largely because the unionists have been defending the status quo. Furthermore,

Protestants are not so ideologically compartmentalized as are the Catholics, so the views of the various Protestant groups slide imperceptibly into one another. At the risk of great over-simplification, one can specify three alternative positions held by unionist leaders. One group has affirmed the action of the United Kingdom government in suspending Stormont and willingly accepts a future course of increasingly complete integration into the United Kingdom. Surprisingly, one of the most influential spokesmen for this view is the Reverend Ian Paisley, formerly in the forefront of rock-ribbed Ulstermen, but of late increasingly given to moderation (almost alone among members of the unionist right wing, he opposed internment). Second, there is a bloc whose adherents range from liberal Alliance Party to old unionist politicians desperate to get back to office, who want Stormont reinstated, but who are willing to accept quite radical reforms in its constitution, such as proportional representation and the establishment of a dual-party system of control. Third, there is an undefined body, of greatly varying strength, in favor of defying the United Kingdom authorities. There are undercurrents of a unilateral declaration of independence in many statements by right-wing unionists. To these three versions of Northern Ireland's future must be added that of a fourth group who simply hope for a return to things as they were. Like the citizens of eighteenth-century London who demanded, "Give us back our eleven days" when the Gregorian calendar was introduced, the times, they find, are eternally against them.

The attention of the United Kingdom government necessarily must focus on the immediate future: whatever the private convictions of British politicians they all must give public allegiance to the democratic principle of respect for the wishes of the majority. At present it would be a waste of time and probably counter-productive for those who project a united Ireland to do so publicly. The mechanics and tactics of direct rule are not very complicated. William Whitlaw, Secretary of State for Northern Ireland, is in control, subject only to the direction of the United Kingdom cabinet. He has a troika of assistants who fill the role previously held by the Northern Ireland cabinet. The Northern Island civil service reports to these men just as it previously reported to the Stormont cabinet. The government's goals and tactics are equally simple: re-establish civil order by convincing the bulk of the Catholic population that it will receive fair treatment and that it should accordingly refuse to countenance further Provisional IRA activity. This will automatically extinguish the chance of a Protestant backlash. While this is going on, the script calls for large dollops of patronage in the forms of bridges, schools, roads, and so on, all underwritten by the British Exchequer. Then, with peace prevailing, obviously something will have to be done about the Stormont government—probably its resuscitation in a form more acceptable to the Catholic minority than was the original northern parliament.

XII Southern Ireland in the Commonwealth and in the World

Under the terms of the Anglo-Irish Treaty of 1922 the Irish Free State was a member of the British Commonwealth of nations. Her entire history within the Commonwealth can be summarized as one long attempt to escape from the fetters of dominion status. Two contrasting tactics were used in pursuit of this goal. The government of William Cosgrave sought to modify the definition of dominion status so greatly that such status would be indistinguishable from complete independence. The de Valera government simply cut ties with the Commonwealth.

It is easy to forget that when the Free State was formed in 1922 it seemed as if the powers of the United Kingdom government vis-à-vis the dominions were more than merely vestigial. As discussed in Chapter IV, the Anglo-Irish treaty placed several imperial obligations upon the Free State, some of which were symbolic, while others appeared to be functional. The Free State undeniably was a member of the British Commonwealth, its freedoms being equated with those of Canada. In theory the United Kingdom government retained the right to disallow legislation by the dominions, although this right was no longer exercised. It was possible for certain British laws (such as those affecting shipping) to directly affect the dominions. The judicial committee of the Privy Council was the supreme court of the Commonwealth, although the leaders of the Irish Free State claimed from the beginning that the United Kingdom government had accorded them the same position with respect to the judicial committee as South Africa, namely, that appeals would be allowed only in cases which affected other members of the Commonwealth. All dominions were limited as to the amendment of their own constitutions. On a less functional level, the crown was represented in the Free State, as in the other dominions, by a governor-general, and an oath of allegiance to the crown was required of members of the legislature.

The government of the Irish Free State, more than those of the other members of the Commonwealth, was unhappy with dominion status. Unlike the other dominions, the Saorstat was not a transplant from the mother country, but the reinvigoration of an ancient civilization whose historical roots went much deeper than those of the mother country itself. (Remember that Ireland, unlike England, never came under the Romans and that there was no Irish equivalent of the Anglo-Saxon conquest.) Bedrock issues of sovereignty were involved. Did the Free State government achieve its legitimacy and powers from the parliament of the United Kingdom, or was its legitimacy based on the inherent sovereignty of the Irish people?

Understandably, the most important diplomatic activities of the Free State government were ritualistic in the sense that they were less important for what they achieved than as proof that the Free State had the right to act in diplomatic matters as an independent nation. Thus, in 1924 the Irish Free State appointed a permanent envoy to the United States of America and, in 1927, the United States appointed a permanent representative in Dublin. These appointments were grudgingly approved by the Imperial government.

The Free State's insistence upon registering the Anglo-Irish Treaty as an international agreement was not a pragmatic diplomatic maneuver but an important ritual affirmation of nationhood. The Irish view of the agreement was that it was a two nation treaty made between two independent governments. The United Kingdom view was that it acquired validity only because it had been affirmed in statute law framed by the United Kingdom parliament. In essence, the British argument was that its own parliament validated both sides of the agreement, not just the one side as in a treaty, with, say, France. To counter this, the Free State established a permanent delegation with the League of Nations at Geneva in 1923 (the first dominion to do so), and this delegation skillfully outflanked the British opposition, the treaty being duly registered in July

1924. The United Kingdom government did not surrender its own views of the treaty, but, nevertheless, in one important world forum the Free State had established itself as a treaty-making power in its own right, not a mere diplomatic satellite of the United Kingdom.

The League of Nations was attractive to the new Free State government, for membership in that body would provide a validation of the nation's sovereignty, while simultaneously providing a network of international relationships not dominated by the United Kingdom. Accordingly, as early as June 1922 the Free State diplomatic authorities resolved to press for League membership, and the Saorstat was admitted the next year. The crucial point in the evolution of the Irish Free State's position in the League came in 1926 when it decided to run for a seat on the League Council. This bid failed, but another attempt in 1930 succeeded.

Successful as were these diplomatic maneuvers, the Free State's most significant achievements occurred within the Commonwealth. A recent study by Dr. D. W. Harkness has revealed that during the twenties and early thirties the Irish Free State was the cutting edge among the dominions, pressing harder and more successfully than any other for liberal redefinition of dominion status. The discussions of the great Imperial Conference of 1926, which set constitutional precedents operative to the present, were dictated to a remarkable degree by the Irish. Out of that conference came the famous Balfour Declaration, which proclaimed that dominions "are autonomous communities within the British Empire, equal in status, in no way subordinate one to another in any respect of their domestic or external affairs, though united by a common allegiance to the Crown and freely associated as members of the British Commonwealth of Nations."

The 1926 report laid down two important principles: first, that the United Kingdom government was not to advise the crown in any matter against the advice tendered by the government of the dominion; and, second, that no legislation of the Imperial Parliament which affected a dominion could be passed without the consent of the dominion concerned. The logic of events thus initiated led by way of the conferences of 1929 and 1930 to the Statute of Westminster, 1931, whereby, in the cases of Ireland and South Africa, the Imperial Parliament renounced, effective immediately, its surviving legislative controls (the renunciatory sections did not come into full effect in the other dominions until later).

Having achieved what was in theory a statement of constitutional autonomy, the government of William Cosgrave had begun to work on the actual implications of this new autonomy in matters such as the oath, Privy Council appeals, and so on, when it was replaced in 1932 by the new government of Eamon de Valera. The diplomatic tactics of the Free State changed abruptly even while the ultimate goal remained the same. Rather than work within the Commonwealth to reshape definitions and practice to fit Saorstat desires, de Valera began a series of unilateral actions designed to reach those goals with a minimum of subtlety and a maximum of efficiency. Thus, in 1933 the oath of allegiance demanded of members of the legislature was removed, and in the same year appeals to the judicial committee of the Privy Council were prohibited. In 1936 the Saorstat constitution was amended to remove the crown from all domestic matters. The only place the crown remained was by virtue of the External Relations Act of 1936 in certain matters related to the recognition of diplomatic and consular officials. By 1936, therefore, the Irish Free State had won complete and incontestable national sovereignty. Ironically, this last dramatic phase, from 1932 to 1936, while less than congenial to the United Kingdom government, was perfectly legal within the rubrics set by the 1931 Statute of Westminster. The new constitution of 1937 simply consolidated matters as the crown was excluded from Irish domestic life. The new Eire government clearly presided over a republic, although for unexplained reasons that word was not used and therefore the public was confused about the actual situation. And what about the Commonwealth? The southern Irish view was that under the External Relations Act of 1936 Eire was still *associated* with it, but not *allegiant* to it.

The ambiguity of Eire's position (was it a republic or not?

was it in the Commonwealth or not?) clearly had to be resolved, and it was the pressure of constitutional logic more than
mere party politics that led the Costello coalition to move forward in 1948. The Costello government repealed the 1936
External Relations Act, thereby cutting the last ties with the
Commonwealth. Thus, within a space of twenty-six years southern Ireland had passed from dominion status to external association to resignation from the Commonwealth. Further, the
Costello government formally proclaimed southern Ireland to
be a republic. The United Kingdom government's reaction was
rather mild. Trade preferences were not abrogated, and the
British government decided to continue to give Irish citizens
living in the United Kingdom the privileges of British citizens
even while recognizing that they actually were not British subjects. To many citizens of the Republic it must have seemed as if
their government and its diplomats had won for them the best
of both the Celtic and the Saxon worlds.

It is possible to argue that the one place where Neville
Chamberlain's policy of appeasement was successful was southern Ireland, for Eire both kept out of war and remained friendly
to the United Kingdom. In 1938 a set of arrangements between
Eire and the United Kingdom ended the economic war which
had been so disastrous for Eire, provided for future trade relations, and returned to southern Ireland full control over certain
"Treaty Ports." Under the Anglo-Irish Treaty the Irish had
ceded to the United Kingdom the defense of the sea around
Ireland (as distinct from coastal defense), and the United
Kingdom had retained the right to use certain strategic harbors
in time of war. Now the British abandoned these rights, and the
ports came completely under the control of the Dublin government. From the viewpoint of the de Valera administration this
agreement was of inestimable importance, for it made possible
a complete and convincing neutrality for the duration of the
approaching war.

The reasons for Eire's neutrality during World War II are
complex and will not be known with complete accuracy until

some future government opens the archives for that period (release of the documents is presently scheduled for the late 1980's or early 1990's). Clearly, prudence and intelligent self-interest were involved. Southern Ireland from its early days as an independent nation was committed to the League of Nations, and de Valera, who acted as his own Minister for External Affairs, was a strong proponent of collective security as the only sensible policy for a small nation. But he knew more clearly than most European statesmen the limits of collective security, for it was he who presided over the League of Nations assembly at the very time the Munich crisis was developing. No one would be protecting the small nations, de Valera realized, and the best hopes for survival lay with those who got safely to the sidelines. Reflecting upon the war, de Valera said in 1957: "We tried to keep out of involvement in the last war because we believed . . . that war would be made in spite of us and without consulting us and that war would be ended without consulting us and that the terms on which the war would be ended would not be the terms we would have wished for but the terms which would suit the interests of the large powers engaged in the war."

It was later charged by David Gray, American minister to Ireland from 1940 to 1947, that even before the fall of France de Valera had become convinced that Hitler would win. Gray produced little evidence to document this assertion so it remains only a thesis awaiting investigation in the distant future when the relevant documents are available. More probable is the less dramatic fact that there was in Eire a great deal of residual bitterness against Great Britain, stemming not only from the distant past but from the more recent "economic war." A military alignment with London, therefore, was far from consonant with the attitudes of the majority of southern Irishmen.

One reason for neutrality put forward with regularity by the Eire government—especially in response to American pressures to join the Allied side—was that Eire did not yet control all her national territory and until partition was ended Eire would not join the British effort. This was both a piece of statesmanship (de Valera's concern with the north was of long standing) and a masterpiece of diplomatic cleverness. By tying neutrality to partition, de Valera was able to make neutrality respectable. All through the war he repeated that England (not the Ulster Protestants) was occupying part of Ireland, a litany which was especially aimed at Irish-Americans, a group which was wholeheartedly committed to American participation on the Allied side and prone to embarrass the Eire government about neutrality unless distracted by other issues.

From a knowledge of southern Ireland's prewar commitment to the League of Nations and the concept of collective security and from a knowledge of Eire's wartime neutrality one could accurately predict its postwar diplomatic patterns: avoidance of military alliance and a thoroughgoing commitment to the activities of the United Nations.

When Eire was invited in 1949 to join NATO, it replied "no." Why? "The reason why Ireland, one of the most democratic nations in the world, is not participating with the signatories to the Treaty in this effort to preserve the democratic way of life: the reason is partition," was the statement of the Department of External Affairs. "Ireland is faced with an insuperable difficulty from the strategic and political point of view," another statement said, "by reason of the occupation of six of her northeastern counties by British forces against the will of the overwhelming majority of the Irish people." Undeniably, concern with partition was high in the years 1948–51 but, as in the case of Eire's neutrality during World War II, it is clear that the partition issue served not only as a reason for the policy of military neutrality but as a legitimation of a policy which was dictated both by expediency—financial reasons for example—and by principle. By the early sixties the Department of External Affairs was able to admit, candidly, that the reason Ireland was not a member of NATO was "*to some extent* due to the Partition situation" [italics mine.] Military neutrality, most Irishmen would admit, was an intelligent policy even without the partition issue.

Eire's desire to preserve its military neutrality made its relations with the United States delicate. It wished neither to join the United States-dominated NATO alliance nor to offend the

American government. Here the Republic's politicians and diplomats were brilliantly successful. The External Affairs people
publicized the sentiment that "the Irish Nation is heartily in
sympathy with the measures sponsored by the United States
for the protection of the Atlantic countries from war, or from
foreign occupation in the event of war." They emphasized that
the Irish people would like to cooperate, and then harked back
once again to the matter of partition. This worked very well.
Not only was the United States government not affronted by
the Irish refusal, but, we have seen, the Irish Republic acquired
millions of dollars in American Marshall Plan aid. Relations
with Washington grew close during the postwar years, the symbol of this development being the decision made in 1950 and
effected in 1951, to raise the United States representation in
Eire from legation to embassy rank. A reciprocal change was
made in the Republic's representation in Washington.

In July 1946 the Republic applied for membership in the
United Nations, but year after year was rejected by the veto
of the Soviet Union. Finally, in 1955 a Big Power arrangement
resulted in its admission. Ireland's representatives took to the
United Nations in the fifties and sixties with the same enthusiasm and success as their predecessors had in the League of
Nations thirty years before. Running through the Republic's
actions in the United Nations were certain matters of style
and principle. First, as Liam Cosgrave, Minister for External
Affairs, said at the time of Eire's admission, "Our aim should
be, I think, to avoid becoming associated with particular blocs
or groups so far as possible." Considerable effort was made to
demonstrate the Republic's independence, especially its freedom
from contractual obligations to the Western military powers.
Second, and in inevitable conflict with the first principle, the
Republic identified itself in a general way with the Western
way of life. "We do not profess or pretend to be indifferent to
the outcome of the East-West conflict, nor present ourselves as
neutral on the ideological issues which now divide the world,"
the Taoiseach, Sean Lemass, said in 1960. "We stand, as a
united people, for the true democratic principles to which the

free Western nations proclaim their allegiance—which are no-where better expressed than in our own constitution—and in opposition to the false philosophies of Communism and totali-tarianism." Third—and this was more a matter of style than of principle—the Republic's delegation made itself as visible as possible. Like a newly elected prefect strutting about the school-yard, the Irish delegation moved from issue to issue, now presenting a "solution" to the Middle East problem, next a complicated answer to the question of when and how the People's Republic of China should be admitted to the United Nations, and then a formula for peace in formerly colonial Africa. Far from being affronted by this almost brash self-confidence, the older United Nations members accepted the Irish Republic's actions with equanimity. In 1960 Frederick Boland, permanent U.N. representative of the Republic, was elected president of the General Assembly.

From our distance in time it is clear that wide-ranging though the Republic's U.N. activities were, they concentrated in matters relating to collective security. Continually in speeches and formal resolutions, Eire's representatives pressed for nu-clear test limitations and for nuclear disarmament. These actions by necessity were directed at the major powers for in this area small nations of themselves could do nothing. In other matters of collective security, specifically in U.N. peacekeeping actions, the Irish Republic could and did participate effectively. The role of the Republic's soldiers in the Congo in 1960–62 is de-servedly well known. From 1964 onward troops from the Irish Republic served in peacekeeping activities in Cyprus. Other smaller contributions were made during the sixties by officers serving as part of the watch on the India-Pakistan border.

The effectiveness of the Irish Republic as a freelance in the United Nations was based on one implicit precondition: it could move independently in and out of other people's affairs without arousing distrust and resentment because it was not using the United Nations as an arena in which to pursue di-rectly its own national interests. But in 1969 this situation came to an end, for events in Northern Ireland led the Republic's government to attempt to use the U.N. as an instrument for prosecuting its own national goals.

The reaction of the southern Irish government to the beginning of the crisis in Ulster in 1968–69 was a mixture of opportunism and hysteria, of naïveté and diplomatic sophistication. Before describing her complex response, let us review the past policies of the southern government toward the north. Until the accession to power of Eamon de Valera in the 1930's the Irish Free State's attitudes toward Ulster were simply a reflexive continuation of attitudes toward Ulster unionists adopted during the fight for Irish independence. However, de Valera suggested a plan in October 1938 to reunify Ireland by allowing the Stormont Parliament to retain the same jurisdiction in a reunited Ireland that it then maintained in the United Kingdom. Another way of stating this proposal is to say that the Dublin government would adopt all the prerogatives and responsibilities vis-à-vis the north of Ireland which the Westminster government held, and that everything else would be unchanged. Whatever slight chance de Valera's unity proposals may have had of receiving a sympathetic hearing in Ulster was destroyed when it became clear that southern Ireland would remain neutral in the war.

Significantly, soon after Churchill took office as Prime Minister in 1940 he sent a secret emissary to de Valera with proposals for reuniting Ireland. Simply put, Churchill proposed that Eire should join the Allies. In return, the United Kingdom government would (1) issue a formal declaration accepting the principle of a united Ireland and (2) convene a conference composed of representatives of the northern and southern governments to work out the details. De Valera viewed the United Kingdom offer as illusory. The offer, he noted, made Eire commit itself to a given course at once while obtaining no more than a half-promise with respect to what would be gained in the future. Undoubtedly de Valera was right in his assessment, but the interesting point is that he did not show any enthusiasm for continuing the negotiations on the matter. After a brief exchange of letters the subject was dropped. De Valera's own proposal deserves notice, for he suggested that the unity of Ireland should be re-established by the whole country's being declared neutral. Thus, despite the propaganda prepared for Irish-American audiences, the maintenance of wartime neutrality was a policy adhered to of its own merits and was not solely a function of the country's being partitioned.

Relations between the United Kingdom and Eire worsened after the refusal of Churchill's offer and became still worse when the war was over. The Republic's government began a vigorous anti-Ulster campaign, a campaign which was intensified when the de Valera administration left office in 1948 and was replaced by the Costello coalition. Two themes characterized government rhetoric about the north. The first was that reunification was a primary aim of governmental policy: "It is the main national objective of the Government, indeed of all the people," Sean MacBride, Minister for External Affairs, said in June 1948. "It is the one issue upon which there is complete agreement between all parties, governmental and opposition." The second theme was that the British were still occupying Northern Ireland and that it was Britain's responsibility to reunify the country. Otherwise, "so long as it continues, partition will constitute a definite obstacle to the kind of relationship between Ireland and Britain which it is in the interest not merely of the two countries but of the world as a whole to bring about." Neither the aggressive tone of Eire toward the north, nor the charges against Britain were apt to make reunification easier; nor was the tactless nature of the propaganda which MacBride's ministry sent forth. In one purple sheet MacBride went so far as to remind the inhabitants of Northern Ireland, who were still under severe rationing as a result of the war, that "if they are undergoing shortages and experiencing high taxation, it is also due to the fact that they are cut off from the rest of Ireland."

The southern government's relations with the north became even less cordial after the decision in 1948 to declare that Eire was a republic whose government had no ties with the Commonwealth. This action drove the unionist government in the north into an even more intransigent position than it had held previously. In response to Costello's declaration, the unionists asked for and received further guarantees from Great Britain of Northern Ireland's position within the United Kingdom. An act passed in mid-1949 declared that "Northern Ireland remains part of His Majesty's Dominion and of the United Kingdom and affirms that in no event will Northern Ireland cease to be a part of His Majesty's Dominion and of the United Kingdom without the consent of the Parliament of Northern Ireland." The counter-response from the southern Irish government was vitriolic. The Department of External Affairs founded a regular "information bulletin" whose primary function was to decry the evils of partition. The old themes were reworked. John Costello, the Taoiseach, claimed that Derry and South Armagh were "coerced and are being maintained by British guns and forces." The Department of External Affairs declaimed that the existence of the government of Northern Ireland "is as complete a negation of democracy and of the principle of self-determination as are Russia's actions in the countries behind the Iron Curtain." It also stated that "Britain has taken the great ship building and linen industries; the magnificent harbours of Lough Foyle and Belfast and Lough Neagh, Ireland's largest lake."

When Eamon de Valera returned to office in 1951 the mixture of aggressiveness and self-pity about Ulster which had characterized the Costello government was considerably moderated. The policy of the government of the Republic became bimodal, involving on the one hand conciliatory gestures to the government of Northern Ireland, and on the other continued denunciations of partition. In mid-1951 de Valera replied to a speech of Sir Basil Brooke, Prime Minister of Northern Ireland, calling for "hands across the border" with an assurance of friendship and cooperation in matters of common concern; at the same time he affirmed his government's desire to reunify the country. On a more practical level the de Valera government completed arrangements with the Northern Ireland government for the joint regulation of railway services which served the territories of both countries. Fishery agreements concerning boundary waters also were concluded. As a counter-theme to these practical conciliatory gestures, the Eire government continued to affirm that reunification was its goal, but in tones less apt to frighten the northern unionists than the strident tones sounded by the Costello regime.

The second Costello coalition of 1954–57 was much less shrill in its approach to Ulster affairs than during its previous term in office. Some of the change may be ascribed to the refusal of Sean MacBride (who had been the Minister for External Affairs and leading agitator about the north) to join the coalition. This allowed Costello to place the moderate Liam Cosgrave in charge of external affairs. "I do not believe," said Cosgrave early in his term of office, "that partition can be solved by anything like a high pressure advertising campaign nor do I think that vituperation and violent or exaggerated language directed either against Britain or against fellow Irishmen in the six counties have any useful part to play." The new cabinet's policy was to emphasize cooperative efforts, such as the Foyle Fisheries and the joint operation of the Great Northern Railway as the best path to unification. Simultaneously, the Republic's government continued to think of itself as in some way the protector of the Ulster nationalists and to publicize injustices to the northern Catholics. Significantly, the use of force to achieve reunification was specifically repudiated. Domestic as well as diplomatic considerations were behind the Costello administration's renunciation of physical force: late in the administration the Irish Republican Army had come to life and begun a series of terror raids on the north. The IRA posed a threat to the Eire government internally (besides complicating Eire's relations with the north) because the organization still maintained that the Eire government was not the legal government of Ireland.

In 1957 Eamon de Valera again returned to power and the campaign against physical force was intensified. Government pronouncements condemned the attacks on the north and repudiated force as a means of reunification. More important, the de Valera government invoked an Offenses Against the State Act under which it arrested the leaders of the IRA.

The real watershed in the Republic's attitude toward the north came in 1959 when Sean Lemass replaced Eamon de Valera as Taoiseach. Lemass was the ideal man for bringing the north and south closer together. It was he who, as Minister for Industry and Commerce, negotiated in 1951–52 the first major detente between the two governments, the agreement for cooperation on the trans-border Great Northern Railway. Lemass assumed the office of Taoiseach on 21 June 1957 and by 21 July he had advanced a set of proposals for economic cooperation with the government of Northern Ireland. He candidly admitted that the aim of his proposals was to create a climate conducive to eventual reunification of the country, but there his rhetoric ended. Instead of fulsome statements of Ireland's indivisibility from which the northern unionists recoil, he advocated practical measures of economic cooperation, such as joint tourist promotions and an adjustment in trading relationships. A conference followed between northern and southern businessmen, with the Eire government but not the Ulster government participating. The result was that the Republic made voluntary reductions in tariffs on linen, furniture, electrical motors, and paint manufactured in Northern Ireland. Despite this show of good faith on the part of the south, the Ulster government did not respond.

Coincident with the new pragmatic approach toward the north, the Lemass government shifted the ideological premises on which its northern policy was based. The classic definition of the Northern Ireland situation was that the six counties were being forcibly occupied by the British. This view had been vigorously expounded in the late 1940's but gradually had lost currency during the succeeding decade. In 1964 Lemass laid it to rest: "We recognize that the government and parliament there exist with the support of the majority in the six county area—artificial though that area is." Regarding Britain Lemass said, "I do not believe that there now exists in Britain, either amongst its political leaders or the mass of its people, any desire to maintain partition or any belief that it serves British interests." In keeping with this new ideology (and in line with increasingly close Anglo-Irish economic relationships) Erskine Childers, Minister for Transport and Power, stated that "the natural friendship between English and Irish people in the face of past history was a supreme illustration of nationalism tempered by rational feeling and true Christianity."

The symbol of Lemass's new Ulster policy was the dramatic exchange of visits between Lemass and Prime Minister Terence O'Neill of Northern Ireland. Arrangements were kept almost totally secret in order to avoid their being blocked by IRA men in the south or by Protestant extremists in the north. Lemass, with commendable courage, agreed to make the first visit and on 14 January 1965 he visited O'Neill. News of the visit was not released until Lemass was within Stormont Castle and, naturally, the news caused a sensation throughout Ireland. On the ninth of February O'Neill returned the visit. At the same time conversations were begun between the ministers of both cabinets who were responsible for trading relationships. Apparently a new era of good will between the two governments was beginning.

Crucially, during 1968 the rise of the civil rights movement in the north made the Eire government falter in its good-will policy. Lemass's successor as Taoiseach, John Lynch, at first was predisposed to follow the Lemass policy. This involved continued consultation with the Ulster leaders (Lynch and O'Neill exchanged visits on 11 December 1967 and on 8 January 1968) and a desire not to disturb the status quo. The civil rights movement undercut the Eire government's northern policy by calling attention to nationalist grievances. The publicity given to the injustices suffered by Catholics in the north inevitably brought pressure upon the government of southern Ireland to support in some way the civil rights activists. Perhaps the Lynch government could have maintained its good-will policy toward the north despite the civil rights movement if the violence of spring and summer 1969 had not erupted; but once Belfast and Derry burned and once British troops set foot on Ulster soil, the policy was abandoned.

The Lynch government's reactions to the crisis in the north was sixfold: it bargained directly with Great Britain, appealed to the United Nations, established refugee centers, mobilized its military forces, began a propaganda campaign, and certain members of the government gave arms and government money to Ulster terrorist leaders. The dealings with the British were not directly productive but helped create the impression that the Lynch government was doing its best for the nationalists in Northern Ireland. In May 1969 Frank Aiken, who was then head of the Irish diplomatic corps, was sent to London to call the attention of Michael Stewart, the Commonwealth Secretary, to the probability of violence in Derry on the twelfth of August if the Protestant Apprentice Boys Parade were allowed to take place. On the first of August Dr. Patrick Hillery, the new Minister for External Affairs, flew to London to repeat the warning. In the actual event the fears of the Dublin government were justified, and on 13 August Hillery returned to London to urge the Westminster government to take control of the Ulster situation. The southern Irish proposal was that the British should call in a United Nations force and, failing that, should agree to a combined British-Irish peacekeeping force. The plan was presented directly to Lord Chalfont, Minister for Foreign Affairs, on 15 August. The British rejected the southern Irish proposal, and the Irish then turned to the United Nations. The rebuff from Chalfont was inevitable, but this does not mean that the Lynch policy toward the north was unsuccessful. From the accurate forewarning about the Derry problem the Dublin government could argue that it was more competent than London to judge the temper and condition of Ulster; and since neither the Westminster nor the Stormont governments did anything to forestall the violence it could be further argued that both regimes were either inept or indifferent to the welfare of the people of the north. And even if the visit of Hillery to Chalfont was perhaps overly dramatic, it emphasized before the world that southern Ireland, at least, was willing to go more than halfway to obtain protection for the northern Catholics.

Recourse to the United Nations was another intelligent step in establishing the competence and concern of the Lynch government. Following the violence of April 1969, Frank Aiken, then Minister for External Affairs, flew to New York to discuss the situation personally with U Thant, Secretary General of the United Nations. There were no concrete results, but probably none had been expected. In mid-August 1969 when that year's violence was at its height, Lynch sent a message to the British and transmitted a copy to U Thant, asking that the

British call in United Nations peace forces to help in restoring order. Soon thereafter, on 16 August, Dr. Hillery, who had succeeded Aiken as Minister for External Affairs, flew to New York to press the Northern Ireland issue. Hillery declared that the British had lost control of the situation and that only a United Nations peace-keeping force could restore order. Hillery raised the matter in the Security Council and subsequently sought to have the question placed on the agenda of the General Assembly. The Security Council refused to take steps to create a peace-keeping force, but Hillery was satisfied with delivering a ringing speech to the General Assembly.

Another effective move from a diplomatic viewpoint was Lynch's decision to establish hospitals and refugee centers near the border. The first of these was established in mid-August in County Donegal close by Londonderry. Soon five field hospitals and two refugee centers were in operation. That these hospitals were merely old tents and that they were not overburdened with refugees is irrelevant; their creation simultaneously indicated to the Irish public that their government was doing something and dramatized to the world the severity of the crisis in Northern Ireland.

If Lynch's government was capable of sophistication, it was also capable of losing its sense of perspective. In response to the arrival of British troops in Ulster, the Dublin government ordered a mobilization of 2,000 front-line reserves and sent a small proportion of the Republic's regular army of 8,500 troops to border areas. There was no possible functional reason for this move. An invasion of the north would have been an insanity, and in all probability the troops from southern Ireland would have been unable to overcome the Royal Ulster Constabulary and its auxiliaries and even less the British Army. (Insane as it now seems, the Republic's army did have a contingency plan for invading the north, and certain cabinet members actually desired to put it into operation.) In any case, the arrival of British troops was considered by the Ulster Catholics to be a victory over the Stormont government. Rather lamely, Dr. Hillery tried at first to explain that the troops had been sent to the border on the assumption that the United

Kingdom would agree to a joint Anglo-Irish peace-keeping force, a possibility only slightly less remote than the Republic's army being able to conquer the north. Then, beginning to realize its mistake, the Lynch government explained that the troops had been sent to the border to protect the recently established field hospitals and refugee centers, although precisely from whom never was made clear. Actually, there was no rational reason for calling up the troops, and from a diplomatic point of view the mobilization was dysfunctional, for it cast the Dublin government in the role of an aggressive trouble-making meddler.

Just how impassioned the southern government could become was indicated by a massive propaganda campaign initiated by the Taoiseach. On Lynch's orders fifteen public relations experts from various governmental agencies and state corporations were seconded to prepare a propaganda drive. By the thirtieth of August 20,000 copies of a booklet entitled "The Story in Pictures of the North's Distress" were printed and were being shipped to Irish embassies for distribution throughout the world. The booklet was visual propaganda at its worst. Ten of the twenty photographs were of British troops. The clear implication was that the British troops were in some way responsible for the afflictions of the Ulster nationalists when the truth was that at that time the troops were protecting the Catholics. Lynch's propaganda was so shoddy that it was not even acceptable for consumption within Ireland. The *Irish Times* denounced the pamphlet as did the liberal periodicals. Clearly counterproductive as a diplomatic move, the Lynch administration's propaganda campaign may best be described as emotional therapy for the Taoiseach and left at that.

During most of the crisis period Lynch was content to allow day-to-day policy to be set by a "Northern Sub-Committee" the two strongest members of which were Charles Haughey and Neil Blaney, both of whom (along with Kevin Boland) had favored invading the north. To what extent these firebrands acted with Lynch's approval probably never will be known for sure. What is morally (as distinct from legally) certain is, first, that Haughey and Blaney were involved in a massive effort to smuggle arms to northern guerilla leaders; second, a subsequent Dail investigation revealed that considerably more than half of £100,000 voted by the Dail for relief of the distress of the northern Catholics did not go for the purposes for which it was intended and in all probability was subverted to buy arms; third, it appears that a band of Fianna Fail politicians promised large sums of money for arms to the (then united) IRA if it would cease political activities in the south and concentrate on military actions in Ulster. The Dublin command was hesitant but the Belfast IRA men were affirmative. This widened the ideological and geographical fissures already developing within the IRA and contributed to the ultimate split between Officials and Provisionals.

After the outbursts with the military and the propaganda, Lynch and most of his associates began to recover their sense of perspective. On 20 September in Tralee Lynch stated that his government had no intentions of using force to reunify the country. Reunification remained southern Ireland's goal, he declared, but "it will remain our most earnest aim and hope to win the consent of the majority of the people in the six counties to means by which the north and south can come together." This statement implied that reunification would come only with the consent of the majority in the north, and there were those within his cabinet (notably Neil Blaney, the Minister for Agriculture) who refused to agree that majority approval of the northern population was a prerequisite for reunification. Blaney voiced the classic view (most clearly enunciated in the past by Eamon de Valera) that as long as the majority of the people in all of Ireland wished reunification, the Dublin government would be justified in acting, even if this implied coercing the majority of people in the north. This division of opinion goes to the heart of the issue facing the government of southern Ireland: Do the Ulstermen have a right to be a part of the United Kingdom? If they do, then did they not have the same right in 1920, and was not the policy of southern Ireland until the late 1950's aimed at violating that right? If the Ulstermen have no such right, then why does not the southern government openly support the IRA groups whose aim is to bring down the northern regime?

Just how divisive the northern issue was to the Dublin administration was made clear in 1970 when Lynch announced that Neil Blaney and Charles Haughey had been dismissed from the cabinet for taking part in a plan to smuggle arms for Ulster into the country. (The charges could not be proved.) In the furor which developed it became clear that Lynch could only control his party on northern matters with the greatest difficulty.

As a result of the "republican" sympathy stemming from the arms affray, the Lynch government was in a vulnerable position when the British army decided to move against Catholic rioters in early July 1970. British troops were using force on Irish Catholics, and that was something no southern Irish politician could approve. Lynch's response was to send his Minister for External Affairs, Dr. Patrick Hillery, on a secret three-hour visit to the Falls Road area of Belfast. This move was diplomatically bumptious but politically shrewd, for it allowed Lynch to argue that he was not forgetting the northern Catholics while simultaneously eschewing violence. Then, on the eve of the Protestant celebration (held on the 13 July, the twelfth falling on Sunday), Lynch made a broadcast urging Catholic toleration of the Orange celebration and affirming a peaceful approach to reunification. The speech was praised in London and well-received in Dublin. For the moment the militants in the Dail were in check.

The diplomatic policy of the Republic's government has been a tortuous one and in all probability will continue to be difficult. Too many forces are at work to make a considered policy possible. The government is pulled simultaneously by its own latent anti-British feelings and by the opposing calculation that a radical worsening of relations with the United Kingdom would be both economically disastrous and internationally catastrophic (particularly with respect to entry relationships in the EEC). Moreover, the policy-makers are torn simultaneously by an instinctive and sometimes sectarian identification with the northern Catholics and by the countervailing knowledge that reunification is possible only if the northern Protestants come to trust the southern administration. And every problem is complicated exponentially because every diplomatic move has domestic political impact. Hence, certain policies which might be diplomatically useful (such as a stringent campaign against IRA men in the south) are impossible for political reasons. Conversely, other activities which have no diplomatic rationale (such as Dr. Hillery's ultimatum of October 1971 telling the British army to stop its "infringement" of the unmarked border between the Republic and the north) seem to be aimed at satisfying internal political pressures.

Two separate sequences of diplomatic events in 1972 illustrate the parameters within which the Republic's policy oscillates. Following the shootings of civilians in Derry on 30 January, the Taoiseach personally called the United Kingdom Prime Minister and berated him; the Minister for External Affairs went to New York to present the Republic's interpretation to the U.S. government and to the United Nations; the ambassador to London was recalled; and in Dublin no attempt was made by the civil authorities to stop a large crowd which set fire to the British Embassy.

Yet, two months later, following the suspension of the Stormont government, the Republic's ambassador to London was reposted and the Minister for External Affairs was able to state in the Dail that in relations with Britain, "Light is, at last, beginning to appear." Then on the 26th of May 1972 the Dublin government issued a proclamation which was seemingly at variance with all its past sympathies. The proclamation invoked a section of the 1939 Offences Against the State Act which allowed the government to establish special courts to try political (read: republican) prisoners without juries. Lynch deemed this necessary to deal with the threat to his own government which the northern guerilla movement inevitably implied. Anyone who savors the ironies of Irish life cannot help but note that it is strange indeed that in Belfast republican political prisoners receive a jury trial whereas in Dublin they are denied such a right. And, given the unpredictability of the northern situation and the volatility of southern emotions on the Ulster question, one wonders if a considered long-range policy about Northern Ireland will ever emerge.

Appendix. Facts About Ireland

Table A.1. TOTAL AREA IN STATUTE ACRES EXCLUSIVE OF LARGER RIVERS, LAKES AND TIDEWAYS

REPUBLIC OF IRELAND	
Munster	5,961,806
Leinster	4,851,403
Connacht	4,230,720
Ulster (part)	1,979,768
Subtotal	17,023,697
NORTHERN IRELAND	3,352,263
Grand Total	20,375,960

SOURCE: *Statistical Abstract of Ireland, 1966* (Dublin: The Stationery Office, 1966), pp. 8, 358.

Table A.2. THE IRISH POPULATION IN THE
TWENTIETH CENTURY

REPUBLIC OF IRELAND

Year	Leinster	Munster	Connacht	Ulster (part of)	Total
1901	1,152,829	1,076,188	646,932	345,874	3,221,823
1911	1,162,044	1,035,495	610,984	331,165	3,139,688
1926	1,149,092	969,902	552,907	300,091	2,971,992
1936	1,220,411	942,272	525,468	280,269	2,968,420
1946	1,281,117	917,306	492,797	263,887	2,955,107
1951	1,336,576	898,870	471,895	253,252	2,960,593
1956	1,338,942	877,238	446,221	235,863	2,898,264
1961	1,332,149	849,203	419,465	217,524	2,818,341
1966	1,414,415	859,334	401,950	208,303	2,884,002
1971	1,494,544	880,018	389,763	206,905	2,971,230

NORTHERN IRELAND

Year	Total population
1901	1,236,952
1911	1,250,531
1926	1,256,561
1937	1,279,745
1951	1,370,921
1961	1,425,042
1966	1,484,775
1971	1,527,593

SOURCES: *Census of Population of Ireland, 1966* (Dublin: The Stationery Office, 1967), I, 1; *Census of Population of Ireland 1971, Preliminary Report* (Dublin: The Stationery Office, 1971), p. 6; *Statistical Abstract of Ireland, 1966* (Dublin: The Stationery Office, 1966), p. 350; *Ulster Year Book, 1966–1968* (Belfast: Her Majesty's Stationery Office [HMSO] 1967), p. 7; *Census of Population, 1971. Preliminary Report* (Belfast: HMSO, 1972), p. 9.

Table A.3. RELIGIOUS PROFESSIONS

REPUBLIC OF IRELAND

Year	Total Population	Catholics	Cath. percentage of total population
1926	2,971,992	2,751,269	92.6
1936	2,968,420	2,773,920	93.4
1946	2,955,107	2,786,033	94.2
1961	2,818,341	2,673,473	94.9

Year	Church of Ireland	Presbyterian	Methodist	Other (incl. no statement)
1926	164,215	32,429	10,663	13,416
1936	145,030	28,067	9,649	11,754
1946	124,829	23,870	8,355	12,020
1961	104,016	18,953	6,676	15,223

NORTHERN IRELAND

Year	Total Population	Catholics	Cath. percentage of total population
1926	1,256,561	420,428	33.5
1937	1,279,745	428,290	33.5
1951	1,370,921	471,460	34.4
1961	1,425,042	497,547	34.9

Year	Church of Ireland	Presbyterian	Methodist	Other (incl. no statement)
1926	338,724	393,374	49,554	54,481
1937	345,474	390,931	55,135	69,915
1951	353,245	410,215	66,639	69,362
1961	344,800	413,113	71,865	97,717

SOURCES: Derived from *Statistical Abstract of Ireland, 1966* (Dublin: The Stationery Office, 1966), pp. 52, 350, 358, and *Ulster Year Book, 1966–1968* (Belfast: HMSO, 1967), p. 10.

Table A.4. COMPARATIVE FERTILITY RATES,
SELECTED YEARS[a]

Country	1901	1911	1926	1937	1951	1961
Northern Ireland	283	266	229	198	186	200
England and Wales	236	197	140	119	111	124
Scotland	272	233	184	163	132	148
Irish Republic	292	305	271	254	270	249

SOURCE: *Ulster Year Book 1971* (Belfast: HMSO, 1971), p. 14.

Table A.5. COMPARATIVE ILLEGITIMACY RATES,
SELECTED YEARS

	Illegitimate births per cent of total births				
Country	1951	1961	1966	1967	1969
Northern Ireland	3.1	2.5	3.1	3.6	3.7
England and Wales	4.7	6.0	7.9	8.4	8.4
Scotland	5.1	4.6	6.4	6.9	7.5
Irish Republic	2.5	1.6	2.3	2.5	2.6

SOURCE: *Ulster Year Book 1971* (Belfast: HMSO, 1971), p. 13.

[a]Per 1,000 married women under 45 years, during the 3-year period around each census year.

Table A.6. COMPARATIVE VITAL STATISTICS, SELECTED YEARS

Years	Northern Ireland	England and Wales	Scotland	Irish Republic
Marriage rates per 1,000 of population:				
1926	5.8	7.2	6.4	4.6
1937	6.7	8.8	7.7	5.0
1951	6.9	8 2	8.1	5.4
1961	6.9	7.5	7.8	5.4
1967	7.3	8.0	8.1	6.1
1968	7.5	8.4	8.4	6.5
ª1969	7.7	8.1	8.3	6.8
Birth rates per 1,000 of population:				
1926	22.5	17.8	21.1	20.6
1937	19.8	14.9	17.6	19.2
1951	20.7	15.5	17.7	21 2
1961	22.4	17.6	19.5	21.2
1967	22.4	17.2	18.6	21.1
1968	22.1	16.9	18.3	20.9
ª1969	21.4	16.3	17.4	21.5
Death rates per 1,000 of population:				
1926	15.0	11.6	13.1	14.1
1937	15.1	12.4	13.9	15.3
1951	12.8	12.5	12.9	14.3
1961	11.3	12.0	12.3	12.3
1967	9.8	11.2	11.5	10.8
1968	10.6	11.9	12.2	11.3
ª1969	10.8	11.8	12.3	11.5
Infant mortality rates per 1,000 live births:				
1926	85	70	83	74
1937	78	58	80	73
1951	41	30	37	46
1961	27	21	26	31
1967	23	18	21	24
1968	24	18	21	21
ª1969	24	18	21	21
Deaths from heart disease (all forms) per 1,000 of population:				
1926	2.14	1.65	1.51	1.57
1937	2.89	3.14	2.89	2.65
1951	4 01	4.06	4.22	3.93
1961	4.14	3.89	4 25	4.16
1967	3.66	3.65	3.90	3.68
1968	3.80	3.80	4.08	3.66
ª1969	3.91	3.80	4.15	not available
Deaths from cancer per 1,000 o population:				
1926	1.12	1.36	1.37	1.02
1937	1.30	1.58	1.57	1.26
1951	1.48	1.90	1.86	1.44
1961	1.53	2.09	2.09	1.60
1967	1.57	2.20	2.26	1.69
1968	1.78	2.20	2.32	1.70
ª1969	1.78	2.30	2.34	1.90

SOURCE: *Ulster Year Book 1971* (Belfast: HMSO, 1971), p. 18.
ªProvisional.

Table A.7. OCCUPATIONAL STRUCTURE, REPUBLIC OF IRELAND, 1966

Occupational Group	Numbers in each occupational group		
	Persons	Males	Females
Agricultural occupations	345,008	311,921	33,087
Fishermen	2,292	2,291	1
Mining, quarrying and turf workers	4,810	4,798	12
Coal gas and chemical workers	1,671	1,351	320
Glass and ceramics makers	2,241	1,651	590
Workers in metal manufacture	3,007	3,003	4
Electrical and electronic workers	15,589	13,566	2,023
Machinists, fitters and related workers	38,815	37,697	1,118
Precision instrument makers, watch and clock			
makers and jewellers	1,584	1,509	75
Woodworkers	20,878	20,696	182
Leather workers	8,396	5,034	3,362
Textile workers	14,320	6,080	8,240
Makers of textile goods and articles	20,428	4,621	15,807
Makers of food	14,848	10,664	4,184
Makers of drink	1,009	902	107
Tobacco preparers and product makers	693	185	508
Paper and printing workers	8,976	5,557	3,419
Makers of other products	5,662	3,858	1,804
Building and construction workers	31,214	31,201	13
Painters and decorators	7,846	7,653	193
Operators of cranes, stationary engines and			
excavators	5,454	5,454	—
Labourers and unskilled workers	72,381	71,466	915
Foremen and supervisors of manual workers	10,629	9,577	1,052
Transport and communication workers	58,477	55,702	2,775
Warehousemen, storekeepers, packers and			
bottlers	22,293	13,081	9,212
Clerks and typists	90,336	34,420	55,916
Commerce, insurance and finance occupations	109,689	70,930	38,759
Service workers	83,314	24,989	58,325
Entertainment and sport workers	4,352	2,973	1,379
Administrative, executive and managerial			
workers	14,476	13,653	823
Professional and technical occupations	87,399	43,184	44,215
Armed forces	7,896	7,881	15
Gainfully occupied, but occupation not stated	2,221	1,512	709
Total gainfully occupied (aged 14 years			
and over)	1,118,204	829,060	289,144

SOURCE: *Statistical Abstract of Ireland, 1968* (Dublin: The Stationery Office, 1968), p. 45

Table A.8. DISTRIBUTION OF MANPOWER IN NORTHERN IRELAND FROM JUNE 1963 TO JUNE 1970 (IN THOUSANDS)

	1963	1964	1965	1966	1967	1968	1969	1970
TOTAL IN CIVIL EMPLOYMENT	546	550	557	563	556	557	560	561
Males	369	369	372	372	369	367	366	368
Females	177	181	186	191	187	190	194	193
Agriculture, forestry and fishing	71	68	66	64	61	57	55	54
Mining and quarrying	4	4	4	4	4	4	3	4
Manufacturing industries	174	179	184	189	180	179	184	186
Construction	46	47	49	49	50	53	54	52
Gas, electricity and water	7	7	8	8	8	8	8	8
Transport and communication	29	28	27	26	27	26	25	24
Distributive trades	74	73	72	72	70	69	68	66
Professional services	53	55	58	60	65	67	69	73
Financial and miscellaneous services	54	55	55	55	54	54	55	53
Public administration and defence	35	35	35	37	37	38	39	39

SOURCE: *Ulster Year Book 1971* (Belfast: HMSO, 1971). p. 258.

Table A.9. SIZE OF AGRICULTURAL HOLDINGS, REPUBLIC OF IRELAND, 1965

County and Province	Above 1 and not exceeding 5 acres	Above 5 and not exceeding 10 acres	Above 10 and not exceeding 15 acres	Above 15 and not exceeding 30 acres	Above 30 and not exceeding 50 acres
	Number of Holdings				
Carlow	332	234	158	422	557
Dublin	1,296	629	325	703	470
Kildare	803	546	303	931	933
Kilkenny	592	355	282	843	1,295
Laoighis	556	447	352	979	1,214
Longford	295	406	548	1,680	1,355
Louth	642	633	489	1,016	664
Meath	578	831	527	2,263	1,961
Offaly	543	422	348	1,041	1,449
Westmeath	582	462	415	1,473	1,625
Wexford	962	652	475	1,137	1,474
Wicklow	497	351	249	624	679
LEINSTER	7,678	5,968	4,471	13,112	13,676
Clare	614	546	575	2,604	3,301
Cork	1,995	1,378	1,157	3,721	5,028
Kerry	1,844	1,377	1,194	3,405	3,860
Limerick	1,053	788	531	1,872	2,544
Tipperary N.R.	626	402	278	831	1,420
Tipperary S.R.	650	423	327	1,213	1,502
Waterford	553	337	199	584	732
MUNSTER	7,335	5,251	4,261	14,230	18,387
Galway	1,167	2,162	1,899	6,974	7,255
Leitrim	203	531	926	3,447	2,335
Mayo	1,982	2,599	3,447	10,331	5,155
Roscommon	380	756	1,218	5,231	3,942
Sligo	456	699	1,102	3,823	2,338
CONNACHT	4,188	6,747	8,592	29,806	21,025
Cavan	501	854	1,310	4,030	3,018
Donegal	2,843	3,142	2,285	4,565	3,027
Monaghan	507	909	1,114	3,026	2,105
ULSTER (part)	3,851	4,905	4,709	11,621	8,150
TOTAL	23,052	22,871	22,033	68,769	61,238

SOURCE: *Statistical Abstract of Ireland, 1966* (Dublin: The Stationery Office, 1966), p. 87.

Table A.9 (continued)

Above 50 and not exceeding 100 acres	Above 100 and not exceeding 150 acres	Above 150 and not exceeding 200 acres	Above 200 and not exceeding 300 acres	Above 300 acres	Total Number of Holdings
		Number of Holdings			
776	342	137	101	42	3,101
501	219	108	92	57	4,400
938	464	265	206	176	5,565
1,955	816	368	244	97	6,847
1,459	539	246	165	68	6,025
904	220	74	55	23	5,560
599	209	95	70	44	4,461
1,449	604	348	269	228	9,058
1,544	516	219	154	111	6,347
1,400	450	206	175	120	6,908
2,136	963	394	250	95	8,538
1,117	490	242	170	108	4,527
14,778	5,832	2,702	1,951	1,169	71,337
3,313	841	296	186	138	12,414
7,878	2,918	1,053	532	213	25,873
4,073	1,027	307	225	188	17,500
3,148	960	333	177	62	11,468
1,878	729	315	190	82	6,751
2,006	728	310	220	93	7,472
1,299	666	270	208	105	4,953
23,595	7,869	2,884	1,738	881	86,431
4,109	691	206	167	145	24,775
1,202	171	22	18	17	8,872
2,255	359	96	77	93	26,394
2,116	350	88	62	15	14,158
1,331	217	53	48	43	10,110
11,013	1,788	465	372	313	84,309
1,811	259	73	38	15	11,909
2,715	869	339	258	211	20,254
1,285	208	37	18	7	9,216
5,811	1,336	449	314	233	41,379
55,197	16,825	6,500	4,375	2,596	283,456

Table A.10. EXTERNAL TRADE OF REPUBLIC OF IRELAND AT CURRENT PRICES, REPRESENTATIVE YEARS

	Value of trade at current prices		
		Exports	
Year	Imports	Domestic exports	Re-exports
	000's Pounds sterling		
1925	62,950	42,744	1,008
1930	56,776	43,768	1,178
1935	37,348	19,615	305
1940	46,790	32,700	266
1945	41,073	35,236	260
1950	159,394	70,452	1,939
1955[a]	204,338	106,683 ⎫	
			3,700
1955[b]	207,663	107,152 ⎭	
1956	182,849	104,276	3,851
1957	184,172	127,076	4,265
1958	198,957	126,623	4,670
1959	212,647	126,616	3,991
1960	226,228	147,831	4,872
1961	261,403	175,212	5,261
1962	273,724	168,920	5,470
1963	307,684	191,941	4,599
1964	349,318	217,043	4,961
1965	371,740	214,875	5,900
1966	372,567	236,357	7,966
1967	392,260	276,459	8,627
1968	496,093	323,411	9,064
1969	589,753	358,531	12,909
1970	653,607	416,422	15,197

SOURCE: Central Statistics Office, *External Trade Statistics, 1970* (Dublin: The Stationery Office, 1971), pp. 1–2. In 1955 the statistics were revised to take into account parcel post trade. It was, however, impossible to backdate the revision.

Table A.10 (continued)

| Total | Import excess | Annual Index numbers of the volume of trade base: year 1953 = 100 | |
		Imports	Total exports
000's Pounds sterling			
43,751	19,199	78.2	100.2
44,945	11,831	87.4	118.2
19,920	17,428	73.5	84.7
32,966	13,824	56.8	70.2
35,496	5,577	31.8	51.5
72,391	87,003	101.2	74.6
110,383	93,956		
		107.6	95.3
110,851	96,812		
108,127	74,722	93.0	98.1
131,341	52,831	88.7	116.9
131,293	67,664	100.2	114.3
130,607	82,040	109.6	109.6
152,703	73,525	114.4	130.2
180,473	80,930	130.9	155.6
174,390	99,334	137.2	149.1
196,539	111,144	151.6	164.9
222,004	127,314	170.7	176.5
220,775	150,965	177.4	173.7
244,323	128,244	177.9	188.9
285,086	107,174	188.6	220.5
332,475	163,617	220.2	239.5
371,441	218,312	251.6	252.5
431,618	221,988	261.2	275.1

Table A.11. EXTERNAL TRADE OF NORTHERN
IRELAND AT CURRENT PRICES,
REPRESENTATIVE YEARS (in £ million)

Year	Imports	Exports	Total trade
1938	54.4	47.1	101.4
1949	188.7	163.6	352.4
1955	299.2	270.2	569.4
1964	470.2	423.3	893.4
1965	512.8	460.6	973.4
1966	523.4	477.9	1,001.4
1967	551.7	507.0	1,058.7
1968	659.6	596.1	1,255.7
1969	727.9	668.9	1,396.8

SOURCE: *Ulster Year Book 1971* (Belfast: HMSO, 1971), p. 262.

Table A.12. HOUSES COMPLETED, RECONSTRUCTED, AND IMPROVED, IN THE IRISH REPUBLIC, 1960–61 to 1968–69.

Year ended 31st March	Houses completed			Grants for houses—	
	Local authority houses	Other houses	Totals	Recon-structed	Improved
1961	1,463	4,685	6,148	9,429	2,337
1962	1,238	4,738	5,976	8,588	2,418
1963	1,828	5,389	7,217	9,461	2,961
1964	1,856	5,975	7,831	9,563	4,124
1965	2,307	7,372	9,679	9,057	6,180
1966	2,989	8,266	11,255	9,474	7,494
1967	4,079	6,905	10,984	8,576	6,747
1968	4,045	7,972	12,017	10,290	8,706
1969	4,613	8,451	13,064	9,724	9,425

SOURCE: *Housing in the Seventies* (Dublin: The Stationery Office, 1969), p. 2.

Table A.13. EXPENDITURE ON BUILDING AND RECONSTRUCTING HOUSES AND ON SUBSIDIES, IRISH REPUBLIC, 1960–61 to 1968–69, (in £ million)

Year ended 31st March (1)	Total capital expenditure from all sources on building and reconstructing houses (2)	Capital expenditure by Government and local authorities on housing (3)	Housing subsidies met from central and local taxation (4)
1961	14.6	8.8	6.4
1962	16.1	9.5	6.8
1963	19.0	11 2	7.2
1964	23.4	12.9	7.6
1965	31.5	15.9	8.2
1966	40.5	21.0	9.2
1967	37.6	22.1	10.1
1968[a]	47.0	25.7	10.7
1969[b]	52.0	29.7	12.0

[a]Provisional. [b]Estimated.

SOURCE: *Housing in the Seventies* (Dublin: The Stationery Office, 1969), p. 2.

Table A.14. NEW PERMANENT HOUSES COMPLETED IN NORTHERN IRELAND, 1949–1970

	Total	Local Authorities	Northern Ireland Housing Trust	Other Public Agencies	Private Enterprise
1949	7,630	2,932	1,928	103	2,514
1959	4,894	1,424	956	56	2,458
1962	8,215	3,071	1,416	317	3,411
1963	8,842	4,188	1,536	195	2,923
1964	9,516	4,107	2,023	216	3,170
1965	8,937	2,789	2,560	225	3,363
1966	10,500	3,588	3,338	299	3,275
1967	11,099	4,088	3,092	149	3,770
1968	12,120	5,493	2,431	121	4,075
1969	11,531	4,950	2,226	142	4,213
1970	11,834	4,734	2,958	104	4,038

SOURCE: *Ulster Year Book 1971* (Belfast: HMSO, 1971), p. 270

Table A.15. HOUSES COMPLETED IN NORTHERN IRELAND, BY SOURCE, 1970

Local authorities	3,806
Northern Ireland Housing Trust	2,958
Development commissions	928
Other public agencies	104
Private enterprise	4,038
Total	11,834

SOURCE: *Ulster Year Book 1971* (Belfast: HMSO, 1971), p. 109.

Table A.16. COMPARISON OF EUROPEAN HOUSING PROVISION

Country	Percentage of dwellings built before 1919	Average no. of persons per room (about 1961)	Estimated average annual population increase rate per 1,000 inhabitants from 1960 to 1970	No. of houses built per 1,000 of population (1967)	Percentage of houses owner-occupied as at a recent census date
Austria	58	1.20	4.7	7.0	37.7
Denmark	n.a.	.69	6.5	9.2	45.0
Finland	21	1.31	8.7	7.9 (1966)	60.5
France	62	1.01	8.1	8.5	41.5
IRELAND, Republic of	58	.90	0.4	4.2	59.8
Italy	n.a.	1.31	6.4	5.1	40.0
Netherlands	36	.76	10.5	10.2	29.3
Norway	34	.77	8.6	8.1 (1966)	52.8
Portugal	n.a.	1.11	5.5	4.9 (1966)	44.5
Sweden	34	.83	5.7	12.7	36.0
Switzerland	n.a.	.69	9.9	n.a.	33.7
United Kingdom	46	.65	4.8	7.6	43.9
West Germany	4	.88	6.2	10.0	35.3

SOURCE: *Housing in the Seventies* (Dublin: The Stationery Office, 1969), p. 52.

Table A.17. COMPARISON OF EUROPEAN HOUSING EXPENDITURE

Country	Per capita GNP (1967) (dollars)	Percentage of GNP spent on housing construction (1966)
Austria	1,460	4.4 (1964)
Denmark	2,320 (1966)	4.3
Finland	n.a.	5.7
France	2,190	6.3
IRELAND, Republic of	1,080	4.1 (1967)
Italy	1,280	6.2
Netherlands	1,810	5.2
Norway	2,200	4.3 (1967)
Portugal	490	4.0
Sweden	3,040	6.0 (1967)
Switzerland	2,620	6.8
United Kingdom	1,980	3.7 (1967)
West Germany	2,030	5.5

SOURCE: *Housing in the Seventies* (Dublin: The Stationery Office, 1969), p. 52.

Table A.18. PARTY COMPOSITION OF THE DAIL,
1922–1973

Election	Total	Republican/ Fianna Fail	Cumann na n Gaedheal/ Fine Gael	Labour	Other
1922	128	35	58	17	18
1923	153	44	63	14	32
1927 (1)	153	44	47	22	40
1927 (2)	153	57	62	13	21
1932	153	72	57	7	17
1933	153	77	48	8	20
1937	138	69	48	13	8
1938	138	77	45	9	7
1943	138	67	32	17	22
1944	138	76	30	8	24
1948	147	68	31	19	29
1951	147	69	40	16	22
1954	147	65	50	19	13
1957	147	78	40	13	16
1961	144	70	47	16	11
1965	144	72	47	22	3
1969	144	75	50	18	1
1973	144	69	54	19	2

Table A.19. MINISTERS FOR EXTERNAL
AFFAIRS, 1922–1973, SOUTHERN IRELAND

Name of Minister	Date of appointment
Desmond Fitzgerald	December 1922
Kevin O'Higgins	June 1927
W. T. Cosgrave	July 1927
Patrick McGilligan	December 1927
Eamon de Valera	March 1932
Sean MacBride	February 1948
Frank Aiken	June 1951
Liam Cosgrave	June 1954
Frank Aiken	March 1957
Patrick Hillery	July 1969
Garret Fitzgerald	March 1973

Suggested Readings   Index

Suggested Readings

(1)

For the reader interested in Irish geography one book stands out:
T. W. Freeman's *Ireland: A General and Regional Geography*
(London: Metheun and Co. Ltd., and New York: E. P. Dutton and
Co. Inc., 3rd ed., 1965). For historical geography the same author's
Pre-Famine Ireland (Manchester: Manchester University Press,
1957) is definitive. There are a number of general surveys which
discuss early Irish history. A particularly graceful one is *Fractured
Emerald: Ireland* by Emily Hahn (Garden City: Doubleday and
Co. Inc., 1971). *The Course of Irish History,* ed. T. W. Moody and
F. X. Martin (Cork: Mercier Press, 1967) is succinct and very well
illustrated.

(2)

The most recent study of the passage and structure of the Act of
Union is G. C. Bolton's *The Passing of the Irish Act of Union*
(London: Oxford University Press, 1966). A classic article by
Thomas N. Brown, "Nationalism and the Irish Peasant, 1800–1848"
originally found in *The Review of Politics* of October 1953, has
recently been reprinted for the American Committee for Irish Studies
by the University of Chicago Press. Sean O'Faolain's life of Daniel
O'Connell, *King of the Beggars* (Dublin: Allen Figgis Ltd., paper-
back ed., 1970) is a stirring and memorable work. Denis Gwynn's
Young Ireland and 1848 (Cork: Cork University Press, 1949) is
useful, although uneven. *Isaac Butt and Home Rule* by David Thorn-
ley (London: MacGibbon and Kee, 1964) is a skillful political
biography. Charles Stewart Parnell has yet to find an adequate
biographer, this being largely a reflection of his enigmatic, secretive,
and complex personality. A fascinating analysis of his political
machine is found in Conor Cruise O'Brien's *Parnell and his Party,
1880–1890* (Oxford: Clarendon Press, 2nd ed., 1964). One cannot
discuss the home rule bills without reference to J. L. Hammond's

massive *Gladstone and the Irish Nation* (London: Frank Cass and Co. Ltd., reprint ed., 1964). An interesting, if not completely satisfying, life of the founder of Sinn Fein is *Arthur Griffith* by Padraic Colum (Dublin: Browne and Nolan Ltd., 1959).

The best introduction to the republican tradition is through the writings of the man usually recognized as its founder: *The Autobiography of Theobald Wolfe Tone* ed. Sean O'Faolain (London: Thomas Nelson and Sons Ltd., 1937). *The Unfortunate Mr. Robert Emmet* by Leon O'Broin (Dublin: Clonmore and Reynolds Ltd., 1958) deals successfully with that romantic figure. Because of the clandestine nature of Fenianism it is doubtful if the early history of the organization will ever be adequately written. A useful, if episodic, work is Desmond Ryan's *The Phoenix Flame, A Study of Fenianism and John Devoy* (London: Arthur Barker Ltd., 1937). Ryan also wrote *The Fenian Chief: a Biography of James Stephens* (Dublin: Gill and Son, 1967), as well as assorted appreciations of the Fenians. The political works of both Pearse (Dublin: Talbot Press, reprinted 1966) and Connolly (Dublin: Three Candles, c. 1948–1949) have been collected and republished. There is a large number of books dealing with the 1916 Rising. From a narrative viewpoint the most dramatic is Max Caulfield's *The Easter Rebellion* (London: Four Square paper ed., 1965). It should, however, be supplemented by analytic studies, especially the essays found in *Leaders and Men of the Eastern Rising: Dublin 1916* ed. F. X. Martin (London: Methuen and Co. Ltd., 1967.)

(3)

The most revealing work concerning the dimensions and character of Irish migration to America is Arnold Schrier's Northwestern University Ph.D. dissertation of 1956, "Ireland and the American Emigration, 1850–1900," available from University Microfilms, Ann Arbor, Michigan, subsequently published in book form under the same title (Minneapolis: University of Minnesota Press, 1958). The Irish material profitably can be related to the overall immigrant situation as presented in *American Immigration* by Maldwyn Allen Jones (Chicago: University of Chicago Press, 1960).

There are many studies of the transformation of the Irish migrants into Americans and the vicissitudes along the way. Oscar Handlin's *Boston's Immigrants: A Study in Acculturation* (Cambridge: Harvard University Press, rev. ed., 1959) is central. Some of his other works, notably *The Uprooted* (Boston: Little, Brown and Co.,

1951) and *Race and Nationality in American Life* (Boston: Little, Brown and Co., 1948), shed light, although somewhat more obliquely, upon the subject. Two general studies of Irish-Americans are of interest: *The Irish in America* by Carl Wittke (Baton Rouge: Louisiana State University Press, 1956), and *The American Irish* (New York: Macmillan and Co., 1963), by William Shannon. For a comparative context within which the Irish experience can be judged, the essays in *The Aliens: A History of Ethnic Minorities in America* ed. Leonard Dinnerstein and Frederic C. Jaher (New York: Appleton Century-Crofts, 1970), are of value.

The ugly history of American nativism is brilliantly told in two books: Ray A. Billington's *The Protestant Crusade 1800–1860: A Study of the Origins of American Nativism* (Chicago: Quadrangle Books, 1964) and John Higham's *Strangers in the Land: Patterns of American Nativism 1860–1925* (New York: Atheneum, rev. ed., 1963).

A varied and interesting collection of articles has been edited by Philip Gleason under the title *Catholicism in America* (New York: Harper & Row, 1970). A fascicule of the *History of Irish Catholicism,* entitled *The United States of America* has extended essays by Thomas T. McAvoy on "The Irish Clergyman" and by Thomas N. Brown on "The Irish Layman" (Dublin: Gill and MacMillan, 1970). Revealing background information is found in David J. O'Brien's *American Catholics and Social Reform: The New Deal Years* (New York: Oxford University Press, 1968). A modern classic is Will Herberg's *Protestant-Catholic-Jew: An Essay in American Religious Sociology* (Garden City: Doubleday and Co., rev. ed., 1960).

The role of the Irish-Americans in the politics of the United States is an endlessly fascinating tale which merges into the larger story of American politics in general. Daniel Patrick Moynihan's chapter on the Irish in *Beyond the Melting Pot* (Cambridge: M.I.T. Press, 1963), written by Moynihan and Nathan Glazer is a tough-minded summary. A recent study with strong historical overtones is *The Irish and Irish Politicians* by Edward M. Levine (Notre Dame, Ind.: University of Notre Dame Press, 1966). Highly readable and revealing is *Al Smith and His America* by Oscar Handlin (Boston: Little, Brown and Co., 1958). The political behavior of the Irish-Americans should be compared to that of other immigrant groups: see *American Ethnic Politics* ed. Lawrence H. Fuchs (New York: Harper & Row, 1968).

It is sometimes said that, had it not been for politics, the Irish-

Americans would have vented their feeling of alienation in violence against American society. This potential for violence is revealed in Wayne G. Broehl Jr.'s *The Molly Maguires* (Cambridge: Harvard University Press, 1965). A gripping account of the Irish participation in the great New York draft riots during the Civil War, made all the more interesting by its anti-Irish bias, is found in *The Great Riots of New York 1712–1873*, originally published in 1873 and reissued in 1970 by Bobbs-Merrill Co., with an introduction by Thomas Rose and James Rodgers.

On Irish-American nationalism one book stands head and shoulders above all others: *Irish-American Nationalism 1870–1890* by Thomas N. Brown (Philadelphia and New York: J. B. Lippincott Co., 1966). There are useful vignettes in Charles C. Tansill's overenthusiastic *America and the Fight for Irish Freedom: 1866–1922* (New York: Devin-Adair Co., 1957), and summary material in John B. Duff's *The Irish in the United States* (Belmont, California: Wadsworth Publishing Co. Inc., 1971).

The diplomatic mainstream against which the leaders of Irish-American nationalism tried to swim is depicted in Bradford Perkins' *The Great Rapprochement: England and the United States, 1895–1914* (New York: Atheneum, 1968). It can profitably be read in tandem with Alan J. Ward's excellent *Ireland and Anglo-American Relations 1899–1931* (London: Wiedenfeld and Nicolson, 1969). The position of immigrant groups in the international diplomacy of the United States is discussed in *The Hyphenate in Recent American Politics and Diplomacy* by Louis L. Gerson (Lawrence: University of Kansas Press, 1964). "Woodrow Wilson, Irish Americans, and the Election of 1916" by William M. Leary, found in the *Journal of American History* (June 1967) is an important revisionist article. The same journal (December 1968) has a valuable piece by John B. Duff entitled "The Versailles Treaty and the Irish-Americans." One is reminded that the Irish-Americans were not the only group of American citizens who had a stake in the peace settlement by *The Immigrants' Influence on Wilson's Peace Policies*, ed. Joseph P. O'Grady (Lexington: University of Kentucky Press, 1967).

(4)

The standard history of the years 1916–1923 is Dorothy Macardle's *The Irish Republic. A Documented Chronicle of the Anglo-Irish Conflict and the Partitioning of Ireland, with a Detailed Account of the period 1916–1923* (New York: Farrar, Straus and Giroux, American ed., 1965). This massive work has a strong anti-treaty bias, but contains many documents and details not available elsewhere. The bias can be corrected by reading a balanced general history of Ireland such as J. C. Beckett's *The Making of Modern Ireland 1603–1923* (London: Faber and Faber 1966) or the impressive new volume by F. S. L. Lyons' *Ireland since the Famine* (London: Weidenfeld and Nicolson, 1971). There are several valuable essays in *The Irish Struggle, 1916–1926,* ed. Desmond Williams (London: Routledge & Kegan Paul, 1966).

Eamon de Valera (London: Hutchinson, 1970) by Lord Longford and T. P. O'Neil is a badly written, semiofficial biography which adds little to one's understanding of de Valera's actions. The most insightful picture of the man still is found in *De Valera* by Sean O'Faolain (Hardmondsworth: Penguin Books Ltd., 1939). I have argued that de Valera's political beliefs usually have been misinterpreted in "Was Eamon de Valera a Republican?" *Review of Politics* (April 1971), pp. 233–253. (Grateful acknowledgment is made for the editor's permission to use some of the material from the article in this book.) A fascinating biography of Michael Collins by his fellow Corkman is Frank O'Connor's *The Big Fellow: Michael Collins and the Irish Revolution* (Dublin: Clonmore and Reynolds, rev. ed., 1965). The original edition of 1937 was released in the United States under the title, *Death in Dublin.* Some new material on Collins is found in Margery Forester's *The Lost Leader* (London: Sidgwick and Jackson, Ltd., 1971). One of the most misunderstood men of the civil war period was the Free State stalwart, Kevin O'Higgins, whose biography has been written by Terence de Vere White (Tralee: Anvil Books ed., 1966).

The classic account of the Anglo-Irish treaty negotiations is Frank Pakenham's *Peace by Ordeal* (London: Geoffrey Chapman, 3rd ed., 1962). Also illuminating is *The Anglo-Irish Treaty* by Frank Gallagher (London: Hutchinson, 1965).

The only available chronicle of the framing of the Free State constitution is found in a series of articles by D. H. Akenson and J. F. Fallin published in *Eire-Ireland* beginning in the Spring 1970 issue under the title "The Irish Civil War and the Drafting of the Free State Constitution." A fine analytic study of the completed constitution is Leo Kohn's *The Constitution of the Irish Free State* (London: George Allen and Unwin Ltd., 1932).

(5)

T. W. Moody and J. C. Beckett have edited two highly readable collections of B.B.C. radio talks under the title *Ulster since 1800.* The first set of talks was given in 1954 and deals with political and economic history; the second, given in 1956 and 1957, discusses social history. Both are published by the British Broadcasting Corporation. Recently, J. C. Beckett and R. E. Glasscock have edited another useful series of B.B.C. talks, *Belfast. The Origin and Growth of an Industrial City* (London: British Broadcasting Corporation, 1967).

Among the monographs on Ulster history, two stand out as especially relevant to the present Ulster problem. They are Hereward Senior's *Orangeism in Ireland and Britain, 1795–1836* (London: Routledge & Kegan Paul, and Toronto: The Ryerson Press, 1966) and A. T. Q. Stewart's *The Ulster Crisis* (London: Faber and Faber, 1967). Stewart's volume deals with the events of 1912–1914.

An interesting study of the Ulster Presbyterians in America is *The Scotch-Irish. A Social History* by James G. Leyburn (Chapel Hill: University of North Carolina Press, 1962). A more specialized study is R. J. Dickson's *Ulster Emigration to Colonial America, 1718–1775* (London: Routledge & Kegan Paul, 1966). *Essays in Scotch-Irish History* (London: Routledge & Kegan Paul, 1969) is a well-chosen selection edited by E. R. R. Green.

(6)

A comprehensive discussion of the Free State constitution is Leo Kohn's *The Constitution of the Irish Free State* (London: George Allen and Unwin Ltd., 1932). Other contemporary commentaries of value are: J. G. Swift McNeill, *Studies in the Constitution of the Irish Free State* (Dublin: Talbot Press Ltd., 1925); and Barra O'Briain, *The Irish Constitution* (Dublin: Talbot Press Ltd., 1929).

A contemporary discussion of early Free State politics is *The Irish Free State: Its Government and Politics* by Nicholas Mansergh (London: George Allen and Unwin Ltd., 1934). Less objective and consequently more informative is Donal O'Sullivan's *The Irish Free State and its Senate: A Study in Contemporary Politics* (London: Faber and Faber, 1940). The militaristic overtones of politics in the thirties is treated in Maurice Manning's *The Blueshirts* (Dublin: Gill and Macmillan, 1970).

The most comprehensive survey of the Republic's politics is *The Government and Politics of Ireland* by Basil Chubb (Stanford:

Stanford University Press, 1970). J. L. McCracken's *Representative Government in Ireland: A Study of Dail Eireann, 1919–1948* (London: Oxford University Press, 1958) is highly analytic. More descriptive are James O'Connell's *How Ireland is Governed* (Dublin: Institute of Public Administration, 1967, and Morley Ayearst's *The Republic of Ireland: Its Government and Politics* (New York: New York University Press, 1970). Cornelius O'Leary's *The Irish Republic and its Experiment in Proportional Representation* (Notre Dame, Indiana: University of Notre Dame Press, 1961) is a readable specialized study. An illuminating recent study is A. S. Cohan's *The Irish Political Elite* (Dublin: Gill and Macmillan, 1972).

(7)

A concise and accurate discussion of the Irish economy is David O'Mahony's *The Irish Economy: An Introductory Description* (Cork: Cork University Press, 2nd ed., 1967). Also valuable is *Ireland in World Commerce* by Charles Hultman (Cork: Mercier Press Ltd., 1969). An excellent historical discussion is L. M. Cullen's *An Economic History of Ireland since 1660* (London: B. T. Batsford, 1972). Comprehensive discussion of agriculture is found in Raymond D. Crotty's *Irish Agricultural Production: Its Volume and Structure* (Cork: Cork University Press, 1966). *Irish Agriculture in a Changing World* (Edinburgh: Oliver and Boyd, 1971), ed. I. F. Baillie and S. J. Sheehy is a wide-ranging symposium. For useful, full journalistic discussions of the economy at different points in time see *The Statist* for 24 October 1953 and *The Economist,* issue of 29 March 1969, and *Hibernia,* 31 March 1972. Definitive statistical information is found in the annual *Statistical Abstract of Ireland* (Dublin: The Stationery Office) and the quarterly *Irish Statistical Bulletin* (Dublin: Central Statistics Office). A good deal of economic information is found in the *Bulletin of the Department of External Affairs,* begun in 1949.

The introduction of government planning, probably the most important development in Ireland's economy since World War II, is best approached by reading the plans themselves. Whitaker's *Economic Development* (Dublin: The Stationery Office, 1958) is crucial, as is the original *Programme for Economic Expansion* (Dublin: The Stationery Office, 1958). These can then be compared to the *Second Program for Economic Expansion* (Dublin: The Stationery Office, part I, 1963, part II, 1964) and *The Third Program for Economic and Social Development* (Dublin: The Stationery Office, 1969). A very helpful survey of Irish planning through 1965 is Loraine Donaldson's *Development Planning in Ireland* (New York: Frederick A. Praeger, 1965) which, however, has been largely superseded by Garret Fitzgerald's excellent *Planning in Ireland* (Dublin: Institute of Public Administration, 1968). Also useful is *Economic Policy in Ireland* (Dublin: Institute of Public Administration, 1968), ed. J. A. Bristow and A. A. Tait.

Readers interested in specific problems of the Irish economy should consult the published research papers of the Economic and Social Research Institute, Dublin. Each of these papers, over fifty in number, focuses on a discrete issue, ranging from tariffs to wage inflation, to the Irish brain drain. For an illuminating discussion of present-day labor management problems see George F. Daly's *Industrial Relations: Comparative Aspects with Particular Reference to Ireland* (Cork: Mercier Press, 1968).

(8)

The organization of the Roman Catholic church in Ireland is detailed in Jean Blanchard's *The Church in Contemporary Ireland* (Dublin: Clonmore and Reynolds Ltd., 2nd ed., 1963, original French ed., 1960). For historical background see *A History of Irish Catholicism,* presently being published in fascicules by Gill & Son, Dublin. *A Short History of the Presbyterian Church in Ireland* by John M. Barkley (Belfast: Publications Board, Presbyterian Church in Ireland 1959) presents Presbyterian history with admirable conciseness. R. Lee Cole's addition to the *History of Methodism in Ireland* (vol. IV) covers the years 1860–1960 (Belfast: Irish Methodist Publishing Co., Ltd., 1960). A useful short history of the Anglicans is *A History of the Church of Ireland* by Thomas J. Johnston, John L. Robinson, and Robert Wyse Jackson (Dublin: A.P.C.K., 1953). For an insight into attitudes and problems of the upper-class Protestants in the Irish Republic, read Brian Inglis' *West Briton* (London: Faber and Faber, 1962). A revealing pamphlet on Protestants in the Republic is Michael Viney's, *The Five Percent* (Dublin: *Irish Times,* 1965).

A major pioneering work is J. H. Whyte's *Church and State in Modern Ireland, 1923–1970* (Dublin: Gill and Macmillan, 1971). Also helpful is R. Dudley Edwards' article "Church and State in Modern Ireland," found in *Ireland in the War Years and After, 1939–1951* (Dublin: Gill and Macmillan, 1969), ed. Kevin B. Nowlan and T. Desmond Williams, pp. 109–119.

Although there is no book available which discusses the southern

Irish moral system in detail, the following popular books about modern Ireland have interesting observations and interpretations: *The Irish* by Donald S. Connery (New York: Simon and Schuster, 1968); *Ireland since the Rising* by Timothy Patrick Coogan (London: Pall Mall Press, 1966); *The Irish Answer* by Tony Gray (Boston: Little, Brown and Co., 1966); *Ireland* by Terence de Vere White (London: Thames and Hudson, 1968).

For historical background on the interplay of religion, economics, and sexual morality see "Catholicism and Marriage in the Century after the Famine," in K. H. Connell's *Irish Peasant Society* (Oxford: Clarendon Press, 1968). Also very important are two classic studies: Conrad M. Arensberg's *The Irish Countryman. An Anthropological Study* (New York: Macmillan Co. 1937) and Conrad M. Arensberg and Solon T. Kimball's *Family and Community in Ireland* (Cambridge: Harvard University Press, 2nd ed., 1968). Notable (and, to the Irish, disturbing) work on Irish sexual behaviour has been done by John C. Messenger. See his "Sex and Repression in an Irish Folk Community," in Donald S. Marshall and Robert C. Suggs (eds.) *Human Sexual Behavior: Variations in the Ethnographic Spectrum* (New York: Basic Books Inc., 1971), pp. 3–37, and see also his "The Lack of the Irish," in *Psychology Today* (February 1971), pp. 41–42, 68. Dorine Rohan's *Marriage Irish Style* (Cork: Mercier Press, 1969) is a disjointed, impressionistic volume which nevertheless often hits the mark with some very astute observations.

A balanced and readable account of the development and operation of the censorship system is Michael Adams, *Censorship: The Irish Experience* (Dublin: Scepter Books, 1968). Desmond Fennell's *The Changing Face of Catholic Ireland* (London: Geoffrey Chapman, 1968), while focusing on change in the modern church, sheds a good deal of light upon the essentially conservative nature of Catholicism in Ireland. In *Is Ireland Dying: Culture and the Church in Modern Ireland* (London: Hollis and Carter, 1968), Michael Sheehy argues that the low cultural horizons of modern Ireland are the result of the Jansenistic nature of Irish Catholicism. *Personality and National Character* by R. Lynn (Oxford: Pergamon Press, 1971) is full of intriguing statistics and odd facts relating to southern Irish life. Most readers, however, will have difficulty following the author's racial explanations of national differences.

(9)

The most recent Irish census report (for 1966) is of course the best source of data on recent demographic developments (Dublin:

The Stationery Office 1967). The 1971 report is presently being processed, but a preliminary report is available. For a detailed study of eighteenth- and nineteenth-century population patterns see K. H. Connell's *The Population of Ireland 1750–1845* (Oxford: Clarendon Press, 1950). *New Dubliners* by Alexander J. Humphreys (London: Routledge & Kegan Paul, 1966) is an interesting study of the adaptation of Irish countrymen to metropolitan life. For an evocative journalistic account of the depopulation of one rural community see John Healy's *The Death of an Irish Town* (Cork: Mercier Press, 1968).

An excellent, concise, readable survey of Irish social welfare programs is P. Kaim-Caudle's *Social Policy in the Irish Republic* (London: Routledge & Kegan Paul, 1967). It can profitably be read in conjunction with Desmond Farley's *Social Insurance and Social Assistance in Ireland* (Dublin: Institute of Public Administration, 1964). *The Civil Service* by Ian Finlay (Dublin: Institute of Public Administration, 1966) provides information on the organization of government agencies including the welfare agencies. *The Dynamics of Irish Housing* by Paul A. Pfretzschner (Dublin: Institute of Public Administration, 1965) is largely theoretical. *Housing in the Seventies* (Dublin: The Stationery Office, 1969) includes a survey of present-day housing policies, while Elizabeth R. Hooker's *Readjustments of Agricultural Tenure in Ireland* (Chapel Hill: University of North Carolina Press, 1938), covers the early history of governmental housing activities. In order to keep Irish social programs in international perspective see Pauline Gregg's *The Welfare State: An Economic and Social History of Great Britain from 1945 to the Present Day* (Amherst: University of Massachusetts Press, 1969).

For a thorough, if somewhat unsympathetic, treatment of the itinerant community see *Report of the Commission on Itinerancy* (Dublin: The Stationery Office, 1963).

Reliable material on Irish primary and secondary education is regrettably scarce. T. J. McElligott's *Education in Ireland* (Dublin: Institute of Public Administration, 1966), is a helpful summary of the modern situation. A more recent work is Norman Atkinson's *Irish Education: A History of Educational Institutions* (Dublin: Allen Figgis, 1969). The two reports of the Council of Education are good indicators of the reasons for the educational stagnation of the nation from the 'thirties through the early 'sixties. The first, on primary education, was published in 1954 by the Stationery Office, Dublin, the second, on the curriculum of the intermediate schools, in 1960 by the same office. A highly revealing document is the two volume *Investment in Education* (Dublin: The Stationery Office, 1965), the importance of which is explained in the text. Also of interest is Patrick Duffy's *The Lay Teacher* (Dublin: Fallons, c. 1968).

(10)

The material on modern Irish nationalism is diffuse and difficult to pursue. There is an excellent chapter on the IRA in T. P. Coogan's *Ireland since the Rising* (London: Pall Mall Press, 1966). The same author's *The I.R.A.* (New York: Praeger Publishers, 1970) is a brave pioneering effort. So too is J. Bowyer Bell's thorough and witty *The Secret Army: A History of the I.R.A. 1915–1970* (London: Sphere Books edition, 1972). For a rollicking, often hilarious view of the IRA, see Brendan Behan's *Confessions of an Irish Rebel* (London: Hutchinson, 1965).

For an introduction to the structure of the Irish language, David Greene's *The Irish Language* (Dublin: published for the Cultural Relations Committee of Ireland at the Three Candles Ltd., 1966), is highly recommended. An uneven collection of essays, which includes some excellent selections, is *A View of the Irish Language,* ed. Brian O'Cuiv (Dublin: The Stationery Office, 1969). O'Cuiv's article "Education and Language," in *The Irish Struggle, 1916– 1929,* ed. Desmond Williams (London: Routledge & Kegan Paul, 1966), is also valuable. Another very helpful article is Donal Mc-Cartney's "Education and Language, 1938–1951," in Kevin B. Nowlan and T. Desmond Williams (eds.), *Ireland in the War Years and After, 1939–1951* (Dublin: Gill and MacMillan, 1969). No informed view on the Irish language revival can be formed until one has read John Macnamera's *Bilingualism and Primary Education: A Study of Irish Experience* (Edinburgh: Edinburgh University Press, 1966). For census data relating to the Irish language question see *Census of Ireland 1961,* vol. IX, *Irish Language* (Dublin: The Stationery Office, 1966).

(11)

The early political history of Northern Ireland is contentious, especially on the border question. For the southern Irish interpretation see Denis Gwynn's *The History of Partition (1912–1925)* (Dublin: Browne and Nolan Ltd., 1950). For a northern viewpoint on politics and partition see St. John Ervine, *Craigavon, Ulsterman* (London: George Allen and Unwin Ltd., 1949). Hugh Shearman's

Anglo-Irish Relations (London: Faber and Faber Ltd., 1948) gives the northern interpretation of Ulster's relations with Great Britain and the Irish Free State through 1948. In 1970 the Irish University Press (Shannon) republished the *Report of the Irish Boundary Commission,* 1925, a document which had been secret for decades.

The basic documents for determining Northern Ireland's original constitutional position are found in Sir Arthur S. Quekett's two-volume work, *The Constitution of Northern Ireland* (Belfast: HMSO, 1933). Matters of domestic as well as constitutional law are treated in Harry Calvert's *Constitutional Law in Northern Ireland: A Study in Regional Government* (London: Stevens and Sons Ltd., and Belfast: Northern Ireland Legal Quarterly Inc., 1968). *The Government of Northern Ireland: A Study in Devolution* (London: George Allen and Unwin Ltd., 1936) remains the most important study of the structure of the Ulster government.

The vexed question of the financial relations of the government of Northern Ireland with the government of the United Kingdom are discussed in R. J. Lawrence's illuminating book, *The Government of Northern Ireland: Public Finance and Public Service, 1921–1964* (Oxford: Clarendon Press, 1965). A treatment of the same topic intended to reveal the financial weakness of the six counties' government is *Ireland: Finances of Partition* by Labhras O'Nuallain (Dublin: Clonmore and Reynolds Ltd., 1952).

An excellent study, which is definitive for the period it covers, is *An Economic Survey of Northern Ireland* by K. S. Isles and Norman Cuthbert (Belfast: HMSO, 1957). For a picture of the exurban sector see John M. Mogey's fascinating *Rural Life in Northern Ireland* (London: Oxford University Press, 1947).

There are two volumes of note published officially by the Northern Ireland government. These are the *Ulster Year Book* (Belfast: HMSO, published annually) and Hugh Shearman's *Northern Ireland* (Belfast: HMSO, 1968). Both these publications contain valuable information, but both should be treated with considerable caution: they are official government publications and they ignore the pressing problems which have confronted the north.

The following general studies of Northern Ireland are still of value even though conditions have changed considerably since they were written: *Ulster under Home Rule: A Study of the Political and Economic Problems of Northern Ireland* ed. by Thomas Wilson (London: Oxford University Press, 1955) and *The Northern Ireland Problem: A Study in Group Relations* by Denis P. Barritt and Charles F. Carter (London: Oxford University Press, 1962).

The next two books, published long before the present troubles, are a great aid in maintaining perspective on the Ulster situation for they are controversial in the best sense, forcing one to re-evaluate the fundamental assumptions with which one approaches the subject: *Divided We Stand. A Study of Partition* by Michael Sheehy (London: Faber and Faber, 1955) and *The Irish Border as a Cultural Divide* by M. W. Heslinga (Assen: Van Gorcum and Co., first published 1962, republished 1971). For a most illuminating and even-handed study of the northern problem by the Belgian League for the Defense of Human Rights see Claude Mertens' "Report on Civil and Social Rights in Northern Ireland," in *Revue de Droit International et Compare,* vol. III, no. 3 (1969). It should be read in conjunction with the *Report of a Commission of Inquiry* into the special powers act conducted and published by the English National Council for Civil Liberties (originally published 1936, republished 1972). An objective pamphlet is *Orange and Green: A Quaker Study of Community Relations in Northern Ireland* (Sedbergh, Yorkshire: Northern Friends Peace Board, 1969). Much less objective, but filled with revealing statistics is *Northern Ireland: The Plain Truth* (Dungannon: Campaign for Social Justice in Northern Ireland, second edition, 1969). *Governing without Consensus* by Richard Rose (London: Faber and Faber, 1971) is based on extensive interview data collected just before the recent violence began and provides many surprising insights into attitudes of the two religious communities. Much less revealing is *Ulster: A Case Study in Conflict Theory* by R. S. P. Elliot and John Hickie (London: Longmans 1971).

The recent troubles have produced a flood of literature. Much of it is exploitative, seeking to press a particular ideological viewpoint, or, presumably, to make some quick royalties for the author. A discriminating ascerbic review of this literature by J. Bowyer Bell is found in *Eire-Ireland* (Spring 1972), pp. 28–38. If one has the time and a taste for sorting out conflicting evidence the most useful sources are the reports of the various commissions set up to examine specific events—the "Cameron," "Scarman," and "Widgery" reports (Belfast: HMSO, 1969–1972). The only source which is continually reliable and analytic about the Ulster situation is *Fortnight,* a Belfast review of independent stance.

(12)

The literature on Irish diplomatic policy is severely limited. One excellent monograph is in print, however: *The Restless Dominion: The Irish Free State and the British Commonwealth of Nations,*

1921–1931 by D. W. Harkness (London: Macmillan and Co., 1969).
Two classic essays on the Free State by Sir Keith Hancock are found
in *Survey of British Commonwealth Affairs: Problems of Nationality*
(London: Oxford University Press, 1937). Related material is found
in Nicholas Mansergh's *Survey of British Commonwealth Affairs:
Problems of External Policy, 1931–1939* (London: Oxford University
Press, 1952). Relevant material is found in the volumes Mansergh
edited under the title *Documents and Speeches on British Common-
wealth Affairs, 1931–1952* (London: Oxford University Press, 1953).
Other useful articles by Nicholas Mansergh are: "Ireland: External
Relations, 1926–1939," in *The Years of the Great Test, 1926–1939,*
ed. Francis MacManus (Cork: Mercier Press, 1967), pp. 127–137;
"Irish Foreign Policy, 1945–1951," in *Ireland in the War Years and
After, 1939–1951,* ed. Kevin B. Nowlan and T. Desmond Williams
(Dublin: Gill and Macmillan, 1969), pp. 134–146; "Ireland from
British Commonwealth towards European Community," in *Historical
Studies* (October 1968), pp. 381–395. A useful collection of docu-
ments for keeping Irish developments in perspective is *The Develop-
ment of Dominion Status, 1900–1936* ed. Robert MacGregor Dawson
(London: Frank Cass and Co. reprint edition, 1965, originally pub-
lished 1937).

For the postwar period the most useful source of information on
foreign policy is the information sheet published several times a year
by the Department of External Affairs. Conor Cruise O'Brien's *To
Katanga and Back* (London: Hutchinson, 1962) is illuminating and
controversial.

Index

The American Foreign Policy Library